BEYOND
A REASONABLE
DOUBT

BEY●ND
A REASONABLE
DOUBT

Convincing Evidence of the
TRUTHS OF JUDAISM

Rabbi Shmuel Waldman

edited by Yaakov Astor

FELDHEIM 🕎 PUBLISHERS
JERUSALEM   NEW YORK

First published 2002

Copyright © 2002 by Shmuel Waldman

ISBN 1-58330-540-8

FELDHEIM PUBLISHERS
POB 35002 / Jerusalem, Israel

202 Airport Executive Park
Nanuet, NY 10954

www.feldheim.com

Printed in Israel

RABBI REUVEN FEINSTEIN

ר"מ תפארת ירושלים ד'סטאטען איילאנד

500C GRAND STREET
NEW YORK, N.Y. 10002

(212) 777-7935

הנה תלמידנו הרב שמואל וואלדמאן שי' המשמש בקדש
בישיבה גדולה "קרעל הרבאר" כמשגיח רוחני וכבר הגיע שם
שמועותיו וגם לפני הרבה בני תורה בדרך קביעות. וגם
בהרבה אסיפות של בני תורה, בעניני אמונה בה' שהוא
הבורא העולם ומנהיגו ואשר הכל בידו. אשר למרות רוב פשיטותן
יש הרבה בני אדם שנכשלים בעניינים אלו ובייחוד גם
יראי ה' ותלמידי הישיבות. והוא משום שאנו שרויין בגלות
בין העמים ומושפעים מדעותיהם הרעות והנלוזות. ושמעתי
משומעי לקחו שדבריו בעניינים אלו מועילים מאוד ושכבר
השפיע על הרבה בני תורה באופן גדול אשר על כן רצונו
להעתיקם כדי לפרסמם ויהא מוכן ביד כל הורה ומורה
תשובות מספיקות להשיב לבניהם ולתלמידיהם בעניינים אלו.
ובכל זאת אני מבקש, שאל יחשבו שיצאו ידי חובתן על ידי שיגיע
הדברים שיתן בהספר כפשוטן, כי בכל עסקי תורה צריכים לאר
והדבר להגיע את הדברים באופן שיקבלו התלמידים כראוי ושישרשו
דו לאורך ימים, עיין עירובין נד:, ולפי זה שונה לכל א' וא' ולפי
תלמוד ותלמיד ולשון הקרא חנך לנער על פי דרכו גם כי יזקין
לא יסור ממנה. והדברים בעניינים אלו שספר [illegible] עליהם
[illegible] ולא [illegible] אחרי [illegible]
לפי [illegible] אחד [illegible] לו האדם זה. [illegible]
הדברים בלשונם ובאופן ההסברה שנוח להם ויודעים שעל ידי כך
יתקבלו הדברים על לב התלמיד וישתמשו בספר זה רק [illegible]
עינים בעניינים אלו. ואם [illegible]
ולשונם [illegible] אל ליבו דוקא יתן ספר זה להתלמיד עצמו.
ואני מברכו שיזכה להוציא ספרים אחרים להגדיל התורה ולהאדירה
ושנזכה כולנו במהרה לימים שנמלא הארץ דעה את ה'.

ראובן פיינשטיין
כ' סיון תשנ"ט

Approbation from
HaGoan Rabbi Mattisyahu Solomon *shlit"a*

I have seen the *sefer* that Rabbi Shmuel Waldman has written. It is truly a [relatively] short work, which contains much quality. The author has merited to "hit the target" with words which will be very useful, and acceptable upon the hearts of our youth, who so sorely lack guidance in these issues.

I have personally "tested out" this *sefer*. There was a young teenager who was very perturbed, and he did not wish to accept upon himself the ways of our Torah, nor did he wish to attend Yeshiva anymore. However, after he read this *sefer*, his eyes lit up, he found peace of mind, and he accepted upon himself to follow the ways of our Torah. After such an episode, one does not need any other testimony, or approbations [about the value of this *sefer*], since even one such episode proves more about the *sefer* than a thousand words of approbation. Therefore, I come to express my gratitude to Rabbi Waldman and to bless him, that his words should spread, and he should merit to teach Torah to our youth with tranquility, security, and with peace of mind.

בס"ד

ג' פ' יצא חקת בלק תשל"ו

פה לייקווד יצ"ו

ראיתי הקונטרס לתכן הרב שמואל וואלדמאן שליט"א
הגון והוא באמת מטפל הקשיות ורב האיכות כי
בא לתקן את הסתרה דפמים טובים ומועילים
מתקבלים על לב הצעיר הלזן אשר על כל אחד ואחד
הדורו בעמינו. ראיתי נסיון יהדולית את הקונטרס
הלז לבחור אחד אשר ה' נבוך וסרב לקבל דרך
אבותיו ולא רצה לבוא לישיבה ואחרי קראו את
הקונטרס אורו עיניו ונתיישב דעתו ויקבל עליו על עצמו
ומזה נעשה כעה אין לביתינו כאשר וגם נעשה אמרית
כי נעשה אחד נוכח יותר נאמן שליח כן בא' כל דבר
לחבירו טובה לחרב הלז ולברך אותו שליטו במעינותיו
חוצה להרבי ועוד לצאן הקודש מתוק מנועת
ונסף הקהל ובות

נאון הכ"ח לכבוד התורה
מרביצ"ה ומגלה

נתתי מ"ר פלועין.

Approbation from HaGoan Rabbi Yisroel Belsky *shlit"a*

I have reviewed your sefer on matters of Emunah, and I find it to be a beautiful work. The ideas are written in a very clear fashion, with words that will penetrate the hearts of your readers. It is written in an easy fashion so that it can be understood properly. The main pillars of Judaism are dealt with in this *sefer*. I am sure these words will be well accepted by the those whose souls thirst to know the Word of G-d, and it will open their hearts to the straightforwardness of our beliefs. Emunah is the last foundation that the Jewish nation will have left upon which to "lean." As the Talmud brings (Tractate *Makos* 24a), the Prophet Chavakuk came and based it [the keeping of the Torah] on one prerequisite: Emunah. The righteous shall live [according to the Torah] through their [firm] belief.

Rabbi Y. Belsky

506 EAST 7th STREET
BROOKLYN, NEW YORK 11218

ישראל הלוי בעלסקי

941 - 0112

לכבוד מו"ר שליט"א שלומכם וכל אשר לכם י"י

באהבה

צרת א בהוורס גר"ל שושנס אתרג י' וראיתיו שוב וגם
ונגבר הר' לגברים ובראיונות מסוגרים גוואל ואת אוגרים של
לסב, ואשרק בפשוט לצין הקורן הכב' שיעשו א וכאן
יסואל ולהילאם ונדואמים הרוש אל עולם, ולא יתקבלו וזל
נשוון הכמאוא לעהר ף יצאתו זהות פואש שהם גבל גוש
בעאהו"ל עשור ושילו הכל רעו בואשרים אל גן תמוקוק
והאן ... אל סאל ובר

ב"ג האתר סיל עולם ... ... בא ברוקלן נויו יארק
ושום לכם גםלן

בס"ד

TALMUDICAL YESHIVA OF PHILADELPHIA

6063 Drexel Road
Philadelphia, Pennsylvania 19131
215 - 477 - 1000

Rabbi Elya Svei
Rabbi Shmuel Kamenetsky
Roshei Yeshiva

27 Nisan 5756

Dear Reb Shmuel שליט"א,

   Your manuscript is a beautiful appreciation of Hashem's presence in all his works on this world. Although you took the מושגים from comparatively recent sources, the ראשונים had already compacted the מושג כל into the basic יסודות upon which you elaborate.

   This ספר will surely be a great asset for גדולים as well as קטנים in providing the proper הדרכה for עבודת in יראת שמים. Studying the wonders of the בריה enhances our recognition of the great חסדים that are bestowed upon the world every moment. In addition, such a ספר will strengthen our אהבה of הקב"ה, which is a foundation of our עבודה.

   May you be Zocheh to be included in the צדיקים יושבים ועטרותיהם and may the רבש"ע grant you the opportunity to be נהנה מזיו השכינה.

Sincerely yours,

Rabbi Shmuel Kamenetsky

RSK:sm

הרב דן זאב הלוי סגל
ירושלים עיה"ק תובב"א

בס"ד.

כבוד ידידי היקר וכו' אשר רוחו היה כרב ... ...

... שמעתי ... כי הנך ... ...

... ... את ... הראשונה ... ...

וכו'.

והנה כל גדולת ... הראשונים הוא ... ...

... של ... הם ואנחנו ... כדי ... ...

... ... הראשונים דבריהם ... כי יפה ... ...

... ... והאחרונים ... ...

ואנחנו ... ...

... ...

... ...

... ... כמו ... ...

... ...

... ...

... ... כמו ... ...

בברכה רבה

פלטיאל הלוי סגל

לז"נ

אבי ומורי
הרב צבי אלימלך
בן
ר׳ שמואל ז"ל
וואלדמאן
Rav Herschel Waldman, z"l

צער ויגון אחזתנו
בהוסר הנזר מראשינו
יתומים היינו ואין אב

את ה׳ כיבד מגרונו
לכל היה משמח בניגונו
יגע הרבה להבין עומק חומש ורש"י
מחדש חידושים היה
לכל היה אהוב
כל שרוח הבריות נוחה הימנו
רוח המקום נוחה הימנו
ת.נ.צ.ב.ה.

ולז"נ זקנתי מרת שיינדל בת ישראל ע"ה
ת.נ.צ.ב.ה.

לז"נ

זקנתי
האשה החשובה וצנועה
רודף צדקה וחסד כל
ימי חייה
מרת חנה בת יצחק שרגא הלוי ע"ה
ע"ה Chana Papernik

From her son-in-law, daughter & grandchildren
Yiddel and Clara Friedman

Rochel & Avi Meyer
Ari Friedman
Naomi Friedman

לז"נ

משה חיים בן אברהם יהודה

ואת

רחל בת ישראל

Contents

Preface

For nearly ten years I have been privileged to teach Talmud at a ye-shivah high school. During that time I have become convinced that many of us involved in Jewish education have, at least in one respect, failed our students. All too often the fundamental philosophic and quasi-philosophic principles of Judaism — the hashkafah of Yahadut — are glossed over as if through some magical osmotic process the student will unconsciously absorb them. This is a luxury which we can ill afford. Many unarticulated but nevertheless very real ques-tions remain unanswered and, therefore, continue to plague students and occasionally undermine their faith.

(MICHAEL HECHT, *HAVE YOU EVER ASKED YOURSELF THESE QUESTIONS?*, SHEINGOLD PUBLISHERS, INC.)

I couldn't agree more.

This book originated from my own research, where I endeav-ored to provide myself, and others, with a wealth of evidence that would verify the truths of our Jewish Faith. After much re-search I finally felt satisfied that I indeed had substantial evi-dence to "prove" the truth of all the main branches of Jewish be-lief. I had strong evidence that there is a God, that our Torah is truly of Divine origin, that God controls the world, and that there is a World to Come. In the course of my research, I came across additional evidence that would show how many other Jewish doctrines were all true.

Then, years later, as *mashgiach* (spiritual mentor) in Yeshivah Mercaz HaTorah of Belle Harbor, which is a yeshivah high school, I prepared lectures, based on my previous research, on *emunah* (faith) for the student body — upon which this book came to be based. Although the yeshivah had quite a religious student body, I still gave lectures on the basics of *emunah*. Why, you ask. Because for more then a decade I had the privilege of dealing with teenage boys from different religious camps and yeshivos, and I noticed that a great number of them had many questions of *emunah*. This convinced me of the necessity to teach about *emunah*, and so I gave lectures on *emunah*, and the boys really gained from them. Many of those students suggested that I write a book on *emunah*. Also, some of our foremost Torah authorities have personally told me of the need to increase the amount of *emunah* taught in yeshivos and day schools. In fact, Rabbi Moshe Feinstein, *zt"l*, states emphatically (*Igros Moshe, Yoreh De'ah, Chelek* 3, *Siman* 71) that teachers today must endeavor to instill in their students with all the important Torah philosophies, and *actively look* for ways of explaining the *foundations* of our faith, and not to rely only on *emunah peshutah* ("simple faith"). Their words, and the words of Rabbi Feinstein, *zt"l*, have also helped inspire me to write a book on *emunah*.

Yes, it's true that many students come from homes with parents who have very deep faith and fear of Heaven, others have been lucky enough to have learned from those select few teachers who are qualified to teach the basics of *emunah*, and some of our students are capable of getting by with what's called *emunah peshutah*, which means simple, pure faith, without any real understanding of it.

Indeed, the famous Rabbi Moshe of Kobryn, and many other outstanding scholars, have always pointed out how in the inner recesses of one's God-given soul all Jews believe in God and the spiritual world of the Torah; it's just that the soul has been covered over with dark clouds of uncertainty due to its exposure to a world of impurities and heresy. Therefore, it's no wonder that a large number of Jews, including the majority of students of today's yeshivos and day schools, sorely need a basic course in *emunah*.

And, let's face it. Anyone in contact with the average Jewish teenager knows that *"emunah peshutah"* can't be the whole answer. The outside world presents challenges that no previous generation has ever had. Whether it's from the bad influences that come from the TV, newspapers, videos, the Internet, magazines, or even school textbooks, virtually no one can claim to be untouched by these outside influences. Once a child has tasted from these forbidden pleasures, it takes a lot of *emunah* to draw him away from them. Many times it's these outside influences that cause subconscious questions of *emunah* to surface, and they start to trouble the child. And unfortunately, most of the time the child has no one to turn to, to ask his questions. In passing, I would like to point out the tremendous adverse effects that come about when rebbeim or teachers avoid teaching about *emunah*. As years and years go by, with students *rarely* hearing a rebbe or teacher discuss vital *hashkafah* topics, inevitably the student subconsciously gets one, or all, of the following three messages:

1. Obviously these topics aren't too important, or else my rebbe or teacher would spend more time discussing them.
2. Maybe my rebbe or teacher isn't capable of explaining these topics too well (and very often that's the truth).
Or worse:
3. Maybe my rebbe or teacher has some of the same questions and doubts of *emunah* that I have.

It's a terrible shame if any of our students should ever have to come to such thoughts about their rebbeim or teachers. Our students must at least sense that their rebbe or teacher is well-versed in these topics. And hopefully our students are able to sense that their rebbe or teacher is always ready to cheerfully discuss such topics with them. What an improvement it would be if rebbeim and teachers would be able to encourage the discussion of such topics without the fear of being unable to answer most of the basic questions. Unfortunately, the opposite usually happens. Usually when a child gets up the guts to ask a question of *emunah*, the child is scorned, since with such a question he (or she, for that matter, though it's well-known that females seem to manage much better with *emunah peshutah* than males do) has shown a lack of *emunah peshutah*. Such a thing should never happen to an innocent child who asks a legitimate *emunah* question.

Therefore, another reason for writing this book, was to make easily available a *sefer* for any rebbe or teacher who wishes to know more about the issues surrounding the topic of *emunah*. This book will hopefully serve as a "teachers' edition" which will supply teachers with loads of ammunition to answer most *emunah* questions that their students may ask. It will provide enough *emunah* information that will enable a rebbe or teacher to feel comfortable enough about their *emunah* knowledge that he or she will not be afraid to answer a student's question, and hopefully it will give educators enough information that they will feel comfortable enough to actually be the ones to initiate the *emunah* discussions in their classes. (Many of our educators have obviously managed to remain solid Jews with just *emunah peshutah*, but as mentioned above, that won't be good enough for today's average student, so we hope that this *sefer* will help enhance the educator's ability to provide evidence to the truths of our faith.)

As I said previously, the material of this book originated from talks that I delivered to teenage boys. And teenagers were originally my target audience. They were, and still are, the ones I personally want most to read this book. The earlier they read this, the better their chances of leading their lives in a Torah-true way. However, unfortunately, because *emunah* isn't being discussed enough, we find all too often people who are past their teenage years who have not developed and deepened the roots of their *emunah*, thereby resulting in their going as far as to completely discard their Torah observance. And even those who do not go so far as to totally discard their Torah observance, nevertheless such people fall much more easily into the quagmire of quasi-observance, and it is such people whose main pursuits in life revolve around material pursuits, with little, if any, spiritual pursuits, all as a result of their lack of a deep-rooted *emunah*. Therefore we have written this book to help Jews in our modern world better understand how the principal beliefs of Judaism are indeed true beyond a reasonable doubt.[1] Because there is such a diversified audience that needs strengthening of their *emunah*, this book was written in a way that will greatly enrich the *emunah* of *anyone* searching to know more about his Judaism, young or old, religious or not. This book was written with the intent to appeal to educated adults from all sectors, and from all educational backgrounds. And for that achievement — and for the natural, easy flow of the writing — I have to thank R. Yaakov Astor, the editor, whose extensive experience in writing and editing numerous books and articles in the fields of both *kiruv rechokim* and *kiruv kerovim* is clearly evident. He has greatly enhanced the presentation of this work. It has been a pleasure working with you.

As to the permissibility of writing a book on *emunah*, we find that throughout the centuries there always seemed to be a need for books on such topics for the general public. Starting from Rabbi Saadiah Gaon, who wrote *Emunos v'De'os*, Rabbi Yehudah ha-Levi wrote his *Kuzari*, the Rambam (Maimonides) wrote *Moreh Nevuchim*, Rabbenu Bachya wrote *Sefer Chovos Ha-Levavos*

---

1. Of course, we cannot account for *unreasonable doubt*. To the person looking for something to defend his God-given right to remain skeptical — whose first commandment is "Thou shall not believe" — this book will probably ultimately prove to be unsatisfying. To such a person no evidence is going to be good enough. On the other hand, there are many sincere, reasonable, and, as of yet, non-believers who will read this book. We encourage you to fully examine all the evidence of this book, and you'll be surprised how quickly your belief will be strengthened. If you have any comments or questions, please feel free to contact the author through the office of Feldheim Publishers.

(in many parts of his *sefer* he addresses *emunah*), Rabbi Yosef Albo wrote *Sefer Ha-Ikkarim*, and Rabbi Menasheh ben Israel wrote *Sefer Nishmas Chayim*. All of these great people found it necessary to write major works on *emunah* where the express purpose of their *sefarim* was to provide a rational basis for our *emunah*. So too, the greatest Jewish leaders and thinkers of this past century have also trumpeted the cause. The Alter of Kelm (Rabbi Simchah Zissel Ziv, 1824–1898), for instance, in his classic *sefer Chochmah u'Mussar*, writes again and again in his essays (#18, 19, 20, 21, 22, just to mention a few) that we must do whatever we can to increase our *emunah*. In our generation, the Steipler Gaon, *zt"l*, emphasized the importance of meditating on the rational arguments for the foundations of *emunah* (see the introduction to his *sefer Chayei Olam*, and see chapters 1 to 13 of his *sefer*, where he elaborates on these subjects). Rav Chatzkel Levenstein, *zt"l*, was also well-known for his efforts to try to strengthen his generation's *emunah* with every opportunity that he had.

(An important disclaimer: In no way or fashion do I, the author of this book, have the audacity to assume that I am on the same, or even a remotely close, level as the above-mentioned people. However, sometimes when one sees a need for something to be done, even if it's really not befitting his status to do such a thing, and he gets the consent of the great people of his generation to go ahead with the project, as I have, then he has permission to do so, and so I did. And another disclaimer that I feel is very important to mention, is that just about every single thought mentioned in this *sefer*, I either heard, or read, from reliable sources. Nothing that I have written is my own. In fact, I highly recommend that you check the suggested reference materials found in the back of this book to see where most of my information came from. I especially recommend doing so for those that wish to have as much evidence as possible to the truths of our Torah, since I could only bring "samples" of the many pieces of available evidence.)

The author is also aware that the fact that we have written

about some touchy topics, such as Christianity and the Holocaust, can open us up to heavy criticism. (It's easy to lift oneself up by criticizing the work and efforts of somebody else.) We also realize that some topics may be problematic if brought up, since they might bring questions into the minds of the readers that they may not have had otherwise. However, as should be expected, we were very careful with how we worded things, in order to avoid these problems as much as possible. Nevertheless, certain topics couldn't, and probably in this generation, shouldn't, be avoided, and therefore we chose to speak about them despite the above possible problems. And to explain why we still chose to speak about such topics, we bring two examples from the *gemara* that back up its permissibility. In *Bereshis* 1:26, the verse says, "Let us make man," which implies that there was a partner with God in the creation of man. Indeed a very misleading verse. In fact, the *Midrash Rabbah* in *Bereshis* 8:7 notes how when Moshe Rabbenu wrote down this verse, he asked God why He was putting a verse in the Torah that would give an opening for non-believers to point to as a proof to their heresy. To this, the midrash has God answering, "Those who wish to err can err, but I have an important lesson to teach with this verse."

In a similar vein, we find that the *sefer Chovos Ha-Levavos* brings in its chapter *Sha'ar Yichud Hama'aseh* a *gemara* from *Bava Basra* 89b which discusses how Rabbi Yochanan Ben Zakkai had doubts about teaching certain tricks involving money matters. These were tricks which he wanted his students to know so that they would be aware of the swindler's behavior. He said, "Woe to me if I say them — for swindlers will learn new tricks; and woe to me if I don't say them — for the swindlers will say that the *talmidei chachamim* don't know of their tricks [and they will persist with their tricks]." The *gemara* concludes that they should be taught, and quotes a verse in *Hoshe'a* (14:10): "For the ways of God (i.e., the words of His Torah) are straight, the righteous ones follow them, and the wicked ones stumble through them."

So we see that sometimes things have to be taught, said, or written, even though there exists the possibility of a problem coming from them. Of course, it's our hope that no damage comes from this book, but that only the strengthening of *emunah* comes from it. We write about the Holocaust — although we realize it's a touchy topic — because today's youth are quite removed from it as far as psychological scars go; but as for the obvious *hashkafah* questions that arise from the Holocaust, to that our youth are quite near. For such people, a partial answer is better than no answer at all. When people see that you completely avoid a subject, they become suspicious and start thinking that maybe you are hiding something from them, or even worse, that maybe you have the same questions as they do. Therefore, we chose to shed some light on the topic so that rebbeim and teachers can discuss the subject. As for Christianity, it's only briefly touched upon, and we hope that the little we said was enough to bring out the farce of Christianity; it's too bad that we couldn't expose its fallacies more than we did. Again, great care was taken as to what, and how, we wrote about it.

And so, with great trepidation we present this book in the hope that it will help bring about the strengthening of faith which this generation so sorely needs.

The first three chapters of this book cover the main principles of our faith, which, according to one of the truly classic works on Jewish belief, *Sefer Ha-Ikkarim* (written by Rabbi Yosef Albo), are: 1) belief in God; 2) belief that the Torah is from God; and 3) belief in reward and punishment, given by God in this world, and in the World to Come. These topics are dealt with in Chapters 1, 2, and 3, respectively. In addition, Chapter 4 discusses the uniqueness and immortality of the Jewish people, and Chapter 5 expounds upon the concept of Divine Providence (*hashgachah pratis*). Besides these five main chapters, there are also several appendices which address other relevant issues of *emunah*. In particular, there is Appendix G, called the Downfall of the Theory of Evolution, for those who need more extensive discussion on that topic. If we include all of the appendices, this *sefer* discusses the first, second, and sixth through the thirteenth principles of the *Yud-Gimmel Ikkarim*, the thirteen main principles of our faith, as enumerated by the Rambam.

The Torah states, "You shall *know* this day and cause it to *dwell in your heart*, that Hashem is God in heaven above and on the earth below; there is none else [besides Him]" (*Devarim* 4:39). There are two requirements of knowledge which this verse mentions: "knowing" and "causing it to dwell in your heart." The first has to do with abstract knowledge. The second has to do with the heart — knowing something deeply, internally, experientially. It's not enough to conclude at an early age that you believe, and then stop there. It's necessary to reinvigorate your belief through knowledge so real, that it actually can be called an experience. That's why the study of nature (*nifla'os ha-Borei*), meditation on rational arguments, scientific facts (as opposed to theories), proper study of Jewish history, etc. — which are all provided in this book — will prove to be valuable tools to strengthen our belief, thereby helping us live our lives as proper Jews more than ever before. The Talmud in *Makkos* 24a cites the Prophet Chavakuk, who stated that the keeping of the whole Torah is dependent on one aspect: *emunah*, as it says in the verse *V'tzaddik b'emunaso yichyeh*, "The righteous man will live with his belief" (*Chavakuk* 2:4). The clearer and more sure of the truths of Judaism we become, the more our lives as Jews will improve. Better belief is more than just a good idea. It's even more than just an obligation. It's something which will make our lives infinitely richer.

The author would greatly appreciate readers' responses, positive or negative, as long as the purpose is constructive. Please contact the author through the publishers.

Acknowledgments

Mah ashiv la-Hashem kol tagmulohi alai. How can I repay God for all the kindness that He has bestowed upon me? (*Tehillim* 116:12). First and foremost, I must thank Hashem *Yisbarach* for having given me the merit of writing this book, and for His giving me the perseverance to see this project to completion. May He always continue to send His blessings to me, my family, and all of *Klal Yisrael.*

As this book was going to publication, the untimely passing of my father, Rabbi Herschel Waldman, may his memory be blessed, occurred. He was very proud that I was writing this book, and he helped extensively with the financial aspects of it. He also helped with his constant encouragement. May the merits that come from the reading of this book be a merit for his soul.

To my mother, Mrs. Faige Chesir, and my parents-in-law, Rabbi and Mrs. Yankel Applegrad, I must express the greatest appreciation for all they have done for me and my family, and for all of their constant encouragement and guidance. May God grant them good health and *nachas* for many years to come.

Many thanks to my uncle, HaRav Yitzchok Waldman, *shlita*, of Bnei Brak. The *hashpa'ah* that you had on me many years ago had a truly lasting impression.

To HaGaon Rabbi Dan Segal, *shlita*, HaGaon Rabbi Mattisyahu Solomon, *shlita,* HaGaon Rabbi Yisroel Belsky, *shlita,* Ha-Gaon Rabbi Shmuel Kamenetsky, *shlita,* and HaGaon Rabbi Reuven Feinstein, *shlita,* I owe a great debt of gratitude for their having reviewed parts of the manuscript, and for writing letters of endorsement. It was a great *chizuk* to me.

It would be impossible for me to adequately express how indebted I am to *Rabi u'mori,* HaGaon Rabbi Avigdor Miller, *zt"l.* The *emunah* and *hashkafos* that he taught have influenced my life enormously. The entire style of this book can be attributed to his style of explaining (wherever possible) the rationale of our *emunah.*

I've also been privileged to learn under many other wonderful rebbeim who have had their *hashpa'ah* on me. My former rebbeim from Yeshivah of Staten Island, Rabbi Gavriel Bodenheimer, *shlita,* Rabbi Moshe Boruch Newman, *shlita,* Rabbi Yisroel Ginsburg, *shlita,* and the Rosh Yeshivah HaGaon Rabbi Reuven Feinstein, *shlita,* and the *menahel,* Rabbi Gershon Weiss, *shlita.* I've also been privileged to be among the many *talmidim* who still keep a *kesher* with the yeshivah, and especially so with Rabbi Chaim Mintz, *shlita,* who has constantly provided me with *chizuk* and advice throughout the years.

In the Mirrer Yeshivah, I had the privilege to learn under Rabbi Avraham Nelkenbaum, *shlita,* and Rabbi Herschel Kaminsky, *shlita.*

I am also *zocheh* to still have an especially close relationship with the former *mashgiach* of the Mirrer Yeshivah, HaGaon Rav Dan Segal, *shlita.* His teachings have also made a great impression on me. May Hashem pay all of my rebbeim their due reward.

To HaRav Levi Dicker, *shlita* and HaRav Chaim Zelikovitz, *shlita,* my sincerest thanks for your having had confidence in me and letting me work for your yeshivah as *mashgiach.*

To Reb Ephraim Isralowitz of the Mirrer Yeshivah Kollel, how can I thank you enough for introducing me to the tapes of HaGaon Rabbi Avigdor Miller, *zt"l*? You have a great share in this book.

Many thanks to my good friend, Rabbi Meir Birnbaum, *mashgiach* of Yeshivah Gedolah of Bayonne, author of the *sefarim* on *tefillah* called *Kuntres Avodas Ha-Tefillah*, who has constantly spurred me on to make sure that I finish this book.

To Rabbi and Mrs. Yaakov Goldwag, you got the "ball rolling" by transcribing the material for this book, which originally was on tape. Your initial enthusiasm for the need for such a book was also a big *chizuk* for me.

Reb Avi Shulman, of Torah U'mesorah, also encouraged me to write a sefer on *emunah*.

A special thanks to Rav Nissan Schwartz of Lakewood, N.J., for his constant *chizuk* and encouragement, and for his helping me raise funds to help pay the costs of editing this book.

A special thanks to Reb Yisroel Segal and his brother, Reb Mordechai, who were especially helpful in the initial stages of the writing of this book.

A special thanks to Michael Danzinger for his last-minute help in proofreading this book.

To my father, *z"l*, and to my mother, to my aunt and uncle, Mr. and Mrs. Yidel Friedman, my uncle Mr. Benny Papernik, my aunt and uncle, Mr. and Mrs. Naftali Waldman, my aunt Mrs. Chany Liberman, my cousins Mr. and Mrs. Avi Meyer, and to my cousin Naomi Friedman, my greatest thanks for your substantial financial help in the publishing of this book.

To the great people at Feldheim Publishers: What can I say about the great *chizuk* you gave me when you agreed to publish my book. I am grateful for the merit of having my book published by such a renowned publisher.

Acharon acharon chaviv — I would like to take this opportunity to express my deep appreciation to my wife Shayna Rochel, *shetichya*, for the *chizuk* that she gave me throughout the writing of this book. There were many times that this project might have fallen through the cracks if not for her constant encouragement. May God grant her much *nachas* from me and all our children.

I ask forgiveness from anyone I may have left out, and from anyone that I may not have thanked properly.

May we all merit to quickly see the time when the world will be filled with the knowledge of God and His Torah.

Shmuel Waldman
Cheshvan 5762
November 2001

1

Compelling Evidence

—— of a ——

CREATOR

WHEN ONE CONTEMPLATES THE ASTONISHING depth of design in the natural world, from molecules to plants, to animals, to humans — the world screams: "Something Intelligent created me! I didn't just pop into existence randomly!"

In this chapter we will show how science can be a wonderful lens for viewing the Divine wisdom and architecture found in nature. Science, when *used properly*, will help us focus on the fact that this world could not possibly have come about by mere random factors. This world demonstrates a complex design — and where there is complex design, a Designer exists. Examining nature with all of its wonders is considered by many to be the fastest, easiest, and best way to recognize God. Studying nature with the use of some basic scientific texts will supply us with abundant evidence that this world *must* have a Creator. And believe it or not, many scientists have come to this conclusion too!

Let us then begin with something so complex, and yet so very simple, that we tend to overlook its great message.

Let us begin by studying a simple orange.

THE ORANGE

The simple orange proves beyond a reasonable doubt that God exists. By the time we finish analyzing the orange tree, you will feel so convinced of God's existence that you will start to look around for Him so that you can say hello to Him.

Let's start by considering the actual trunk and branches of the orange tree. (Of course, the following not only applies to the orange tree, but to other trees as well.) They're wood. But where did the wood come from?! From the water? Obviously not. Wood and water are two entirely different substances. Did the wood come from the sunlight, then? Of course not. How about from the orange pit? That can't be either, since the pit is also not made of wood. So it must have come from the earth, right? Well, besides the fact that wood is not the same material as earth, there's another problem with this assumption. Let's do a little experiment. Say you placed an orange pit in 500 pounds of earth and waited fifteen years or so for a well-developed orange tree to grow. If you measured the dirt surrounding the tree fifteen years later, guess how many pounds of earth there would be? That's right, about 500 pounds.

Where, then, did this ton or so of wood come from? How did this complex combination come about? How did the microorganisms, which live in the earth, know how to combine completely unrelated materials into a "live" tree? The human equivalent would be an incredibly huge factory with dozens of highly trained and skilled technicians (the microorganisms) working to create a car using only some paper, rubber bands, and paper clips (the water, sunlight, and pit). It's highly unlikely that they would succeed no matter what machinery or chemicals they would use. Yet, without any tools or machinery, the little orange pit produces a large tree with hundreds of fruits on it. Fruits that even have the ability to reproduce themselves! Somehow, one pit turns into thousands. It's truly amazing. It's a miniature factory, yet it has no foreman, no blueprints, no electricity, and still it works!

Let's examine this "accident" a little further.

Imagine that a friendly alien from outer space landed on earth and you were chosen to be the one to show him around our planet. You assume that he doesn't know much about this planet because our world is completely different from his. The first thing you decide to show him is our orange tree. You begin by informing the alien that the tree developed from nothing more than water, soil, an orange pit, sunlight, and time — and you show him a sample of water, an orange pit, and soil.

"You don't expect me to believe," he says, "that this big tree here came about from those things, do you?"

"What's so hard to believe?" you ask.

"For starters, where did all the wood come from?"

"From all the elements in the ground, in combination with sunlight, and water which fell from the sky, water we earthlings call rain."

"But how can that happen if they are made up of such completely different elements?"

"It's called nature."

"Nature?" the alien asks. "Is that the whole explanation?" As an average American with something like fifteen years of schooling behind you, you confidently nod your head yes.

The visitor continues. "And those green things (the leaves) — where did they come from? Who attached them to the tree?"

"No one attached them. They grew out of the branch."

"That's amazing. How can anything come out of something solid?"

"It's not so amazing."

"What do you mean? Sure it's amazing!"

"No, it's not."

"Why not?"

"It just isn't, that's why. Anyway, if you think that that's amazing, let me tell you a real shocker. All human beings on this planet are alive because of those leaves."

"Are you serious?"

"Yes. You see, there's this process called photosynthesis. It works as follows: Water gets sopped up by the tree roots and is then sent up to its highest leaves."

"How can the water get all the way to the top? I thought this planet has gravity pulling things down."

"What do you mean?"

"I mean, things don't just float up by themselves. Getting that water to the upper leaves defies gravity, so how does it get there?"

"Don't ask such ridiculous questions. It will only confuse the matter. Somehow the water gets to the top. That's all. Anyway, back to photosynthesis. You see, there's a green pigment called chlorophyll in the leaves."

"Chlorophyll?"

"Yes, and it works as follows. When the light of the sun strikes the leaf some of the sun's energy is absorbed in the chlorophyll. The chlorophyll then "somehow" causes a chemical reaction to take place which splits the water found in the leaf (you know, the water that somehow rose from the roots of the tree, to its tip-top leaves) into hydrogen and oxygen. (A water molecule has two molecules of hydrogen and one molecule of oxygen.) The oxygen goes out of the leaf through pores, special holes, on the bottom of the leaf, and guess who happens to need this oxygen? Human beings and animals. Lucky, aren't we? Without oxygen we couldn't breathe. So you see, leaves are not so simple. They just happen to produce the gas that sustains all human and animal life."

"Who designed such a wonderful system?" the alien asks.

"Design? It's a lucky accident. That's what Science teaches us."

"An accident? That's impossible to believe."

"Impossible? What's so impossible to believe?"

"You're not amazed by the whole process?"

"Nah."

"What happens to the other molecules?" the alien then asks.

"The hydrogen?"

"Yeah."

"Well, the hydrogen is combined chemically with carbon dioxide."

"What is carbon dioxide?"

"It's also a gas."

"And where does it come from?"

"It comes basically from humans and animals. You see, after we inhale oxygen it gets processed by the body, and then is exhaled as a waste product in the form of carbon dioxide. Trees, on the other hand, just "happen" to need carbon dioxide. This carbon dioxide is taken in by the pores in the leaves. Of course, the carbon dioxide by itself is useless, but when the chlorophyll stimulates the carbon dioxide to combine with the hydrogen, a simple sugar is produced. Don't ask me how that happens, but somehow carbon dioxide and hydrogen are turned into a sugar which dissolves in water and then is transported throughout the tree — and that is what gives the tree the energy it needs to continue to grow. Then the plant takes this simple sugar and converts it into more complex sugars and starches, which when eaten, are such an important part of a human's diet."

"You mean this gas, which is a waste product of human beings and animals, is vitally important for trees to help them grow?"

"Yes."

"And in turn, the tree is vitally important to human beings and animals in order to enable them to breathe and to supply them with food?"

"Yes."

"And you say this awesome cycle happened by accident?"

"Yes. Why do you seem so amazed?"

"Why? Because according to what you just said it comes out as follows: If you didn't have the sun, photosynthesis would never be able to work. And if you didn't have photosynthesis, animal life couldn't exist. And if you didn't have animal life, trees couldn't exist. For all of these lucky, unrelated events to work together in such harmony, thereby enabling life on this planet to exist — it's anything but an accident!"

"Yeah, I guess you're right. And thank God for it, too." The alien looks at you in a funny way, so you say, "Maybe photosynthesis was the wrong place for us to start. Why don't you ask me a different question?"

"Okay," the alien says, looking over the tree. "What are those round green things hanging up there?"

"They're called oranges. They're an example of the food we humans eat."

"If they're called 'oranges,' why are they green?"

"All fruits and vegetables of the entire planet start off green."

"You mean they don't stay green? They change color?!"

"Yeah, what's so incredible?"

"Well I don't know how things are here, but where I come from — let's say you have a room that's green. Unless someone decides to paint it, the room is going to stay green. And yet here you have this green fruit and without anyone painting it you are telling me that it's going to turn orange?"

THE BANANA

"Well, if you put it like that it does sound a little miraculous. But that's because you're naive. Let me educate you a little and you will learn to take it for granted, just like me. You see, all unripe fruits are green. Here's a banana, for instance." You hand the alien a dark green cluster of bananas. "Try pulling one banana off the bunch."

"Hmm. It's a little difficult."

"Right. Let me help you." Both of you struggle together for a moment and manage to pull one off. "Now," you say, "try to peel it."

"It doesn't go," he says.

"Here, take this sharp knife," you say. "Cut off the top, and then try peeling off the peel."

He tries. "It won't go," he finally says. "The peel is almost as if it's stuck to the banana . . . Oh, wait, I think I have it now." Finally, he pulls off the peel. "Is this inside part the stuff you eat?"

he asks.

"Yes," you reply. The alien begins to put it in his mouth, but before doing so, you grab it from him. "Don't do that! The banana is still very hard and it doesn't taste good yet!"

"I don't mind. I just want to know what it tastes like."

"No, you don't understand. If your digestive system is anything like ours, then you can get a stomachache if you eat it."

"A stomachache? Thanks for telling me. But answer me this: Why would humans ever have these things around the house if you can't eat them?"

"That's what I've been trying to tell you — these bananas are in a stage called 'unripe.' Many people buy them in the unripe stage and then store them in the house for a few days or more."

"What happens then?" the visitor asks.

"They turn yellow."

"Yellow?! How do they turn yellow?"

"They just change colors, like the orange changes colors. That's just the way it goes. Anyway, I see you're anxious to taste one. Here's a bunch that's ripe, so they're edible."

The visitor looks at the bunch and gingerly pulls off one banana. "Hey, that was easy," he says.

"Yes, that's what happens when the banana changes from green to yellow."

"You mean, it not only changes colors, but quality too? When it's not ripe it's almost impossible to peel, but when it ripens it becomes easy to peel?"

"Yes, and now try tasting it."

"I don't want a stomachache," he says.

"It's ripe now. It won't upset your stomach. Go ahead, give it a taste."

The visitor from outer space takes a cautious bite. "Oh, what a sweet, soft, delicious taste."

"And don't forget nutritious."

"Incredible. Miraculous."

"It's incredible and miraculous only the first time you see it. Once you have it all the time it's not so incredible."

"I don't care how many times you've seen it. How can you say that it's not incredible? It's obvious that this banana — this plant life that has no brains — "somehow" knows that you humans exist, and it knows how you humans work too."

"What do you mean?" you ask.

"The banana changed colors when it turned ripe. It must have known that you humans have eyes that are capable of detecting color changes. Also, it became easier to detach from the bunch and peel, so it must have known that you have hands. Furthermore, it knows you have a tongue and that you like sweet things, because somehow it changed its taste in order to suite your taste buds. And even beyond that, the banana must have known that you have a stomach, and what upsets your stomach, and it actually cares about you, so that when it wasn't ripe it made itself difficult and untasty to eat. It's just incredible!"

"I think you are taking this a little too far."

"Not at all. Think about it. You told me that green is the universal symbol for being unripe. So first of all, the green color helps camouflage it by allowing the unripe fruit to blend in with the green leaves so that you shouldn't be interested in taking it yet. After all, it's not ripe yet. But as soon as it starts turning ripe, its color changes to help you see it better, and its texture, taste, and nutritional value have also changed, and now they are perfectly suited for human consumption. Whoever created the banana obviously also had in mind the human beings that would be eating them."

"You're mistaken, my friend. It only seems like someone created it, but I assure you it was all a lucky accident. Anyway, I see you're having problems with the banana, so let's go back to the orange. Let's take a ripe one off the tree and open it up."

"Okay."

You open the orange.

"Hey! What's all that orange water spilling out?"

"It's called orange juice."

He takes a closer look at it.

"Fascinating."

"What's so fascinating?"

"First of all, how did the rainwater turn into a colored, sweet tasting, nutritional drink? Second of all, who sat down to individually wrap each tiny drop of orange juice?"

"What are you talking about?" you ask.

"Ah, you've been eating oranges since you're a little kid, so you're too familiar with them to realize how amazing they are. Why don't you look a little closer. Look how each slice of this orange has hundreds of drops of orange juice, and each separate drop is remarkably contained in its own special wrapper. It must have taken ages to make just one orange, and look how neatly packed all these wrapped-up drops are. Who spent the time to pack them so neatly? It must have cost a fortune to produce a single orange."

"I don't know what you're talking about. It doesn't cost a fortune. No one wrapped the drops. They wrap themselves, dumbbell. I told you already, it's all an accident. An orange tree, with its oranges and leaves, all came about by itself. You can ask any scientist or professor if you don't believe me."

"Look, I don't know who these scientists or professors are, but if they say that an orange tree is the result of an accident, I really can't say I agree with them. I wonder if some of them may have had ulterior motives which led them to make such statements."[1]

At this juncture, we must point out that any sarcastic com-

---

1. As one scientist said, and he was expressing the feelings of many of his contemporaries, "I had motives for not wanting the world to have meaning; consequently assumed that it had none, and was able without any difficulty to find satisfying reasons for this assumption. . . . For myself, as no doubt, for most of my contemporaries, the philosophy of meaninglessness was essentially an instrument of liberation. The liberation we desired was simultaneous liberation from a certain political and economic system, and liberation from a certain system of morality. We objected to the morality because it interfered with our sexual freedom." (REPORT, June 1966. "Confession of Professed Atheist," A. Huxley)

ments that we may make about the theory of evolution, isn't in any way or form meant to minimize the great importance of science, and what scientists have done for the betterment of mankind. Nor do we wish to cast doubts with regard to the honesty of most scientists. However, we will demonstrate with the words of evolutionists themselves, that they themselves have serious doubts that our world came about by accidents caused by *macro*evolutionary processes. A significant minority of first-rate biologists have never been able to bring themselves to accept the validity of Darwinian claims because of the great complexity and ingenuity that they found in nature.[2] This is a fact which many otherwise educated college graduates do not know. [See Appendix G of this book, where we write about the problems of the theory of evolution, we explain at length the difference between *micro*evolution and *macro*evolution. In a nutshell the difference is as follows: Microevolution is the process of very small mutational, evolutionary changes that take place *within* each individual specie. Microevolution is a recognized fact that no one can deny. Macroevolution describes the process where, supposedly, vast changes have taken place, bringing about the transformation of one specie into an *entirely different* specie, all through random (accidental) mutations. It is macroevolution that has very serious scientific problems, and we shall bring quotations from many scientists who express their grave doubts as to whether it ever could have taken place. Also, the stupendous change from inorganic (dead) matter, into organic (live) matter, is so vast that it too has many scientists doubting the ability of any random process of evolution to be able to bring about such changes.] In fact, Darwin himself admitted that "The eye, to this day, gives me a cold shudder," being that it's an "organ of extreme perfection."[3]

---

2. Michael Denton, *Evolution: A Theory in Crisis*, London: Burnett Books, 1985, pp. 326–29.

3. C. Darwin (1860), in a letter to Asa Gray, in F. Darwin, ed., *Life and Letters of Charles Darwin*, vol. 2, London: John Murray, 1883, p. 273.

We must also realize that lack of scientific discussion regarding the possibility of there being a Creator is not because of lack of evidence, because no matter how many questions will be brought up against evolution, and no matter how much evidence will be brought which clearly points to the existence of a Supreme Creator, science by its very definition cannot acknowledge it, since science only discusses and validates things which actually can be seen, studied, and examined. Again, we don't mean to negate science, or scientists, in any way, shape or form. In their private lives, many scientists do actually believe in a Creator. However, in order to help minimize any of our readership's prejudice to their belief in evolution, we have taken the liberty to give a little extra poke at this theory.

We resume the above dialogue.

"If the orange and banana are not enough evidence that a Higher Intelligence designed them, then I don't know what is. Hey, wait a second, I even have absolute proof to what I'm saying," the alien suddenly says.

"Absolute proof? What do you mean?"

"Yes. I happened to notice on the peel of the orange the name of the Higher Intelligence who created it."

"What do you mean?"

"The Being who created the orange left Its signature on each fruit."

"What name are you talking about?"

"Sunkist. The Holy Sunkist."

"You're naive, my alien friend. Sunkist is just the name of the company that owns the orange groves where these oranges grow."

"Hmm. Well, maybe the Designer's name is not Sunkist," the alien replies, "but He clearly left His signature on every orange. It's the most obvious thing in the world."

The orange and the banana are just small examples of the *nifla'os ha-Borei*, the "wonders of the Creator." Random accidents,

even if they ever were to combine to produce one positive outcome, which they haven't done yet, certainly could never produce such purposeful products. The orange reveals to us the
Higher Intelligence Who created them.

CARNIVOROUS PLANTS

Let's turn from oranges and bananas to another type of plant life.

One of the most amazing marvels of nature is the Venus' flytrap, a plant which eats insects. According to common scientific
theory today, the Venus' flytrap (and other carnivorous plants),
by a series of random accidents, not only developed the means of
catching insects, but also developed the digestive system necessary to digest the insect for its nutrients.

Think about this. Insects, in general, are very hard to catch,
especially flies. I have a hard time killing flies even with a fly
swatter. Yet, this "accident," the Venus' flytrap, is faster at catching flies than you and I, and does a great job of it. It just snaps its
mouth closed, and boom! Fly dinner.

How does it do it? First, let me describe the plant to you. [4]

Imagine a clam-like structure − which is green on the outside and red on the inside − with its mouth wide open. The upper and lower outer edges of the "mouth" are studded with soft,
thin, teeth-like protrusions. The teeth are designed in such a way
that when the mouth closes, the teeth interlock, like fingers of
one hand would interlock with fingers of the other hand. That's
how the outside of the Venus' flytrap looks.

The inside of this mouth is a red rose or pink color, a perfect
color to attract insects. Furthermore, the center of the mouth
emits a scent that attracts insects. Along the inside of this red,
fragrant center are tiny, sensitive hairs. They're called trigger
hairs. If an insect, or anything else for that matter, touches one of

---

4. Information for this section is taken from *ABC's of Nature*, Readers Digest
Press, 1984, pp. 116–17.

them, the mouth won't close. But, if two of them are touched, the plant quickly snaps shut and the fly is caught.

If that isn't amazing enough, the plant has digestive juices which can digest the insects. Now, you just can't digest insects with anything. You need the exact digestive juices, and the whole system has to be developed in a way that the plant can actually utilize the nutrients from the insect. (I know it doesn't sound too appetizing, but bear with me.)

Now, how could the Venus' flytrap have developed as it did just by chance? If any of its features were missing, it would have been unfit to survive. It couldn't have "evolved slowly." It needs all of its components together at one time for everything to function properly. It has to have the "teeth" to enable the plant to lock shut. It has to have the bright colors and the right scent to attract the flies. It has to have the trigger hairs and the spring mechanism that closes it up fast enough, and then, after all that, it has to have a fully developed, specialized digestive system. All of this had to come together at the same time or the whole plant could never function properly. How could all of these things have developed "randomly," yet at one time?

And the Venus' flytrap is not the only plant of its kind. In totally different and isolated sets of "happy accidents," several other carnivorous plants "developed" in other parts of the world. One of them is called the sundew plant.

The leaves of the sundew are covered with bright red or orange hairs. On the tip of each of these hairs is a shiny drop of glue which looks like honey. The insect is attracted to this "honey" and is caught by the glue. Then it starts struggling to get away, of course. The more it struggles, though, the more the surrounding hairs are stimulated. Eventually, these hairs curl over the trapped insect and soon the insect becomes fully coated with this glue-like "honey" until it suffocates.

Now, this "accident" obviously "knew" the following: It "knew" that there are insects in the world and it also "knew" that insects are attracted to honey. And, by the way, the honey isn't real honey. The plant doesn't create honey; it just creates something that looks like honey. And what's the function of this "honey"? It's glue! "By accident," it "knows" how to create a deceptive glue that looks like honey. (I don't know how to make Elmer's Glue. Do you? But, the sundew plant just happens to "know" how to create glue — a glue that just happens to look like honey which insects just happen to like. It's a smart accident! It's a genius!)

The sundew also "knew" that it had to suffocate the insect in order to kill it. So it "knew" that the insect breathes and is going to try to get away. After all that, again this plant — which the scientists admit did not evolve from the Venus' flytrap or vice versa — also happened to develop the exact enzymes necessary to digest insects.

There are more carnivorous plants. Another one is the pitcher plant, so called because it's shaped like a thin water pitcher. The lip of the pitcher, just outside on the top, is very colorful. (Again, somehow, by accident, it "knows" that insects are attracted to bright colors.) Along the edges, on top of the plant, are cells which secrete a very sweet nectar to attract insects. However that's not enough, since the digestive enzymes are on the bottom of the "pitcher," so we must come up with a system which will bring the insect to the bottom of the plant, and somehow make sure it stays there. So this "accident" had to develop a totally different system. This plant somehow "knew": (1) that there are insects, and (2) that insects have hooks and suction cups on their legs, which allow them to grip onto almost any surface and stand sideways, upside-down, or however they want. (I don't know about you, but I never knew about these hooks and suction cups until I read about it in a book on insects — yet this "dumb" plant "knew" it on its own.) Consequently, the pitcher plant developed (by "accident") wax secreting glands that secrete a very slippery wax to prevent the insect from "getting a grip" with its specially designed feet, causing it to slide down the walls of the plant.

So, here comes an insect, which lands on the pitcher plant (because it's attracted to its color and nectar). Then, ZOOM! — it slips on this super-slippery wax, which is on top of the sloping plant, and it slides down to the bottom of the plant, right down the chute, as if it were going down a slide. Of course, the insect doesn't give up yet. It tries to fly or crawl up the slippery walls — but lo and behold, this accident had the foresight to build a barricade. Toward the middle of the "pitcher" there's a barricade of stiff, *downward*-pointed, dagger-like hairs which line the narrow neck of the "pitcher," thereby thwarting the attempts of any insect to escape!

Eventually exhausted from its struggle to escape, the insect sinks to the bottom of the plant. The really bad news for the insect is that the pitcher plant, as its name suggests, is shaped like a water pitcher and, therefore, rainwater collects at the bottom of it, which conveniently drowns the exhausted insect. Of course, as I mentioned, this plant also "accidentally" has the proper enzymes with which to digest its victims.

Thus, this happy accident, also somehow "knew" so many things of its outside environment. It "knew" that there are insects, and it "knew" of their ability to escape. It "knew" that insects are expert climbers, except when it comes to waxy surfaces. It also somehow "knew" *how* to create a very slippery wax surface. It "knew" that insects can breathe, and that they can be drowned. It "knew" it had to make dagger-like hairs and to have those hairs face downward in order to form a bug barricade! And, of course, it also "knew" how to digest its catches.

All three of these carnivorous plants have completely different mechanisms for catching their prey. No one has the audacity to claim that one plant developed from the other, being that they are so different from each other. Three separate, awesome "accidents" indeed.

INSECTS

Until now, we have illustrated the incredible, undeniable genius behind the relatively simple life-forms of the plant kingdom. Now, let us discuss insects. [5] We'll start with the spider.[6]

First of all, it has been said that weavers have learned secrets of weaving from watching spiders spin their astonishingly intricate webs. (We have to take sewing courses to learn how to sew. But, a tiny spider — just out of its egg — can spin the most intricately designed webs; webs professional weavers can learn from!) How are webs made? Spiders "by accident" developed in themselves a factory which created the necessary mechanism to produce a miraculous liquid compound. This liquid is secreted from its abdomen through little organs called spinnerets. When this liquid comes in contact with air, it miraculously turns into the strongest known organic fiber in the world. What an accident! Furthermore, each spider is able to produce an unbelievable amount of webbing. One scientist wanted to see just how much web you could pull out of a spider, so he started pulling and pulling... and he kept pulling...ten feet...twenty feet...thirty feet...one hundred feet...two hundred feet...three hundred feet...four hundred feet! At 450 feet he got tired and stopped. (But the tiny spider was not tired. It was still going strong after 450 feet!)

THE HONEYBEE

Let's now turn to another common insect — the honeybee.[7] How do they make honey? First they gather nectar from flowers. Then the bee goes back to the beehive and passes the nectar, a thin fluid, to another bee. The nectar, in turn, is mixed with glandular secretions in the bee's mouth and loses some of its water. Then

---

5. *ABC's of Nature*, pp. 194–95 and from *The Fascinating World Of Spiders*, BARRONS, 1992.
6. Actually insects are categorized as those that have six legs, and spiders have eight legs, but for our purposes we'll classify them as insects.
7. *ABC's of Nature*, pp. 192–93.

the bee deposits this still watery honey into an open cell (a tiny storage area) within the wax comb, otherwise known as a honey-comb. For about three days, other bees have the job of fanning the open cells with their wings, evaporating the remaining water in the honey, and thereby finishing the transformation of nectar into honey. Then they fill the cell with an airtight plug of wax storing the honey until they need it for food. Who "taught" the bees how to transform nectar into honey?!

And where did they get the wax which encases and preserves the precious honey? Luckily, by accident too, of course, a honey-bee has built-in wax producing glands on its abdomen. In other words, it has a wax machine on its stomach! The bee removes the wax with its legs. Then it chews it to make it soft and pliable. Eventually it's shaped into the honeycomb.

And the bees are lucky they happen to know how to make and shape wax, because the wax is essential for the storing of their eggs which later hatch and develop slowly into adult bees. Also, survival of the bees' colony during the cold winter months depends on an ample supply of honey, which as we said is pre-served in these wax-encased cells. And so, by accident, every-thing developed exactly the way it needed to.

Another puzzler is that bees just happen to know how to shape the wax into small hexagonal (six-sided) cells, which is considered to be the most efficient way of maximizing the hive's limited space. Where did bees learn to make a honeycomb? Wow, so many happy accidents.

BIRDS AND THE MIRACLE
OF MIGRATION

There is much more to talk about in the insect world (such as the extraordinary transformation of an "ugly" caterpillar into a beautiful butterfly), but let's go on to the next level: the bird. We all know that birds migrate south during the winter. Nothing special, right?

Wrong.

Scientists have called it the "mystery of migration,"[8] and they are amazed at how every winter many species of birds take a tremendously long trip, year after year, and arrive at some faraway destination very often on the same date and at the same exact location as the previous year. Scientists want to know: How can birds travel thousands of miles without getting lost, and how can they be so accurate in pinpointing the exact location that they went to the year before? Well, here's one of the answers that they provide. They say that birds have the ability to direct themselves by reading the stars at night, and during the day, if it isn't too cloudy, they orient themselves via the location of the sun.

Now maybe you're not impressed by this answer, but imagine it's a clear night and you and I are traveling along the road. All of a sudden we realize we're lost. Lost? No problem. We can find our way home by looking at the stars, right? Well, I don't know about you, but to me there's the Big Dipper, the Little Dipper, and there's a plate, and there's a spoon, and there are some forks, etc. You get the idea. When it comes to star navigation, I don't know the first thing about it, and probably most of us don't either. Yet, here's this bird — this bird brain — and it knows how to read the stars (supposedly). And even if they know how to read the stars, which is highly doubtful, that would only help them get to a large general area, but it could never get them to any precise location. However, it is well-documented that many birds migrate year after year to the exact location as the year before. How can the sun or stars get them there? And how do they get around by day, if for days on end it is extremely cloudy? So, the scientists theorize, "There's evidence that certain species are tuned into the earth's magnetic field."

Science has taken millennia to develop very sophisticated technology to identify and measure the earth's magnetic field. Yet, according to this theory, long before satellites with their multimillion-dollar antennae orbited the earth, birds were

---

8. *ABC's of Nature*, pp. 166–67.

"tuned into the magnetic field."

Now, if you're a scientist and for some reason didn't like this explanation, there's another one. A much better one: Birds are somehow "tuned into polarized light." (I'm not even sure what polarized light is, but, according to these scientists, birds know all about it.) If you don't like the "polarized light theory," then maybe you'll like their next theory— that birds are "tuned into the earth's infrared rays." And if you didn't like those theories, there are still others. Maybe they are "tuned into slight changes in barometric pressure." Now, usually you need a sensitive device to measure barometric pressure. But birds, through their feathers I suppose, are able to pick up all these invisible signals.

I relay this information to you from an article called, "The Mystery of Migration."[9] At least they are honest enough to call it a mystery. In some places they even use the word miraculous: ". . . extraordinary sensitivity that makes migration all the more miraculous to instrument-dependent man." What is truly "mysterious" and "miraculous" is to conclude that birds came about by random accidents.

The anatomy of birds is also truly incredible.[10] First of all, their bones are different than the bones of any other species. All mammalian bones are solid, more or less. The bones of birds, however, are basically hollow. They only have extremely thin crossbeam-like structures which keep up the top and bottom of the bone. These "beams" keep the bone strong, yet very light since the bone itself is mostly hollow. If not for these specialized bones, birds could not fly; they would be too heavy. How these bones could have developed by accident is truly unexplainable. Who hollowed out their bones?

Another amazing feature of a bird is that it can, on the average, beat its wings several times a second, and yet it can fly for over ten hours straight, baking in the sun, without getting tired!

---

9. Ibid.
10. *ABC's of Nature*, pp. 208–11.

We'd collapse after twenty minutes, probably less. How do they manage that? By a unique process.

You see, when we humans breathe in, we inhale oxygenated air. When we breathe out, we exhale deoxygenated air. We cannot simultaneously be inhaling oxygenated air and exhaling deoxygenated air. That's why we fatigue easily when we exercise; while we exercise, our muscles need an increase of oxygen, but they can't get a continuous supply, since while exhaling there's a break in our intake of oxygen. However, when birds inhale, half the oxygen goes immediately into the lungs, like with humans, but miraculously a unique system "accidentally developed" whereby half the oxygen bypasses the lungs and goes into a series of air sacs which act as reserve air tanks. Then, somehow, when the bird exhales, it has an amazing system that sucks the extra air which is in this "reserve tank" straight into the breathing tubules of its lungs, which enables the bird to obtain oxygen during inhalation and exhalation! No mammal has such a system! Our blood and organs can't receive oxygen at the same time that we exhale deoxygenated air. But birds do. And they are "very lucky" for that, since if not for this "miraculous" system, they would be unable to fly for the hours and hours it takes to migrate over oceans in order to come to a warm climate. But because they have a built-in mechanism which keeps them supplied with a double dose of oxygen, they can flap their wings vigorously for all those hours and hours without getting fatigued.

The digestive system of birds also differs from that of mammals. The bird's digestive system is especially geared for the rapid processing of food, digesting the extra "baggage" very quickly, which also enables them to take very long flights. There is no other creature like this. Yet, Science wants us to believe it came about exclusively through a series of happy accidents.

BATS

Let me tell you about another amazing accident: the bat.[11] Do you know how blind bats get around? (Not all bats are blind, but many are.) Believe it or not, "by accident" they developed a radar system. (If you live in a dark cave long enough, perhaps you, too, will evolve your own radar.) A radar system, called echolocation, enables them to avoid obstacles, and it helps them locate food. High-pitched sounds emitted by an insect-eating bat (which humans can't hear), are sent out at a rate of *200 per second*; they hit the objects in front of the bat and then they bounce back to the bat. The bat's brain, with supersonic speed, is able to analyze these high-pitched sounds as they bounce back to it, and it can tell exactly where, and exactly what, that object is. All in about half a second!

Now, imagine a bat flies into a lecture hall and sends out its radar, which hits a tape recorder. The echo bounces back and the bat says to itself: "Oh, there's something there." Immediately, it nose-dives and attempts to take a big chunk out of the tape recorder. It would be in big trouble because it would break its teeth. But, don't worry. Built into the bat's brain, by accident of course, is the ability to tell by the way the radar echoes back to it exactly where and what that object is. Somehow it knows that a tape recorder is not a soft banana. (Bats like bananas.)

How an "accident" could develop such an amazing system is your guess as well as mine.

The fact that a radar system developed "by accident" in one species is really impossible according to naturalistic explanations. However, we find that whales also have the same type of system and whales are completely unrelated to bats, i.e., no one suggests that one evolved from the other. Imagine, twice this "accident" happened! And, believe it or not, there are even scientists who say that seals, which are a completely different species

---

11. *ABC's of Nature*, pp. 240–41.

from whales, also developed this complicated system by accident. How can this accident happen three times in three separate species?!

Obviously, there are so many mysteries and miracles in the plant and animal kingdoms it is presumptuous to stop here. However, this book is not meant to be an encyclopedia on these topics, so let's move onto the next level.

THE HUMAN BODY

Before we begin, since we will be discussing four or five aspects of the human body, I just want to put into proper perspective what is involved when we're talking about the awesome human body. As the editors of a book on the human body put it:

> The most incredible creation in the universe is you, with your fantastic senses and strengths, your ingenious defense systems, and mental capabilities so great you can never use them to the fullest. Your body is a structural masterpiece more amazing than science fiction.[12]

I'll give an example that will give us a little insight into the above statement. Let's contemplate the following. Imagine a person who is a very ambitious fellow. He likes money and he wants to make it really big, so he decides that he's going to buy out and take over the entire postal service of the United States of America. That means that besides buying the regular U.S. Postal, he is also going to take over Federal Express, UPS, Airborne Express, etc. (He's even going to take over the service called G.O.D., Guaranteed Overnight Delivery.) He figures that this should bring in a decent income.

However, just in case it doesn't work, he wants to have a back-up source of income so he decides to also take over the entire garbage pickup industry. He's going to pick up all the gar-

---

12. *ABC's of the Human Body*, Readers Digest Press, 1987, p. 5.

bage — everywhere, the residential garbage, the industrial garbage, etc. The entire garbage industry of the United States of
America — all fifty states — are under his control. Don't ask
how. Just use your imagination.

And to make things more interesting, he decides to take over
one more industry — every single supermarket in the entire
country: Pathmark, Shop Rite, Grand Union, Key Food, Met,
Waldbaums, etc.

He, and he alone, will run these three industries, coordinat-
ing everything. After all, he wouldn't want to leave such an ambitious project (with such potential financial rewards) in the
hands of anyone else.

Can you imagine what's going to happen next?

The next day, when you come home, the mailman delivers
you a package. You open the package and there's garbage in it.
When you go to the grocery store you find there's mail on the
shelves (and some garbage also). You go to throw out your garbage and last week's garbage is still there. The whole country is
in turmoil. The garbage is not being picked up, everyone is dying of starvation, and nobody is getting important mail. You get
the picture.

Now, how many people are there in the U.S.? Approximately
250 million. But that's nothing compared to the amount of cells
that you have in your body. A single adult human body consists
of some sixty trillion cells — that's a good 240,000 times more
than there are the number of people on our entire planet! (Assuming there are about 4.5 billion people on our planet.) And
every single one of our sixty trillion cells needs its specific diet of
nutrients delivered to it *many times* each day. Sometimes it needs
a little more of one food and sometimes a little less. It depends
on what you're doing at that time. So, if your bloodstream, the
delivery system of the body, would start making mistakes and
by accident deliver the wrong things to the wrong place — for
instance, if it were to deliver some calcium to your brain cells —
you'd be in big, big trouble. You don't want calcium in your
brain cells. You want them in your bones. In your teeth. Not in

your brain.

And not only does your bloodstream deliver the right material to the right cells, but it also simultaneously picks up any waste material that the cell may need to get rid of. Don't take my word for it, though. Let me quote from a scientific text:[13]

> Capillaries [a film-thin vascular connection between the arteries and the veins] are so small that red blood cells must squeeze through in a single file to get through. But in this second or so, while squeezing through, there's a whirlwind of activity. It is like unloading a delivery truck and then reloading it. [You unload the truck which was filled with the groceries and at the same time you reload it with the garbage that had to be picked up.]

Let me explain that. Mixed all together in your bloodstream are waste materials (garbage) and food. However, there is a slight problem: there are no garbage bags, and for that matter there aren't any cartons in which to keep the food, either. Yet, miracle of miracles, they don't get mixed up (even though they are actually mixed together), and they don't contaminate each other either (though they are traveling down the same "stream").

Continuing:

> The big thing to be unloaded, of course, is oxygen. Carbon dioxide, on the other hand, which accumulates from cellular combustion [i.e., the work that the cell does — cells are working!], is the main waste product [and needs to be] loaded into [the bloodstream].

So, again, it's like unloading a delivery truck with food (here being the oxygen), then reloading it with garbage (carbon dioxide). That's a part of the "whirlwind of activity" — this big exchange. But there is much more going on.

> The variety of other merchandise that is delivered to the tissues, is amazing. The shopping lists of individual tissue and organ cells

---

13. J.D. Ratcliff, *Your Body and How It Works*, Readers Digest Press/Delacorte Press, pp. 116–19.

are by no means the same. One cell will want a smidgen of cobalt;
others will call for [either] minerals, vitamins, hormones, glucose,
fats, amino acids, or [just] a simple drink of water. This process is
known as the "capillary exchange."

And all this takes place in a "second or so."

All these materials are floating around together in the bloodstream and the blood delivers exactly what you need, to exactly
the right place, at the right time. We have to thank God that
nothing goes wrong, day in and day out.

Just consider how "smart" your bloodstream is. Has the following ever happened to you? You go to a wedding with eight
people sitting at your table. The waiter comes over for the order,
and tells everyone that they have a choice of ordering either
chicken or meat. Not such a complicated menu, is it?

"All right," he says, "how many of you want chicken?" You
and some others raise your hand. "How many meat?" and the
rest raise their hands.

Later, he comes back and says, "Who ordered the chicken?
Who ordered the meat?" After a little arithmetic, he says, "I
guess I brought the wrong amount of chicken. I'll be right back.
Sorry."

Has that ever happened to you? It has happened to me. Now,
that was only one table with eight people. It wasn't so complicated. Imagine what would happen if he had to serve a table
with sixty trillion hungry guys! And what if instead of just
chicken and meat the menu consisted of nutrients A to Z! And
every single molecule of all these nutrients has to go to the right
place, at the right time, and in the exact amount — daily, and
there's no vacation. Seven days a week, 365 days a year. Winter,
spring, summer, fall. Sixty trillion customers; very demanding
customers with an exact order!

Sound unbelievable? Yes. But all this is accomplished by your
bloodstream, which delivers the exact nutrients to your body
cells even as you read this. And we really have to thank God that
it rarely, if ever, makes mistakes. How does the bloodstream
"know" what each cell needs? Can such a system develop "by

accident"? Such a complex system is simply awe-inspiring. It gives us but a glimpse of the Wisdom of our Creator.

Another example: the liver. The liver is not so large, weighing only three pounds or so, but it's very complex. It is a major organ that has an effect on almost every other part of the body. It provides fuel to the muscles. It helps process your food and helps you manufacture different vitamins. To appreciate it, imagine a large chemical company that has built a huge plant, acres in size, having in it all the correct machinery with different complex chemicals placed in enormous vats with tremendously hot fires underneath them. Such a vast complex would be needed just to be able to do the simpler chemical breakdowns that our liver does. However, no man-made plant could duplicate the more difficult chemical transformations that the liver accomplishes, because the greatest intellects in the world haven't yet figured out how to duplicate such complex reactions.[14]

The average liver produces over 1,000 enzymes which are necessary to process the many chemical conversions needed for nutrient utilization. Yet, the possibility of one enzyme developing accidentally is only a one in 10^{20} chance. This is comparable to having 100,000,000,000,000,000,000 black marbles mixed together with only one red marble and picking out the red marble in one try![15]

In the entire body we have thousands of enzymes which work together with the greatest cooperation and complexity, always producing very purposeful and beneficial chemical reactions. Yet, as another scientist said, [16] "The trouble is that there are about 2,000 enzymes, and the chance of obtaining them all in a random trial is only one part in $(10^{20})^{2000}$ or $10^{40,000}$, an outra-

14. *Your Body and How It Works*, pp. 155–61.

15. Lawrence Kelemen, *Permission to Believe*, Jerusalem: Targum/Feldheim Publishers, 1990, p. 58.

16. F. Hoyle and C. Wickramasinghe, *Evolution from Space*, J.M. Dent and Sons, 1981, p. 24.

geously small probability that could not be faced." Accidents indeed!

But now I really want to turn our attention away from minor "accidents" like enzymes, and direct it to the star of the show — the brain.

Imagine a tremendous skyscraper large enough to house every single telephone exchange of the tri-state area — New York, New Jersey, and Connecticut. And you put all those buildings, every single one of them, into this one enormous skyscraper. Of course, we'd end up with a skyscraper much larger than any in existence today. Can you imagine the network of phone wires crisscrossing all over the place?

Yet, your brain is even more complicated. It's equipped with electrically powered mechanisms for storing, retrieving, and processing information. No computer can replicate all of the brain's innumerable functions.[17] "And whereas a computer can only process information one piece at a time, the brain, with its trillions of cross-linked neural connections, simultaneously processes enormous amounts of information along millions of multidirectional pathways."[18] As we will see a little later, some scientists say that the brain "continuously handles 'traffic' that would swamp the world's telephone exchanges."[19]

Let's explain where some of this traffic comes from. Take the eye, for example. There are over 137 million nerve endings in your eyes! And all 137 million pick up messages that the brain has to process in order for you to decipher exactly what you are seeing; 137 million messages every second and the brain is able to process all of them! We take it for granted, but it's a miracle to top all miracles.[20]

And our ears contribute to the "traffic" as well. Your ears

---

17. *Your Body and How It Works*, pp. 13–20.
18. *ABC's of the Human Body*, p. 47.
19. *Your Body and How It Works*, p. 14.
20. Ibid., p. 33.

pick up sound waves through the tens of thousands of different nerve endings that are in then. These, too, are messages that your brain has to process every single second.[21]

In addition to basic information coming in through the eyes and ears (and the other sense organs), there are enormous amounts of information which the brain has to coordinate for our survival. Take, for instance, the "fight-or-flight" mechanism which is the body's instantaneous and automatic coordination of activity triggered when a person is faced with an imminent potential danger. It's called the fight-or-flight response because the body prepares to either fight what it perceives as an enemy or flee to safety.[22]

To explain this properly, imagine the following. You're walking down the street, minding your own business, completely oblivious to what's going on around you when all of a sudden, you hear a loud crack above you. A branch is falling. We all know what happens. In less than a split second, you raise your hands above your head to block the branch which is about to fall, and at the same time you also start to run from under that tree.

Let's pause here for a moment and analyze what's happened. You're daydreaming. You hear this crack. So what? So you heard a crack? What's the alarm? What are you getting so nervous about? Who said there is something wrong with hearing a crack? You hear many noises, and don't budge for them. And you weren't even listening. What happened here that made you put up your hands and flee from the "scene"?

The answer is that since you were a little kid, your brain has been filing away in your memory banks new experiences. A baby doesn't know what the crack of a tree branch is, so it won't pick up its hands when it hears a crack. (A baby will just give a little shudder, which comes about as a reflexive response.) You, as an adult, however, know what a tree is because this knowl-

---

21. Ibid., p.41.
22. *ABC's of the Human Body,* pp. 84–85.

edge, through experience, was filed into your memory bank. One day, you went outside, and, as little kids do, you bumped into a tree. You found out that trees were hard, and you noticed that they have branches, and as time went on you discovered that when branches break they make a cracking sound. You thereby deduced that a hard, heavy branch falling on you is probably very dangerous. You filed all this information away into your brain's memory compartment.

Then, one day, as you were walking, not paying attention to anything, you heard a loud crack and in less than a split second your brain's filing system was activated. "What's this loud noise? Is it a dangerous noise? Oh no, it's the sound of a branch cracking — a sound which is filed in the 'dangerous noises' compartment." This information was retrieved in less than a second.

Think for a moment how unbelievable that is. The fastest computer cannot react that quickly and efficiently. (And not only does your brain work incredibly fast, thank God that in a healthy person it never "goes down," either.)

Now, not only does your brain size up the situation instantaneously, it also just as quickly sends the correct messages to the exact muscles that are now needed. "Hey, this branch may come crashing down. You have to protect your head. Lift up your arms now to protect it." Your feet don't raise themselves over your head. Your hands do. Similarly, your hands don't start pumping to run away. Your feet do.

Your brain has everything on file, in exactly the right place, and in a split second sends the right messages to the right muscles. That's no small feat. No supercomputer works that fast, that efficiently, all the time. This is called the "fight-or-flight" response. And this explanation only illustrates the external aspects of the response. When we consider what takes place internally during that second or so, we see it's even more mind-boggling than what takes place externally.

For instance, when the danger is first perceived, many different hormones are immediately secreted, which, after some quick chain reactions, automatically cause your heart to pump much quicker. (Hearts just don't pump quickly when they want to. Hormones control the pace of your heartbeat. If the hormones aren't working correctly, you're in trouble.) Then, when your body needs it, the hypothalamus, a certain gland, secretes a substance called CRH, which causes the pituitary gland to secrete a burst of ACTH, which in turn stimulates the adrenal cortex to release certain hormones (the most important among those, cortisol) into the bloodstream. These hormones then go and mobilize the necessary supplies. They pull amino acids out of storage (i.e., from your muscles as well as other tissues) and take them to the liver where the amino acids are quickly converted into much needed glucose, a sugar. This sugar is then released into your blood, ready to give you an extraordinary burst of strength (because you may have to fight or flee now).

Whew!

And this all happens simultaneously, in a split second.

Furthermore, during the same second that you're registering what's going on, and at the exact same second that your muscles are moving, the blood vessels at the surface of your skin constrict (i.e., they get narrower). Why? Because your body is anticipating possible injury, and constriction of the blood vessels means reduced bleeding since it restricts the speed at which your blood can flow out of your body. At the same instant, the pupils in your eyes get larger in order to sharpen your vision. Similarly, your breathing tubes open wider for deeper breathing, enabling you to increase your intake of much-needed oxygen. Your digestion slows down, because digestion consumes a lot of your brain's "concentration," and uses up much of your precious blood supply. Every ounce of blood is now needed to bring an ample supply of oxygen to the muscles in order to be able to fight vigorously and long, if necessary. Moreover, your perspiration increases so that your body will stay cooler while your muscles are working so hard (which increases your body heat).

All this happens in a split second. And everything that happens here is absolutely necessary. Your body needs the maximum strength to be able to fight or flee. What amazing coordination. This is just a small part of the billions upon billions of different nerve connections being processed by the brain every second while you're awake. That is a mind-boggling amount of communication to handle every second. If things went haywire, you'd be bumping into the walls. Literally. We have to thank God from the bottom of our hearts that the brain is processing all these messages correctly, all the time, without any mistakes. Could this system develop "by a series of happy accidents"? According to the above, and the following paragraph, [23] I think you will agree it's somewhat unlikely.

> In terms of complexity, an individual cell is nothing when compared with a system like the mammalian brain. The human brain consists of about ten thousand million nerve cells. Each nerve cell puts out between ten thousand and one hundred thousand connecting fibers by which it makes contact with other nerve cells in the brain. Altogether, the total number of connections in the human brain approaches 10^{15} or a thousand million million. Numbers in the order of 10^{15} are of course completely beyond comprehension. Imagine an area about half the size of the USA (one million square miles) covered with a forest of trees containing ten thousand trees per square mile. If each tree contained one hundred thousand leaves, the total number of leaves in the forest would be 10^{15}, equivalent to the number of connections in the human brain! Despite the enormity of the number of connections, the ramifying forest of fibers is not a chaotic random tangle but a highly organized network in which a high proportion of the fibers are unique adaptive communication channels following their own specially ordained pathway through the brain. Even if only one hundredth of the connections in the brain were specifically organized, this would still represent a system containing a much greater number of specific connections than in the entire communications network on Earth.

---

23. *Evolution: A Theory in Crisis*, p. 330.

Believe it or not, God intended to make the world in a way that one can see Him if one would just take the time to look for Him. As the verse states in *Koheles* 3:14, God created [the world in a way so that we can recognize him enough] that we should [be able to] fear Him.

SOME SIMPLE ARITHMETIC

I end this chapter with an important point. Mathematically speaking, what are the chances of a human being developing by accident? Now, I'm not talking about the chances that our entire, extremely complex world came into being by accident. I'm just talking about the chances that just one of the species of the world, the human being, could have developed by accident. Some scientists have calculated those chances. However, before I tell you how infinitesimally small the chances are, let me help you appreciate what this number is going to mean.

Scientists have estimated the number of electrons in the entire universe. It's got to be a very large number because we're talking about the entire universe, with all its solar systems, and galaxies, etc. (assuming a universe with a 5 billion light-year radius).[24]

Scientists estimate that the number of electrons in the universe is somewhere around ten to the eightieth power (10^{80}). Ten to the eightieth power means a one with eighty zeros after it. Let me bring that number home to you.

A one followed by three zeroes is one thousand. A one followed by six zeros one million. When we say ten to the sixth power (10^6), it is the same as saying one million. Ten to the ninth power (10^9) means one billion. Ten to the twelfth power (10^{12}) means one trillion. Ten to the fifteenth power (10^{15}) is one quadrillion. And so on.

---

24. *Scientific Creationism*, San Diego, California: CLP Publishers, 1974, pp. 60–61.

So, how many electrons are there in the universe? Ten to the eightieth power (10^{80}). That's a one with eighty zeros after it. Whew!

If the universe was 30 billion years old — although even scientists don't assume it to be that old — its age would be only 10^{18} seconds. That's a one with only eighteen zeroes after it. Ten to the eightieth power (10^{80}) is unimaginably larger. (By the way, ten to the one hundredth power (10^{100}) has a special name, it's called a googol. The dictionary says that a child coined that name. It's such an awesome and unimaginably huge number that normal human words are not enough to express it; we are reduced to describing it only in a child's terms — "goo-goo" and "ga-ga" — as we gawk at the indescribable enormity of such a number.) As you can see, then, the number 10^{80}, the amount of electrons in the universe, is a number which is practically impossible to conceive.

And, yet, that number is nothing compared to the chances of a human being developing randomly! What are those chances? Well, based in part on the complexity of the brain and other bodily systems that we touched upon above, and the rest of our complex body which we didn't discuss, some scientists estimate that it's ten to the one quadrillion, two hundred and fifty trillionth power! That's $10^{1,250,000,000,000}$.[25] That's not a chance of one out of one quadrillion. Oh, no. That would merely be a one followed by fifteen zeros. That's kid stuff. This number is a one with a quadrillion zeros after it! (In addition, for good measure, add in another 250 trillion zeros.) The odds of this happening by accident is about the same odds that one has of throwing ordinary dice and rolling a double six 100 trillion consecutive times![26] Highly unlikely, wouldn't you say? And that's the chance of just one human being developing by chance. As one

25. *Permission to Believe*, p. 61.
26. Ibid.

Nobel Prize-winning chemist-physicist said, [27] "The statistical probability that organic (live) structures and the most precisely harmonized reactions that typify living organisms could have been generated by accident is zero!" That is what these numbers mean — statistically speaking, there's zero chance of it ever happening.

And we didn't even discuss how infinitesimally small are the chances that all the other complex creatures and objects found in our world could have developed by accident, such as bats with radar, plants that trap and eat insects, spiders that spin webs, orange pits that make orange trees, etc.

Is it all an accident? You decide.

How great are Your works God, You make them all with wisdom, the world is full of Your possessions (*Tehillim* 102:24).

(Once again we strongly recommend that those who have been tainted by the theory of evolution should proceed to read Appendix G, where we show the side of evolution that you probably weren't told about when you were in school. We are quite sure that you will see that things aren't on the side of the evolutionists — as they themselves attest to.)

This chapter has dealt with what is called the "Teleological Proof," which shows the tremendous plan and purpose that is evident in all of the creatures that are found on our planet. It is widely considered the most effective way of showing that this world has a Creator. However, if the reader wishes to read a number of other convincing arguments that give additional evidence that there must be a Creator, I suggest reading *The Road Back: A Discovery of Judiasm*, by Mayer Schiller pp. 119–152 (Feldheim Publishers, 2001).

---

27. Ilya Prigogine, recipient of two Nobel Prizes in chemistry. See *Physics Today* 25, pp. 23–28.

2

The
Divine Origin
of the
TORAH

OKAY, NOW WE KNOW THERE is a Creator. The next question is how do we know that our Torah is Divine? How, for instance, do we know that Moshe did not make it up or that it wasn't written at some later date by a committee of very intelligent human beings? (Of course, even assuming you have no doubts about any of the above, it would be nice to have quick, surefire answers to help those who do have doubts.)

We're going to address the Divinity of Torah with several different types of arguments:

- The history of strict Jewish adherence to the Torah is explainable only as the by-product of some earth-shattering experience like the Exodus and the Revelation at Sinai
- Christianity's and Islam's claims to authenticity are based on belief in our Torah, thereby strengthening the authenticity of our Torah
- Internal evidence: How Torah laws reflect Divine underpinnings
- Internal evidence: The Divine wisdom of the Torah
- Internal evidence: The unusual, truthful way that the Torah speaks negatively about its greatest leaders
- Through archaeological findings

48

THE PHONE CALL

"Sh, Sh, Sh...Shi...Shimon."

"What?"

"You...You have a phone call."

"Why are you so nervous? And why do you look so pale? Is everything okay?"

"Everything's okay. It's just...It's just..."

"What?"

"I don't know. It's strange. G...g...go answer the phone."

Shimon runs to the phone and hears a very deep, haunting voice say, "Shimon...Shimon...this is the Creator." He wonders if perhaps it's April Fool's Day. He looks at his calendar. No, it's not April Fool's Day. So what's going on, he wonders?

Right away Shimon tries to figure out which one of his friends is the practical joker. Whoever it is, he certainly sounds very convincing. "Yes," Shimon says. "What do you want?"

"I have a very important mission for you. But first I want to prove to you that I am Who I say I am. Therefore, at noon tomorrow make sure you are at the deserted road outside of town. Be there and we'll talk further."

"Who is this?" Shimon says. But the phone line goes dead.

Not knowing what else to do, Shimon goes to the deserted road outside of town the next day. And, sure enough, there's a phone booth there. Suddenly, the phone rings. It's the exact time the voice said it would call. Shimon picks up the phone and hears that very haunting, powerful, booming voice again, which tells him, "I have an important mission for you, but first I have to make it clear to you that I'm truly the Creator of the entire universe. Once you believe that, I'll be able to convey to you your mission."

There's a pause. And then: "In two minutes from now, all of a sudden, out of the clear blue sky, a terrible thunder and lightning storm will occur. A fire will blaze, burning all the way up to heaven. Then, the earth (and the heavens; see *Devarim* 4:35, Rashi and the Ba'al HaTurim) is going to split right in front of you.

And there are going to be tremendous, ear-shattering sounds. Then, finally, you will hear Me speaking to you from the sky in a loud voice. It'll be the same voice that you hear on this phone. And then you'll know that it's Me, the Creator." (See *Shemos* 19:16–20:18 and *Devarim* 4:35.)

Two minutes pass...and then, all of a sudden out of nowhere, the sky is streaked with lightning and it starts to thunder frighteningly. The earth splits open (and the heavens, too), fire starts shooting up to the sky, and Shimon hears that awesome, powerful voice once again. He faints. It's just too much for him.

Eventually, he revives, but he's all shaken up. Trembling from head to toe, he grabs the phone and the voice says, "Okay. That's enough for today. I want you to come here again tomorrow."

Shimon says, "Of...of...of course. Absolutely."

He can't believe it. It's the Creator. There's no question about it. It's as clear as can be.

He returns the next day. Sure enough, as Shimon picks up the phone, the same booming voice on the other end starts speaking to him. He tells Shimon to write down everything he is about to be told. Shimon takes out a pen and paper and does just that. This goes on for one day and then another, until finally after many days the entire message has been fully dictated.

The voice then says, "Shimon, this is a new religion. There's no religion like this in the world and there never will be. I want you to go now and study everything in this notebook. Review it over and over until you know it perfectly. Then, I want you to teach it to your family so that they too can live by these laws. Explain to them that there will be great reward for obeying these God-given laws, and harsh punishments if they disobey. Also, tell your children that in the future, if they see slackening off in keeping these laws, then they must implement all necessary safeguards that will ensure the strictest adherence to these laws throughout all future generations."

Now, if *we* got this phone call, would *we* obey? The earth split. The sky thundered. Lightning streaked across the clear blue sky. The fire reached the heavens, the voice came booming out from the skies — all according to the precise prediction of the voice on the other end. It was proven beyond a reasonable doubt that it was the Creator talking. I think you would agree that anyone who shared that experience would surely believe that the laws and lifestyle which were dictated to him by God were absolutely essential to follow. On the other hand, without such an experience, would we agree to take on the obligations of a new religion that had no precedent, especially if it was a very demanding one? And keep in mind that in the Torah it's mentioned over and over again that the keeping of the Torah and the belief that Moshe is the chosen prophet of God are all based on this colossal event. (see footnote 15). Now, if no one knew the first thing about this event, who in his right mind would keep a word of this difficult Torah if it was obviously based on open lies?

Specifically, would you go home now and make all your dishes kosher, learn how to slaughter animals in a very precise, complicated manner in order to be allowed to eat their meat, stop working on Shabbos (the Sabbath), observe *shemittah* (the Sabbatical year) and *taharas ha-mishpachah* (the family purity laws)? Would you diligently strive to guard your tongue from speaking slander, be painfully honest in business, remove all your idols (idols were *the* big thing in those days), refrain from charging interest, never wear *sha'atnez* (a mixture of wool and linen), keep the laws of *tumah and taharah* (ritual purity), give *terumos* and *ma'asros* (types of tithes), bring sin-offerings, put on *tzitzis* and *tefillin*, put up a *sukkah*, keep Pesach (Passover), etc., etc., etc.? Whew!

And, remember, a lot of these commandments cost money. (See the sub-chapter below entitled, "Money Mitzvos.") Furthermore, they encompass your whole life, every minute of your day. If you have any spare time, you must spend it learning the laws over and over again. No more wasting time. Who in his right mind would ever follow through on such an undertaking?

The answer is: no one.

No one, that is, except Shimon. Only someone who believed

in it like our friend Shimon after his phone call experience would take up such a demanding lifestyle.

For centuries and centuries, the Jewish people have been keeping the Torah in all its detail. (Only in this past century has the phenomenon that the majority of Jews do not keep the Torah arisen. Today's non-observant Jew is not the norm, though, given the overview of Jewish history.) Nowhere in the Torah is there any record of dissenters denying the authenticity of the Torah's claims.[1] Even a late outside source, the Jewish soldier-historian Josephus (who was the chronicler of the Romans' wars with the Jews), wrote the following in his time (the time of the Second Temple): "Even now, there is no one of the Hebrews who does not act as if Moshe was present now" (*Antiquities* III:XV, 3). "For it is no new thing for our captives...to be seen to endure racks and deaths of all kinds, that they may not be obliged to say one word against our laws and the records that contain them; whereas there are none at all among the Greeks who would undergo the least harm on that account" (*Contra Apion* I, 8). "But, we, on the contrary, suppose it to be our only wisdom and virtue to admit no actions nor supposals that are contrary to our original laws" (*Contra Apion* II, 21).

Jews have always kept the Torah with a tenacity and deep faith that defies rationality. Where did this incredible faith come from? Could such conviction have started from a fairy tale, from a man-made Torah? The most reasonable answer is that there had to be a tremendous "hook-up" where everyone — not just one Shimon, but the whole nation — got a "phone call" from God, all at one time. Jews took on the awesome yoke of the Torah because: "You were shown to know that Hashem, He is the

---

1. Of course, the Torah does record the rebellion of Korach (*Bemidbar* 16). However, this only proves the point further, because Korach only challenged why Moshe appointed Elitzafen ben Uziel as the head of the family of Kehus, since he felt he himself was more deserving. Moreover, Korach never challenged the truth of Moshe being the leader of the Jews at Sinai.

Lord, there is none else" (*Devarim* 4:35). Each Jew was *shown* — just as Shimon was shown; they were convinced at least as much as our Shimon was. Otherwise, it would be inconceivable how such a demanding religion could have begun in the first place. (Further on, we will discuss how logic dictates that if God wanted to bring a true, verifiable religion to this world, then He would only have started this religion with a large number of people around, thereby enabling us to verify its authenticity. Based on this, we will later discuss the obvious fallacies of religions that started based on private one-man prophesies.)

The Revelation at Sinai is the single most important event in all history. A whole nation heard the Divine word, which thereby also verified, without the slightest doubt, an immensely important article of our faith, that there is prophesy. Yes, God does speak to humans, and God did indeed reveal His will to humans. An important event indeed. This is the explanation for the tenacity of the Jewish people's stubborn preservation of their faith throughout the centuries.

NON-JEWISH SOURCES: CHRISTIANITY AND ISLAM

Let's not be naive, however. What about Christianity and Islam, you ask? Don't hundreds of millions of people believe in their claims? And if religions like Christianity and Islam could get started, maybe Judaism could have, too? That's a good question; however, once we examine the origins of these religions, we will be more convinced of the authenticity of the Torah because it will become obvious how a man-made religion differs from a Divinely started one. Let's begin, then, by briefly explaining what Christianity is and how it came about. (Note: The author never went through the New Testament, as per the ruling of Maimonides in the *Laws of Avodah Zarah*, Chapter 2:1-3. I'm just bringing verses that Rabbi A. Miller, *zt"l*, brings in his books. For much more detail about the fallacies of Christianity and the Islamic religion, I recommend that you read Rabbi Miller's books, one called *Sing You Righteous*, paragraphs 52-69, and the other called *Awake My Glory*, Chapter 6. He received permission from great rabbis of the previous generation to read through the New Testament and the Koran for the purpose of showing their fallacies. I also read a little from the book *You Take J, I'll Take God: How to Refute Christian Missionaries*, by S. Levine. In *A History of the Jews* (HarperCollins Publications, 1987), by Paul Johnson, who is a recognized historian, I read pp. 124–133, which deals with the "birth" of Christianity from Judaism, and pp. 166–68, which briefly discusses how the Islamic religion also came about through the direct influence of the Jewish people.)

According to the Christian "Scriptures,"[2] the founder of Christianity never claimed to be God, or anything similar. He himself basically kept the Written Law, but was delinquent in fulfilling the Oral Law. It is openly written in the New Testament (*Matthew* 5:17–18) that he had no intention of abolishing a single law of the Toràh. He kept Passover (Ibid. 26:17), made a blessing over bread (Ibid. 26:26), etc. However, the main difference was his claim that the meticulous keeping of the laws of the Torah wasn't so important. If the keeping of a certain law would impede rather than assist you on your road to God, then you didn't need to do it. (In other words, instead of being submissive to God's Torah, and working on overcoming one's desires and one's bad character traits in order to fulfill God's will, he said to forget about it.) He taught that the main point of the Torah is its ethical teachings and not its intricate laws. His audience consisted mainly of ignorant Jews who were looking for an easy way out of fulfilling their obligations towards God. He also privately professed to his disciples that he was the Messiah. His ignorant Jewish followers — and he did not have too many of them— all

---

2. In a book by J. McDowell, called *Evidence That Demands a Verdict*, Here's Life Pub. Bernardino, CA 1979, p. 44, the author quotes others that tell of some 200,000 variations of the New Testament's text, representing 10,000 different places, ... at least 400 of these inaccuracies cause actual doubt about the textual meaning, and at least 50 of them are variations of great significance.

continued to basically keep the Torah, even after his death. (Most of his generation did not believe in him; and the Jewish Sages ignored him, which is why he constantly cursed them. When those who doubted his claims requested a "sign" to verify his truthfulness, he evaded them [*Matthew* 12:39].)

It wasn't until well after his death that another Jew — originally called Shaul and later called Paul — created Christianity, as it has come to be known. Paul's Christianity first became popular only when persecutions against the Jews reached a height. Followers of the early Christian sect, who were mostly Jews, started to disclaim their Jewish identity in order to escape persecution. Many Jews were "looking" for a way to remain "good" Jews, and still be able to abandon the ancient laws of Moshe, which had become so difficult to keep in their modern society. So they gladly embraced the teachings of Christianity. (Christianity didn't start with its founder. He was what we would call today a Conservative Jew. In fact he was quite a learned man, which is what gave him the slightest credibility.) Paul, however, was unsuccessful with gaining a following among his own people, so he turned to the gentiles.

Now, the gentiles of those days were idol worshipers. They projected their own human and immoral character traits onto their gods. Many gentiles were sick of this and were looking for something better. The gentiles of those days lived in very close proximity to the Jews, and they wanted a form of religion similar to what the Jews had, minus most of the difficult laws. Paul preached ethical monotheism, which is the Jewish way of life, but without the difficult laws. It was an idea whose time had come, so it spread quickly among the gentiles. This explains why originally when Paul first came to the gentiles, he met with failure, because the gentiles thought that to be a "Jewish" Christian you had to be circumcised and keep other Jewish laws. Paul was clever, though, and a good recruiter. He said, "To Jews I become a Jew in order to gain Jews...to those outside Torah, I am outside Torah in order to gain them" (I *Corinthians* 9). And so, (in *Acts* 15) Paul claimed a (private) prophesy where God officially abolished the need to circumcise, and God officially abolished the necessity of keeping the Torah laws. This finally brought in many customers. Similarly, many of the Christian holidays are based on pagan holidays, as are their rituals based on pagan rituals. Paul stole stories and rituals from the myths of his neighborhood gentile pagans[3] and ascribed them to his "Messiah" in order to make his religion more familiar and palatable to his new gentile patrons.

There is much more to be said about the fabricated religion of Paul. Thomas Jefferson called Paul "the first corrupter of the doctrines" (*The Mississippi Valley Historical Review*, Vol. XXX, No. 2, Sept. 1943). In essence, it was Paul who made the Christian "Messiah" into a god. And yet, despite that, Paul, and the new religion which today the world calls Christianity, in essence accepted the authenticity of our Torah. We'll soon see why he had to. But first we must know that it's a fact that the Christians and Moslems use the *Five Books of Moses* for most of the foundation of their religions. For instance, the belief that there is a God, that He controls the world, that there is reward and punishment, the phenomenon of prophesy, etc., are all taken from our Torah. The concept of prophesy is especially important to them since both religions claim that they, too, have prophets. And what do you think is the source which verifies that the Creator speaks directly to humans, telling them exactly what He wants done? Both religions point to our Torah, which points to Moshe as the one to whom God was speaking at Sinai. They point to Moshe, the

---

3. In a famous book on pagan rituals, *The Golden Bough* (Chapter 34; abridged), there is a discussion about a god called Attis which was worshiped at the time in nearby Western Asia. It's uncanny how the stories about Attis, and all the rituals around it, are almost identical to the stories that Paul made up about the already dead founder of Christianity. They're a little *too similar* to be considered a mere coincidence. See the book called *You Take J, I'll Take God: How to Refute Christian Missionaries*, by S. Levine, 1990, pp. 39–41; HaMoroh Press, PO Box 48862, Los Angeles, California 90048.

prophet of all prophets, about whom it states: "And there never again would arise a prophet in Israel like Moshe, whom the Lord spoke to face to face" (*Devarim* 34:10). And, whether they like it or not, they *must* turn to our Torah, since it's the only source that verifies the existence of such an unlikely thing as prophesy. (I mean, who says that God is going to speak to us lowly earthlings?! Unless, of course, He has a message to convey to us.) So, Paul, who had to claim prophesy (a private one of course), had to agree to the truth of the Torah. And he did.

In the region of Medina, there were many Jewish settlements. Mohammed liked the Jewish ethical monotheism, so he adapted the Jewish teachings into Arabic. At first Mohammed "officially" accepted the Jewish God and their prophets, and Jewish dietary and ritual purity laws, hoping to get the Jews to accept his "new Torah," the Koran. However, when Mohammed saw that the Jews wouldn't accept his arbitrarily contrived Arab version of Judaism, he turned his religion into a completely separate one. He therefore changed the "day of rest" to Friday, he instituted that prayers should be directed to Mecca and not to Jerusalem anymore, and he abolished most of the strict dietary laws. These changes caused a permanent division between the Arabs and the Jews. Soon afterwards the Arabs embarked on a mission to carry out forced conversions, and they were quite successful at it. Hence, Islam.[4]

Now, when Mohammed founded Islam, he also needed to claim belief in the Torah for at least three reasons:

- As stated, he also wished to claim prophesy
- He claimed that the Arabs, as descendants of Avraham's son Yishmael, were the true Chosen people
- He wanted to adapt the laws of the Torah in such a way that they would fit in better with the lifestyle that his fel-

---

4. Much of the information brought here is from Paul Johnson's book, *A History of the Jews* (New York: HarperCollins, 1987), pp. 166–68.

low Arabs were already used to

Mohammed claimed that he received a prophesy (a private one, of course), that the Moslems are the real chosen people, and that a new set of laws were given to him. Mohammed claimed that since Avraham was chosen by God — as stated in our Torah — Avraham's children are chosen too. He claimed, therefore, that although the Torah says openly to Avraham, "For *only* through Yitzchak will your offspring be considered yours" (*Bereshis* 21:12), the truth would now be told: Really it was the other child of Avraham, Yishmael, who was chosen, and it was the Jews who doctored up the Torah and put the name of Yitzchak there instead. (Hmm, I wonder why the rest of the Torah only discusses the children of Yitzchak? And I wonder why only the children of Yitzchak were privileged with a grand Revelation at Sinai, and not the Moslems?)

Like Paul, Mohammed could only claim that this earth-shattering news came to him in a private prophesy.[5] This is an important admission because it demonstrates the main difference between the other religions' claims to authenticity, and the Torah's claim. In the Torah, when God wanted to reveal His will to humanity, He didn't do it to one person in a private prophesy. He did so in front of masses of people.

> Has any nation ever heard God speaking out of fire, as you have, and remained alive? Has God ever done miracles bringing one nation from the midst of another nation with such tremendous trials, signs and wonders, and war, and a mighty hand and outstretched arm, and terrifying phenomena, as God did for you in

---

5. It's interesting to note that most of his contemporaries did not believe in him at all, as Mohammed himself attested to, until he convinced a couple of brutal guys of his supposed prophecy that he received privately from Allah. (His only witness to that prophecy was his donkey.) It was these brutes who then went to others and said, It's your choice: the Koran (the supposed word of Allah) or the sword. If you don't believe, we will make you a head shorter. Hence, Islam.

Egypt before your very eyes? You are the ones who have been shown, so that you will know that God is the Supreme Being, and there is none other besides Him. From Heaven, He let you hear His voice so as to discipline you, and on earth He showed you His great fire, and you heard His words from within the fire. (DEVARIM 4:33–36)

The Torah was not given to one person, who had a private vision and tried to convince others of its authenticity. It was given in broad daylight, in front of *millions* of people, and at that same event Moshe was clearly selected as *the* leader and Prophet of the Jewish nation. Other religions base themselves on blind faith. Jewish "belief" is entirely different. It's not really even belief. The people of Moshe's time did not have to believe that he had a personal revelation from God telling everyone to follow Torah. They experienced the revelation themselves. *The people themselves heard as God spoke to Moshe.* There was no philosophy or blind faith involved. "And God said to Moshe: Behold! I [will] come to you in the thickness of the cloud, so that the people will hear as I speak to you and [thus] they also will believe in you forever" (*Shemos* 19:9).[6]

These words were said prior to God speaking the Ten Commandments. Subsequently, the entire people were given the privilege of prophesy by hearing the voice of God as He spoke to Moshe.[7] Thus, it was like a "conference call" — everyone was hooked in. This was no private prophesy. All of Klal Yisrael clearly saw that there *is* prophesy — God *does* speak to humans. And it also proved to the people, beyond a reasonable doubt, that God had singled out Moshe to be His chosen prophet.

It had to happen this way. If God wanted to create a viable monotheistic religion, amidst a world of idol worshipers, it would only make sense to reveal Himself to their leader *in the presence of a large multitude*, and then communicate to that leader

---

6. See also *Devarim* 4:9–15, 5:4–5, 5:21–24; *Shemos* 34:32.
7. See Rambam, *Hilchos Yesodei HaTorah*, Chapter 8.

what He wanted His people to do. (Note: Though in general, most humans are not in the proper spiritual state to enable them to experience prophesy, at that time, in order to "start off the true religion on the right foot," and in order that the masses accept the one person [Moshe] who *was* on the proper spiritual level to enable him to be in constant communication with Hashem, Hashem gave the whole nation a taste of prophesy, with Moshe at the helm.) However, if God would have revealed Himself only to one individual, with no one else present, any charlatan or dreamer could have come along with the claim of a revelation. Surely, God would never have expected us to have to guess if our main prophet — the one through whom the Jewish people would receive the rest of the Torah — was a legitimate prophet or not. God would never expect us to have to guess if the Torah is true or not. Therefore, when God wanted to reveal His will of how to serve Him, it was of the utmost importance that: 1) He reveal Himself to the multitude, and 2) that He also reveal to us the individual whom He chose to be the leader and mediator between Himself and the Jewish nation — *which of course also had to be done in front of the entire nation so that we would know who this true leader was.* And this is exactly what happened at Sinai.

The curious thing is that both Christianity and Islam, while they must confirm the revelation, want everyone to believe that they reflect God's "new" will without any new revelation! Both Paul and Mohammed agree that God chose the Jewish people as His special nation by revealing Himself in front of the entire people, and they agree that Moshe was the Chosen Prophet to whom God told His Divine will. In this regard, they make sense. What makes no sense, however, is to then claim that when God supposedly wanted to make a "new chosen people" He did not say "good-bye" to the Jewish people or at least call together His "new people" to reveal Himself to them. I mean, wouldn't such a drastic change necessitate a dramatic, earth-shaking event with a public display that at least remotely matched the events that took place at Sinai? Yet, their own books admit that God (allegedly) only told Paul himself, or Mohammed himself, about such stupendous changes! How could anyone think that God would want to start a whole new religion and dump the old one by telling only one man about it, in private, with no one else hearing a thing? There's not the slightest possibility of verification. And if it was true, then God certainly would want people to be able to verify such a major "change in policy." Obviously they're as false as can be. (Later on we will discuss why God wanted such fallacies to spread.) And so, it's clear why God could not, and would not, make a "phone call" to just one individual without anyone else hearing it. To make a private phone call to just one "Shimon" (or to Paul or Mohammed) would be self-defeating since no one, not even the person's closest relative or friend, could have the slightest way of verifying it. You and I could make the same claims, and no one could prove us wrong. It's common sense that God would never start a religion that way. Now of course the Torah espouses the concept of private prophesies, but 1) you obviously don't start a religion that way, and 2) the Torah gives us rules which tell us the ways to prove the validity of a prophesy. A prophet had to predict, or bring, some type of sign or wonder which would prove his prophesy to be true. (Unless he was already a confirmed true prophet, such as Moshe. See Rambam, *Hilchos Yesodei HaTorah*, Chapter 7:7.) However, Paul and Mohammed didn't bring or predict any signs. And truthfully, there's another fundamental problem with Paul's and Mohammed's claims of prophesy, since their prophesies abolish the existing laws of the Torah. Since they agree that the Torah is the sole source to establish that there is such a thing as prophesy, then with regard to prophesies they must abide by the statements and rules of the Torah: 1) The Torah clearly states that the Torah and its laws are forever. [See *Shemos* 12:14, 17; 28:43; *Vayikra* 3:17; 7:36; 10:9; 16:29, 31, 34; 23:14, 21, 31, 41; 24:3; and *Bemidbar* 15:15; 18:23.] And it clearly states in *Devarim* 4:2 and 13:1 that no one is ever to add or detract from any of the laws of the Torah. So Paul, who claimed a prophesy in which God supposedly stated that the Jews (and he was also Jewish) no longer need to keep most of the laws of the Torah, is in essence saying that Hashem is a liar. 2) It also clearly says (*Devarim* 13:2–6; 18:20–22; 30:11,12) that if anyone will come with a prophesy that is against the Torah, then even if he were to bring signs that verify his prophesy, we are still forbidden to listen to him. The Torah says that anyone who claims such a prophesy is surely a false prophet, and the prophet is to be put to death. So Paul, who told his "prophesies" to Jews, "prophesies" which came to abolish most of the Torah, is obviously a false prophet, and he was therefore deserving of death. No matter how you look at it, Paul and Mohammed do not establish their legitimacy.

Someone might claim that the Jews heard "only" the Ten Commandments directly from God, and the remainder of the commandments we only know from Moshe; so on superficial glance, this would seem to fall under the problem of "private prophecies." In response to this, first we must understand that there are a number of major differences between the prophecies of a legitimate prophet, and the prophecies of Moshe, the Prophet of all prophets.

Prophets are capable of receiving a message from God. And throughout Biblical history many did. However, Moshe had a status that was completely superior, in comparison to all other legitimate prophets. First, God openly chose Moshe to be the mediator between Himself and the Jewish people, as we find by the miracles of the Exodus, and by the Revelation at Sinai. We also find that after the Revelation at Sinai, for about a six-month period before the Tabernacle was erected, Moshe would walk outside the camp of the Israelites, in full view of whoever wished to watch, and would go to a special meeting tent (*Shemos* 33:8–11). As Moshe approached the tent, the "Cloud of Glory" of God would descend on the tent, thereby "greeting Moshe," and God would commune with him in the tent. (See also *Bemidbar* 11:16,17; 12:4,5; 14:10; 16:19.) This was a daily spectacle that all the people saw.

Another daily spectacle seen by all the Jews, was the special radiant glow which shone on Moshe's face at all times, for almost forty years. It was such a real, physical glow that Moshe had to put on a veil at different times, for otherwise the people couldn't look at him. (See *Shemos* 34:29–35.)

They also saw how Moshe wasn't "in it" for his own honor, by the fact that his sons did not receive any positions of importance. They also saw how in many instances Moshe admitted that he didn't know how to rule. (See *Shemos* 18:14–27; *Vayikra* 10:17–20; *Bemidbar* 15:32–36; 25:6; 36:3–1.) Now if you are making everything up anyway, why not make believe that you know absolutely everything.

It's no wonder that when the people of that generation saw how close Moshe was to God — how God performed so many colossal miracles through him, how God spoke to him on a daily basis, and how his face had a constant special Godly shine — no one of that generation doubted the truth of every word that he said. It was as clear as can be, to the people of that generation, that Moshe was God's prophet, who was chosen to relate the will of God to His Jewish people. (This is in addition to the reasons that we will later give to explain why it's not feasible for any human to have written our Torah in the way it is actually written.)

There's another important point to learn from all this, which once again shows the validity of our Torah. You can lie to a few people and try and convince them of your beliefs, but you can't convince a whole nation about something that supposedly happened if that nation never experienced it. And believe me, if it could be done, then surely others would have padded their religions with claims similar to ours.[8] Wouldn't the Christians love to be able to claim: "We had tremendous miracles done for us right

---

8. A rebbe of mine once told my class the following incident that happened to him. Once, while traveling on a train, a priest came over to him and started up a conversation about topics of faith. Amidst the conversation the priest said, "You think you Jews need faith? It's us Christians who really need faith." How true indeed.

in front of millions and millions of Christians"? Don't you think they would have claimed this if they could? But not once do they claim such an occurrence. And the Moslems, too, do not claim any open revelation to the multitudes. To take this point a drop further, we must remember that many of the other miracles that are related in the Torah (such as the Ten Plagues, the splitting of the Red Sea, and receiving manna from heaven for forty years, etc.) also happened in front of millions of people. So if the Jews can make up such "lies," why can't the other religions make up similar lies? I mean, if the Jews could buy such lies, why do the Christian leaders think the Christians won't buy them? It's obvious that they realize that such open lies could never gain acceptance. To the contrary, it's these public miracles that have had a part in convincing the other religions of the truth of our Torah! [9]

Yes, both Christianity and Islam each claim to be the new true religion. But both admit that they started off with the private prophesy of one person and only afterward spread to the masses. Was God not capable of performing a second set of ten plagues or a second revelation at Mt. Sinai? Yet, nowhere in

---

9. And the skeptics can't claim it happened in a historical vacuum. All the events took place smack in the middle of ancient Egypt, perhaps the most famous civilization ever. And they can't claim that it happened to primitive people. Ancient Egypt was such an advanced civilization that it has left its mark on every culture which has followed — their knowledge of mathematics, language, astronomy, architecture (scientists today still can't figure out exactly how they built the pyramids) and other disciplines, continues to impress every scholar who studies the subjects.

And then there's another "small" historical fact the skeptics have to contend with. Everyone agrees that Egypt was once the undisputed world power around the time the Torah's accounts took place. Yet, all of a sudden it disappeared as a significant factor in the ancient world. Scholars stretch their imaginations to come up with a logical explanation for it (other than the Torah's account). Throughout virtually the entire *Tanach*, Biblical Israel is never once threatened by a self-ruling Egypt, despite the fact that they go to war with almost every other neighboring nation. What happened to the undisputed world power?

world history, not even in all the writings of the Christians and the Moslems, has anything like the Exodus from Egypt or the Revelation at Mt. Sinai ever been claimed. Donkeys, prostitutes, a couple of close relatives and friends, a few disciples, etc., may suffice for them as witnesses (attesting to some poorly displayed magic tricks), but nowhere do we find a claim that anyone heard God talk to Paul or Mohammed (which is surely a prerequisite if they wish to claim that God was "changing his entire game plan" and trading off the Jews, His Chosen People, for a new nation). Nor were any open miracles ever done for them in any big way at all.[10] With regard to the few poorly attended miracles that the "founder of Christianity" supposedly did, there are conflicting reports as to who the few witnesses were to these events. Also, these events that supposedly happened, all were first mentioned at the start of Christianity, which was years after these events actually took place, thereby greatly minimizing the ability to verify or disprove their legitimacy. But the most important thing to realize is that one doesn't become a Prophet or Messiah, — and certainly not God — just by performing miracles. Many of our great Prophets and scholars all performed miracles, miracles as miraculous as the reviving of the dead (see *Melachim* II 4:18-37), but that in no way, shape or form gave them any claim to divinity; it just showed that for whatever reason God gave them a temporary power to do supernatural things.

Now, one may be wondering about the tremendous number of followers which both these religions have. In truth, it doesn't mean a thing. We must understand the socio-political structure in those days. When Christianity and Islam began to spread, there was no need to consult the common people. The masses, especially in those days, were completely uneducated. In many places they were slaves who were treated worse than cattle. It was only necessary to persuade the king and his advisors to ac-

---

10. See Lawrence Kelemen, *Permission to Receive*, Jerusalem: Targum/Feldheim Publishers, 1996, pp. 50–75, 206–211.

cept their religion. Once accepted, the multitude who were under their rule had practically no choice but to accept their ruler's religion.

A fact very well-known to historians is that many kings accepted these two religions to use as an excuse to wage "holy wars" with neighboring kings. The history books, however, tell us just how "holy" these wars really were (the Crusades, for example). Beneath the veneer of holy purposes was a rabble of despotic ruffians whose lives were totally meaningless. Often the kings or clergy incited the masses to wage "holy wars" just to keep them occupied, for fear that otherwise their own people might rebel against them. That's what brought about the rapid rise of these religions. By contrast, the Torah is not a philosophy or revelation of one man who then spread his message until it attained wide appeal through political takeover, crusades, and *jihads*. As the Torah attests, Judaism started at one time with one generation. The entire Jewish nation was taken out of Egypt in the most miraculous fashion and led to the foot of Mt. Sinai where it received the Torah — everyone at one time, in front of each other. This is totally unparalleled.

Another fact to keep in mind is that the Christians came along and abolished almost all of the Torah laws. It is one thing to create a new religion which makes great demands on people, and an entirely different matter to copy a sprinkle of the laws and ethics of a religion and nullify all the difficult laws. [11] That's why the Christian religion is called a daughter religion of Judaism, and that's also why we find the term *Judeo-Christian values;* their religion is simply a watered-down version of Judaism. Christianity's big "innovation" was to believe in their savior. Be-

---

11. We find that whenever the Christians feel that certain laws of the New Testament are too difficult to keep, they make a meeting (this goes on to this day) and vote on whether or not to abolish the law. Now if it was a Divinely given law, shouldn't it be applicable for all generations? And how do humans come to vote on Divine laws?

lieve, get saved, and live the rest of your life with a clear conscience. Christianity promised you the rewards of Torah without demanding the sacrifice. How can one compare its acceptance by the masses to the acceptance of the Torah? One has to be truly convinced to keep a religion which requires very specific, clear-cut, personal day-to-day sacrifice.[12]

And let's not forget that the Torah's uncompromising stand against idol worship contradicted the single, most powerful belief in the ancient world. Paganism gripped the masses. Yet, the Torah says in no uncertain terms that one had to kick the habit immediately, without compromise. Keeping the Torah was an uphill battle. We Jews paved the way for the rest of the world, making it easy for other people to accept monotheism. But what gave the Jews the strength of conviction to fight the idolatrous ways of the nations around them? The millions of Jews who kept the Torah had to have had something very convincing performed before them.

And of course the simplest reason for the spreading of Christianity is the plain old reason that God was setting up a tremendous test for Jews, a test that would last for centuries. The power of the Church, and their evil persecutions, would be a solid test to see the strength of the faith of Jews throughout the generations.

The bottom line is that you cannot compare the Jewish people's acceptance of the Torah to the gentile world's acceptance of Christianity or Islam. The numbers of adherents to a religion does not prove a thing. Only by analyzing the initial stages of the birth of a religion can it be possible to discover solid evidence if it is truly a Divinely started religion, or a very suspicious-looking, run-of-the-mill, one-man, private-prophesy type of re-

---

12. It's no wonder then why we find that throughout our history, whenever our Sages saw some Jews start to do things which the Torah forbids, they made strict safeguards in order to make sure that it wouldn't happen again.

ligion which had the "good luck" to spread to the masses.[13]

This reminds me of something my nephew recently told me. He told me that his bus driver, a black man, once remarked, "Hey man, I wish there was a black Moses." Why did he want a black Moshe, I wondered? Why does he need any Moshe? The answer is because he knows that if there is anything to religion at all, it all starts with Moshe and the teachings of the Torah that he received from God. He knows that from Moshe stems all his religious inspiration and values.

Now the fact that the gentiles base themselves on the Torah is a very significant confession. Did they base themselves on the teachings of some tribe in Africa? Did they base themselves on the writings of the ancient Hittites or Sumerians? Did they base themselves on their own independent experiences and teachings? No. They based themselves on the Torah, because they agree that it is really the only source of truth. If they didn't think so, wouldn't it have been much smarter to start their religion based on something else?

In conclusion, Christianity and Islam both agree on two points: 1) that the other of them is a false religion, and 2) the Jews received the true Torah on Mt. Sinai. We agree on both accounts as well: both Christianity and Islam are man-made fabrications, and we received the true Torah on Sinai.

One last important point. Based on all of the above, we Jews have an advantage over all philosophers. Philosophers spend their lives philosophizing whether or not there's a God, who created God, etc. However we Jews have no need to philosophize. We have no doubts at all. When your entire nation experiences open miracles in Egypt, the splitting of the Red Sea, eating manna which falls from heaven, etc., topped off with the most colossal event of history — the actual hearing of the "voice" of

---

13. It wouldn't be far-fetched to say that God let all these false religions spread, in order that they be a test for the Jewish nation, as it actually was during the Middle Ages in Europe.

God at Mt. Sinai, then you don't have any place for such doubts. We Jews don't need any philosophizing; for us it's a pure waste of time. Philosophy is only for those who have doubts, but it's a waste of time for a nation which literally experienced God first-hand. We know firsthand that God exists and interacts with the world that He created.

A LITTLE HEALTHY SKEPTICISM

The Jewish people began keeping the Torah because they, millions of them, were *all* present when God revealed Himself to them. They *all* heard the voice of God firsthand. However, let's take the side of the skeptic and think about this "objectively." Maybe the Torah is man made, no less than Christianity and Islam. The Jewish people may have accepted the Torah, and preserved it with great tenacity, but perhaps if we look into it we will find that the Torah's claim to authenticity is flawed as well. Perhaps things didn't happen the way they're written.

There are only a few possibilities for how the Torah and its acceptance could have come about:

- It actually happened as related in the Torah
- Moshe made it all up on his own and then "sold" it to his generation
- It was made up at a much later date in history, long after the Jews settled in the Land of Israel

Let's take up the second possibility — that Moshe made up all these stories and convinced his generation to believe in him. The problem with this is that if Moshe was smart enough to deceive all the people, how could he be so foolish to write the Torah the way he did? If you want to perpetrate a great lie, the first rule is that you do *not* keep mentioning that lie over and over. Rather, the intelligent strategy would be to try to sneak it by and hope that no one would dwell upon it. Referring to it over and over again would be self-defeating. Yet, the Torah discusses the giving of the Torah at Mt. Sinai, and the miraculous events which took place right before and right after the revelation, numerous times.[14] Moshe keeps reminding the Jewish people of what they saw and heard at Mt. Sinai. They are warned in the strongest terms not to forget the slightest detail of what occurred at that great revelation, and they are commanded to tell it over to their children, who must in turn relate it to their children, etc., on down until today (*Devarim* 4:9).

The revelation becomes the basis for which the Jewish people are expected to listen to all the commandments that Moshe told them in God's name (as we will explain in detail below).[15] Why, then, if Moshe made it all up, would he be so foolish as to repeat it so much and make it the central point of the new religion?

Moreover, if Moshe had made it all up, how could he expect to fool an entire nation into believing a story that they themselves supposedly personally experienced — a story of colossal proportions, a once-in-history event? By basing his credibility on such a brazen, outright lie, how could he expect the people to listen to him and accept such a difficult set of laws? The people would surely rebel against such a person, and maybe even kill him.[16] One thing is certain: the "Torah" this person would try to

---

14. *Shemos* 19:1–25; 20:1–19; 24:1–18; 34:27–35; *Devarim* 4:9–15; 4:32–40; 5:1–30; 9:8–29; 10:1–11; 18:15–22.

15. See *Shemos* 20:19–20; *Devarim* 4:14,40.

16. Although we have seen in recent history how people can be convinced to partake in mass suicides, and we find individuals who willfully commit suicide for a "cause," that can't be compared to the Jews accepting to lead their lives according to the Torah that Moshe dictated to them in the name of Hashem. First of all, it's a lot easier to convince a person to do a one-time act of sacrifice — even if it's the ultimate sacrifice — than to get a whole nation to permanently change their lifestyle.

Another more fundamental difference is that no one would ever commit suicide if the whole reason to commit suicide was based on a leader stating an open lie. If a leader would say to commit suicide because "yesterday, a heavenly voice called out telling you (or us) to commit suicide," and the person he is talking to knows for sure that this is not true, one can be sure that no one would do anything based on such a lie. It's one thing to prom-

teach would never be accepted, even by a single person of his generation.

However, quite the opposite happened. The Jewish people fully accepted Moshe's teachings, taught to them in the name of God. The entire nation studied and kept the Torah, and transmitted it to their children as well. Nowhere do we find the slightest doubt cast on a single word which Moshe uttered. (The story of Korach, if studied properly, is in no way a contradiction to this.) To say, therefore, that Moshe made up the entire story and then tried to "sell" it to the people of his generation is a position which logic does not support.

Let's then, take up the other "fabrication" hypothesis, namely that at some time after the Jews entered the Land of Israel, the Torah was made up. This, however, is also unreasonable to accept. And we will spend the next several pages explaining why.

To begin with, let's not forget that the Torah tells about the Ten Plagues, the splitting of the Red Sea, the great Revelation at Mt. Sinai, and all the other great miracles which took place during the forty years in the wilderness. Such events obviously would have had a profound impact on the nation's consciousness. And, indeed, the majority of the nation's major festivals, and many of its commandments, are all based on those events.

For example, "You shall remember that you too were slaves in Egypt," is stated in the Torah portion which prohibits pervert-

---

ise heaven to those who "die for the cause" (a charismatic leader can convince people of many things that can't be clearly verified — many Jews have been killed because Gentiles were convinced of the "Jewish problem" by their leaders), but it's another thing to try to get people to do difficult things based solely on an open lie. If Moshe would have based adherence to the Ten Commandments and all the other laws of the Torah on a spectacular public revelation that all these people knew for certain never occurred, then no sane person would ever comply with such an open lie. It's an outrageous insult to take people to be such fools. A person like this could be lynched; but even if the people wouldn't kill him, they certainly wouldn't believe, or accept, a single word that he uttered.

ing justice for the proselyte and orphans.[17] In the portion of *leket*, *shikchah* and *pe'ah* (various agricultural tithes) it states: "You shall surely remember that you were slaves in the land of Egypt" (*Devarim* 24:19-22). And again, "You shall remember the day of your Exodus from Egypt all the days of your lives" (*Devarim* 16:3). The reasons given for redeeming the firstborn son, the firstborn animal, and the firstborn donkey are because God skipped over the firstborn Jews and the firstborn of their animals in Egypt (*Shemos* 13:11-15). We have to dwell in *sukkos* (booths) ". . . in order that your generations should know that in *sukkos* I caused the Children of Israel to dwell when I took them out of the land of Egypt" (*Vayikra* 23:43). The entire holiday of Passover, including the prohibition of eating *chametz* (leaven), the laws of *matzah*, the entire *seder* night — are all based directly on the Egyptian experience.[18] Even keeping Shabbos is based on having been redeemed from their servitude in Egypt.

There are numerous other subtle pieces of evidence which indicate that the Torah was written to the generation of those people who actually lived through the events described in it. For instance, it says many times that all the events happened *l'einei kol Yisrael*, "In the presence of all of Israel." Everything happened in front of the entire nation of Israel. The manna fell for forty years in the presence of all Israel.[19] The Cloud, or Pillar of Glory, which lead the Jewish people for forty years by day, and the Pillar of Fire by night were also "before the eyes of all of Israel" (*Shemos* 40:36-38). These are claims which would have been immediately rejected by people who had lived at that time but had never actually experienced them.

Moreover, merely the way the Torah makes statements demonstrates that it was written for the people who experienced everything firsthand. For instance, "Remember what Amalek did to

---

17. *Shemos* 22:20; *Devarim* 24:17-18.
18. *Shemos* 13:3-10; *Devarim* 16:1-8.
19. *Shemos* 16:16-35 (cf. Rashi v. 32); and *Devarim* 8:3-18.

to you," i.e., *you*, not your ancestors. Even the simple command to "Remember . . . don't forget" (*Devarim* 25:17–19) is informative. Why would the Torah say "Remember," if nothing ever happened to these people? It's contrary to all logic to tell people not to forget something if it never happened, because the more you tell someone not to forget an event that never happened the more that person is going to "remember" that the entire incident is a lie![20]

This type of internal consistency runs throughout the entire Torah. Even a skeptic has to admit that the more you delve into the details the more you see that the Torah was written for people who lived through that era of the miraculous Exodus from Egypt. The evidence is so convincing, in fact, that it forced John Bright, a world-renowned scholar, to write:[21]

> But the Bible's own witness is so impressive, that it leaves no doubt that such a remarkable deliverance took place. Israel remembers the exodus for all time, as the constitutive event that had called her into being as a people. It stood at the center of her faith from the beginning onward, as is witnessed by her most ancient poems (*Shemos* 15:1–18) [*Az Yashir*]...as well as by other texts [including the many commandments which refer to the Exodus] too numerous to list.... A belief so ancient and so entrenched will admit of no explanation save that Israel actually escaped from Egypt to the accompaniment of events so stupendous that they were impressed forever in her memory.

Another thought to contemplate: if these miraculous events weren't true, then why would anyone from back then keep the commandments that the Torah explicitly connects to those events? Put yourself in the shoes of those people and imagine

---

20. It's interesting to note that never has there been found in any of the countries that surrounded the Jews, whether it was while they were in the desert, or when they had settled in Eretz Yisrael, any documentation that would refute any of the accounts we find recorded in our Torah.
21. John Bright, *A History of Israel*, Westminster Press, 1981, p. 122.

having a conversation then. Your friend tells you: "Look. It says here: I am God Who took you out of Egypt."

"Egypt?" you reply. "Where's Egypt?"

"You know, the Egypt where the Ten Plagues took place."

"Ten Plagues?"

"You know, the river turning to blood, the frogs, the lice, the killing of the firstborn and all that."

"When did that ever happen?"

"You never heard about it?"

"I just recently heard about it, but I don't believe it. I mean, did your father, or your grandfather ever mention anything about that stuff?"

"No."

"Your great-grandfather?"

"No."

"Well mine neither. And yet these people expect us to keep the whole Torah based on the most unbelievable claims that none of us have ever heard of? Who are they kidding?"

Who is going to keep this demanding Torah if the whole thing is based on an easily exposed lie? Not one person. No one would take up the difficulty and expense of the Torah lifestyle if it were based on easily refutable outlandish claims. No one.

Yet, the Torah says, "You must be on guard and guard yourselves exceedingly, lest you forget the things that your eyes saw" (Devarim 4:9). If no one saw this — if everyone is saying, "I didn't see anything, did you?" — then no one is going to keep the Torah. Another passage (Devarim 8:2-4) tells us how Moshe was telling the Jews to remember the manna that they themselves ate, and the clothing and shoes that they wore for forty years which miraculously didn't wear out. Again, it's obvious that the Torah was given to a generation that actually experienced these events. And if these stories are being told to a later generation, then they would have had to have heard these stories from their ancestors, and if they didn't, then certainly no one would believe them. Such open mockery would only bring the Jews to forsake the Torah.

Also, to say that someone made up the Torah at a later date and revealed it as our long lost Torah to the Jews of his time, and from there it spread, is also a theory that can't be accepted for all the above reasons, and: (1) Surely it's unlikely that the whole Jewish nation would have completely forgotten about its amazing past as depicted in this Torah that he had "found." Therefore it's highly unlikely that they would have believed this person; (2) If such a person had existed in our past, then his name surely would be emblazoned in our current history. Who could forget such a person whose contribution to our nation would have remained unmatched? Who could be a greater hero, then the one who would have given back to our nation its old way of life? However, even though we have thousands of ancient manuscripts, no where in any of our writings has such a person ever been mentioned.

As long as we are talking about the miracle of the manna, let's analyze it for a moment. In many ways, the manna falling from heaven is the most impressive miracle recorded in the Torah — it has elements which make it even more impressive than the giving of the Torah on Mt. Sinai, the Ten Plagues of Egypt, and the splitting of the Red Sea. True, those were awesome miracles that happened in front of millions of people, but they were each basically one-time events. Manna, in contrast, fell *continuously* for forty years — day in and day out, over and over again; the people had to eat something for those forty years in the desert. It's inconceivable how someone could have gotten away with writing that the manna fell uninterrupted for forty years in the desert for millions of people if, in fact, the people had not eaten it.

A skeptic might say, "What do you mean? Maybe the first generation living in the Land of Israel made it up after the generation in the desert died out. The Torah itself testifies that the generation which left Egypt did not enter the Holy Land. No one was left to testify, so the first generation of settlers in the Land of Israel could have made it up."

However, that claim cannot be taken seriously because only

the males from twenty to sixty years of age died in the desert. The males under the age of twenty and over the age of sixty left Egypt, lived forty years in the desert, and then entered the land. Picture, for instance, a young man who was nineteen when he left Egypt. He was only fifty-nine when he entered the land. The best years of his life were spent in the desert. How are you going to convince him that millions of people were fed manna in the desert if it didn't happen? And take all the 58, 57, 56...45 and 44-year-old males who would have remembered the manna. Furthermore, most of the women went in. Thus, the forty- and fifty-year-old men, as well as women of all ages, experienced the daily miracle of manna. They all knew the stories firsthand. They taught it to the next generation. If no one had ever heard of the manna, would they have accepted the Torah's claim? And remember, we are told that the manna was put in a special jar to bear witness to the miracle, and that this jar was in existence at least until the time of Yirmeyahu (*Shemos* 16:32–34).

From the little we have already pointed out thus far (and the remainder of the chapter will add to the evidence),[22] it should already be apparent that the "late fabrication" hypothesis is a far-fetched theory. To say that the religion of the Jewish people could have come about by fabricating the stories of the Exodus, the Plagues, and so forth takes a much greater leap of faith than admitting their authenticity.

One more important point. The laws of writing a Torah scroll are extremely stringent. When writing a Torah scroll it is forbidden to write a *single* letter by heart; every letter must be written while reading out of an existing kosher Torah scroll (Rambam, *Laws of Tefillin, Mezuzah, and Torah Scrolls*, Chapter 1:12). To add

---

22. For instance, in the section on archaeology we will cite quotes like the following (from Dr. Y. Aharoni): "..No author or editors could have put together or invented these stories, hundreds of years after they have happened. There is no serious Bible scholar remaining who can argue with the fact of these historical events."

or subtract even one letter is strictly forbidden, and it would render the entire Torah scroll invalid (Rambam, *Laws of the Torah Scroll*, Chapter 10). Because of these strict laws it is well-known that Torah scrolls from all parts of the world have always been found to be identical to one another.

It is no wonder that Josephus wrote thirteen hundred years after the Torah was given (about two thousand years ago) (*Against Apion* 1:8):

> How firmly we have given credit to those books of our own nation is evident by what we do; for during so many ages as have already passed, no one has been so bold as either to add anything to them, or take anything from them, or make any changes in them. All Jews imbibe with their mother's milk the belief that these books are of Divine origin, as well as the resolve to remain faithful to them, and willingly, if need be, to die for them. For it is no new thing for our [Jewish] captives, many in number, and frequently in time, to be seen to endure racks [a form of torture] and deaths of all kinds in their theaters, rather than be forced to say one word against our laws, and the records that contain them.

We must ask ourselves, what was it that gave Jews this firmly entrenched belief?

In the beginning of Rambam's introduction to his *Mishnah Torah*, he writes of how our laws and traditions (and as explained above, our Torah Scrolls as well) have been handed down from Moshe, in an unbroken chain, through the times of the Prophets, down to the post-Temple era, down through the period of the Mishnah, and down through the period of the Talmud. Following the Talmudic period was the period of the Geonim, which was quite close to the times of the Rambam himself. The Rambam lists the names of each generation's leaders, and the names of their disciples, who in turn gave over the laws and traditions to their disciples. It's this well-known, unbroken chain that goes back to Moshe himself, together with the tradition of the Great Revelation to the Jewish people at Mt. Sinai that has kept us so strong and unwavering in our beliefs.

So once again, we see how unlikely the "late fabrication theory" is, since we see how our traditions go all the way back to Moshe, without a single break in the chain. Furthermore, we see how strongly the Jews believed in their tradition, by their willingness to undergo terrible tortures rather than say a word against their Holy Torah. Such a tradition could never have been made up "midway" through our people's existence. This is common sense.

THE COMMITTEE

Ignoring everything said above, maybe someone nevertheless wants to claim that the Torah's laws were man-made. Even granted that something miraculous happened in Egypt and that God revealed Himself at Sinai, a skeptic might still claim: Who says that the laws of the Torah were not made up afterward? After all, it's not so hard to imagine a committee of very intelligent human beings getting together and creating a constitution and laws. Maybe the Torah was put together by such a committee.

In response, let's put ourselves in the place of those people who supposedly were appointed to such a committee, a committee created specifically to make up the laws of the Torah. You've got to win millions of people over to your new man-made religion. How would you go about doing it? Would you put it together the way the Torah is put together?

I think I can show you that you would never write the Torah the way we actually have it today.

Let's begin, then. Imagine that you are a committee member trying to set up a bunch of laws which you and your fellow committee members will have to set forth as the laws of the first pilot religion. Naturally, if you wanted others to take up a lifestyle tailored after your own ideas the first thing you would do is make sure you kept the new laws down to a bare minimum. Remember, you're trying to sell a religion. The first rule is: Don't make it too difficult. That's common sense.

But the Torah doesn't do that.

The Torah has 613 commandments. No sane committee person would dream of enacting so many commandments. And, remember, our Torah consists of much more than just 613 commandments. The Ramban and the Rambam (and other respected commentators) differ over exactly which commandments make up the 613,[23] but all agree that technically there are many more Biblical commandments than 613.[24] Thus, the sheer number of commandments is the first piece of evidence against a man-made Torah.

But let's not stop here. Let's analyze several of the actual commandments and see if anyone would include them as basic tenets of their new religion.

Imagine someone getting up at the committee meeting and proposing another commandment (assuming, as we have been saying, that this is a man-made Torah). The commandment is *shemittah*, the "sabbatical" year — letting the fields lie fallow for one out of every seven years (*Vayikra* 25:1-24). After it is initially proposed, you, as a member of the committee, think, "Hey, a sabbatical. That's a pretty good idea."

In a split second, you think to yourself: How should we do it? Hmmm. Maybe we should divide the land into seven parts. That's it. In year one, one seventh of the land will lie fallow; year two, the second seventh will; year three, the third seventh, and so on. The more you think of it, the more you like the idea. Every year, six-sevenths of the land is being worked while one-seventh rests. Furthermore, those who are working have to give a portion to those who are not working. Everyone chips in to give the sabbatical group a livelihood. Great idea.

However, imagine if the committee leader would propose the

---

23. We have a tradition that there are 613 mitzvos (commandments), so although technically there are many more mitzvos, the commentators show us how to isolate exactly which fit into the select 613 mitzvos.

24. For a commandment to be part of the "613" it needs certain technical qualifications. Not having those qualifications doesn't disqualify the law from being classified as a Biblical commandment, so in essence there are many more than 613 commandments.

following: "In our *shemittah* year no one is going to plant during the seventh year. Nobody. The entire land will remain unplanted. You'll have to leave your land free — *hefker*, 'ownerless' — and everyone will be allowed to come into your field and take whatever he needs."

Stunned by the irrationality of it, you stand up and protest, "Mr. President, sir, the concept is good, but I'd like to suggest a modification. Let's make it that each year only one-seventh of the land lies fallow. Over a seven-year period, then, everyone will experience one *shemittah*." Proud of your idea, you sit down.

However, the President says sternly, "The whole land at once! Or none at all."

You retort: "But what are we going to eat that year, not to mention the year after *shemittah* when the new crop is first growing, if no one in the entire land is allowed to plant during the seventh year?"

"Oh, I'll tell you what we'll do," he says. "We'll promise everyone a bumper crop in the sixth year. The land is going to grow so much in the year before *shemittah* that they'll have plenty for the seventh and eighth years, until finally late into the eighth year they'll have their new crop." (See *Vayikra* 25:20–22.)

"Begging the President's pardon, sir," you reply, "but who are you to make that promise? Can you control the land? How can you promise a bumper crop?"

The President sticks to his guns, though. "Everyone lets their fields lie uncultivated or no *shemittah*." Your comrades on the committee side with you. "There's no shortage of commandments, Mr. President. Let's drop it. It's too difficult. No one's going to go for this one."

Now, let's not forget that we are talking about an agricultural society where there were no factories and just about everybody was a farmer who depended upon a plentiful harvest. All of sudden, you are telling them to stop working for a whole year! A whole year! Does that make sense? Clearly a committee of sane people would never pass it.

However, in the Torah it explicitly states that everyone has to let his land lie fallow in the seventh year. Everyone. No exceptions. But don't worry, the Torah says, because a bumper crop in the sixth year is promised. Ridiculous! No one is going to keep it. Unless the one who promises the bumper crop in return for nationwide *shemittah* is God. Then the people could accept such a law. And it's clear that no one but God would ever dare make up such a law.

But, we're not finished with this commandment. Let's return to our committee meeting and take things one step further.

Yovel, the Jubilee year, occurs after the completion of seven *shemittah* cycles (*Vayikra* 25:8–24). In addition to letting the fields lie fallow the seventh year of the seventh *shemittah* cycle, i.e., the forty-ninth year, you also have to let the fields lie fallow during *yovel,* the fiftieth year. Two years in a row of fallow fields! A man-made law would never go so far. You reluctantly succumbed to the pressure and agreed with the President of the committee to pass the *shemittah* laws, but now he expects you to add the stipulation of *yovel*? Is he out of his mind?

"We're trying to sell a new religion, sir," you tell him. "No one is going to buy into it. It's too difficult. You're going to lose all your new dues-paying members."

"But *yovel* is a good idea," the President says. "All it really amounts to is two years in a row of *shemittah*."

"Two years! Are you crazy!? Who's going to keep it? You know, if we thought they were going to rebel when they heard *shemittah,* this one will really get them. They're just going to forget the whole Torah that we're presenting to them. It will undermine all the other commandments that we've worked so hard to put together. You're pushing your luck."

Nevertheless, the President persists. "And I'm not done," he says. "There is another law I've connected with *yovel.* Every landowner has to return his field to its first original owner at the beginning of the fiftieth year of the *yovel* cycle, no matter how many times it was bought and sold over the prior fifty years." (See *Vayikra* 25:14–17, 23.)

"What?" you cry out, protesting to the President. They have

to give back all the fields to their original owners?! Are you kidding? Imagine the average person of those days who owns a few fields, and he has been there for thirty-five years or so. Here's what he would think to himself about such a law. 'Move?! But I'm accustomed to it here. I built my house here. I've invested everything in these fields. I have great neighbors. Now you want me to give it all back? I have to move?! No way!' Do you think anyone is going to want to do that? Excuse me, sir, but use your brains. You have a house for many, many years; you put in a new carpet; you put in this and you put in that; and now you have to give it all back?"

"Well, you can expect to be reimbursed for the improvements you made."

"How much does that really amount to? And besides, that's not the point; the bottom line is that I put my heart and soul into these fields for so many years and you tell me I have to give them back? They have sentimental value to me, and, furthermore, moving is a big headache. Who are you to tell me to do so? You're just another human being."

There's no question about it. No one would listen to him. No one would be crazy enough to put into a Torah something that's going to ruin the whole religion.

On the other hand, if God says you must do so "Because to Me belongs all the earth" (*Vayikra* 25:23), only then can it start to make sense. That's exactly why Hashem designed the mitzvos of *shemittah* and *yovel*, in order to remind us that God is the Boss. The mitzvos of *shemittah* and *yovel* were not given only because of the agricultural gains of letting fields lie fallow. They were given so that every seventh and fiftieth year we learn to break our dependency on our fields, and learn to rely on God in a very big way. Even more so, every fiftieth year we have to relinquish our land that we may have worked for decades. There's an important lesson that God wanted to impart with this mitzvah too. In essence, God is telling us: Do you think you're the boss? Do you think you're going to stay here forever and forget about the real purpose of life? Thus, in order that we not get too haughty, and in order that we not become too involved with our fields, our business, and our livelihood, God shakes us from our spiritual sleep every once in a while. God wants to teach us that only the spiritual commodities are truly worth pursuing. And of course, it reminds us who the Real Boss is. It's a reminder for us to pledge our allegiance to the One and Only Boss.

But it's quite obvious that no human being would ever have enacted such commandments. And there are many other commandments whose very logic reflect the Divine nature of Torah as well. Let me bring to your attention just a few more.

Mei sotah, the "waters of a *sotah*," is a special drink given to a woman suspected of adultery (*Bemidbar* 5:11–31). The Torah spends a lot of ink telling us how to deal with a woman whose husband warned her that she shouldn't be seen in private with a man whom she recently had been seen with a lot. It says in the Torah that if indeed she violated the warning, and was caught with that man, then we give her the special *sotah* waters to drink, and if she did sin with that man then the waters will cause her to die in a horrible fashion. However, if she didn't sin, then the waters will not harm her; on the contrary, they will cause her much blessing.

Now, if God made such a law, there is no problem. Of course it will work and it will create the necessary deterrent that it was intended for. However, in a man-made Torah it would be crazy to include such a law. First of all, since the committee knows that this is a man-made Torah, they certainly know that there's no way that these waters will work, so why make up such a poor deterrent. And on a practical note, they should be worried that since they know that these waters will never work, then it's inevitable that after a few ladies (known to be guilty) drink it but nothing happens, eventually word would get out that one can sin without worrying about any consequences, and this would lead to a national catastrophe. Also, they should realize that failure of the waters to work will sooner or later cast doubts on the validity of this law, and subsequently will bring doubts about all the Torah laws. Surely it would have been a much more effective deterrent simply to give this man and woman some type of severe punishment, such as a severe flogging, if they should ever be caught together in a suspicious setting. This would have helped as a deterrent, and it would have been a lot less risky in terms of exposing the Torah as a man-made law. Thus, if you're on the committee making up the laws, this one will surely never do. Either this law was written by God, or it is one of the most easily refutable laws a person can think of.

Another law which shows that Torah was not authored by a human being is the thrice-yearly pilgrimage to Jerusalem (aliyah l'regel). The Torah says: "Three times a year all able-bodied males[25] must come up to Jerusalem" (Shemos 34:23, 24; Devarim 16:16, 17).[26]

First of all, it's a big hassle for everyone to come up to Jerusalem. It really is. People don't like to just drop everything and leave their families. It's a tremendous nuisance and sacrifice. No human being is going to think of asking people to do this three times a year. And even if they would, people would ask, "What about our enemies? We have nations surrounding us who are just waiting for us to leave our border towns and territories unguarded in order to attack us. Who's going to watch the borders? Who's going to watch our families? Who's going to watch our businesses, our livestock, our fields?"

"Oh, don't worry," Mr. President says. "I'll promise them the following: 'And no one will desire your land when you go up to

---

25. Of course, based on certain technical leniencies or physical handicaps, some males were exempt. However, the majority did make the trip to Jerusalem thrice yearly.

26. Although it really doesn't matter if subsequently the Jews actually carried out this mitzvah or not, it's still good to know that there's an extensive amount of proofs showing that the Jews kept this commandment. See "HaAliyah L'Regel During the Second Commonwealth," by Professor S. Safari (Am HaSefer, 1965), pp. 10, 58. Our main point is that we must realize how such impossible and improbable commands could never have been made up by a human.

see the Presence of Hashem, your God, three times a year' (*She-mos* 34:24). So, don't worry. None of your enemies will think of coming in." Can a human being make such a ridiculous promise?

Who can promise that...but God? Which human being would have the audacity to say, "You know, the next commandment I want to suggest for this big Torah is that everyone must be *oleh regel* three times a year."

"Are you out of your mind? People aren't going to want to do that. It's national suicide. Thanks, but no thanks." People can trust God with such promises, but not humans.

And who can understand why a committee would come up with forbidding meat cooked in milk (*Shemos* 23:19), if both by themselves are permitted. The same holds true with the prohibition against *sha'atnez* (*Devarim* 22:11), where it's forbidden to wear wool woven with linen although both are permitted when they are worn in separate garments. And so, too, it's prohibited to plant together wheat and barley, even though they may be planted by themselves. These laws make no sense, so why risk rebellion by pushing them? A last point to contemplate: What humans would go so far as to try to regulate not only our every spoken word — that it be free of gossip, etc. (*Shemos* 23:1; *Vayikra* 19:16) — but even what we think, desire, and what we are allowed to look at (See *Shemos* 20:14 and *Bemidbar* 15:39). What chance is there that humans would make up laws governing areas that everyone knows are impossible to enforce? Why even give such commandments? Suggestions you can give, but it's ridiculous to think that anyone would feel any obligation to observe them if they were man-made Biblical commandments. Thus, only God who can detect everything, can realistically demand of us such behavior, knowing full well that we know that God is even aware of our thoughts, desires, and what we are looking at. And if you think about it, it probably would take a God, who truly knows the inherent greatness of the human race that He created, to hold us to such high and noble standards.

EXPENSIVE MITZVOS

You may be satisfied with the above, but a truly stubborn skeptic might not be. For his sake, then, we have to take this a bit further.

One of the most annoying, and sometimes difficult, aspects of keeping the Torah is the expense involved. People like their hard-earned money. They work very hard for it so they want to keep it. Can you expect to sell a religion that costs so much money if people thought it was man-made?

Of course, there are plenty of commandments one can agree to, even if they cost a little money. And you could even include some mandatory charity if it doesn't tax one too much.

But with commandments that cost lots of money, and time, and effort — and there are so many of them — who would agree to keep them? And more important: who would dare try to "sell" such an expensive religion? Consider the following: For starters, when we lived in our Land of Israel during the times of the *Beis Ha-Mikdash*, every year there was an obligation to give *ma'aser rishon* to the Levite.[27] *Ma'aser rishon* is a tax amounting to a tenth of a person's hard-earned produce.[28] And on top of that, every third and sixth year (of the seven-year *shemittah* cycle) you had to give *ma'aser ani*, a tithe to the poor. (*Devarim* 14:28, 26:12) Thus, in addition to the 10 percent of *ma'aser rishon* given every year, you had to give away another 10 percent of your produce every two out of seven years. Now, that really hurts. Then, after all that, there was still an obligation every year to support poor people if it was within your means. If the Torah was man-made, who would tolerate that? And who would dare demand such great sacrifices when trying to start up a religion in its "experimental stage?"

---

27. *Bemidbar* 18:21–24; *Devarim* 14:22, 26:12.
28. Of course, even before giving a tenth to the Levite, a person was obligated to give *terumah* to the Kohen. *Terumah*, admittedly though, was a minute amount according to the strict letter of Torah law.

And then there is *orlah*: all benefits from the produce of the first three years of a fruit tree's life are prohibited. "At least let me receive a little benefit from it," we can hear people say. "I worked so hard planting these trees. If you won't let me eat the fruit, at least let me sell it. Let me make a few bucks on it."

"Nothing doing. It's forbidden to benefit in any way, shape, or form from fruits of the first three years. You have to burn it."

Imagine planting an orchard of hundreds of trees which produce thousands of bushels of produce, and for three years in a row you cannot get any benefit at all from them! That's what the Torah law of *orlah* demands.

And by no means does it stop there. A Jew owning a field is commanded to set aside for the poor *leket*, *shikchah*, and *pe'ah*, which entails relinquishing control over parts of one's produce (*Vayikra* 19:9-10). Again you have to give away your money. Your hard-earned money.

And it doesn't stop there either. Consider Shabbos (*Shemos* 31:13-18, and many more verses). The committee announces in the marketplace the following decree: "You cannot work on the seventh day. We don't care how poor you are; you cannot work on Shabbos."

"Listen," you say, "I realize that this resting business is a great idea, but, if you don't mind, I'd like to have the option to work if I want. Hey, I need the money. Business is not going so well lately. Besides, I want to work. I enjoy working. I'm a workaholic."

"No. You have to sit and relax. No work whatsoever."

And what about *shechitah*, the laws of ritual slaughter, and eating only kosher food (*Devarim* 12:20-21)? If you slaughter an animal in the wrong way you cannot eat it. That's expensive. A whole cow. True, you can give it to a gentile. However, it's not always so easy, and even then it's sold at a loss.

Ribis, interest. Taking interest from a fellow Jew is strictly prohibited (*Shemos* 22:24; *Vayikra* 25:35-38; *Devarim* 23:20,21). "With this one you have gone too far, Mr. Committee President. Until now, I had been lending with interest. Now you say, however, that charging interest is prohibited?! I don't deal too often with gentiles. I deal primarily with Jews.[29] What's really wrong with charging them interest? Look, a friend asks me to lend him money: So, I decide to lend him the money. Why shouldn't I have a right to ask him to give me back a little extra? Besides, I don't take interest money unless the borrower agrees to it — in fact, many times it's the borrower's idea in the first place, so what's wrong? By lending him money, I'm losing an opportunity to use the money for an investment or to earn interest in a bank. So, why can't I expect him to compensate me? It's the normal thing to do. The whole world does it."

"It doesn't matter. No lending with interest."

Korbanos, sacrifices (*Vayikra,* Chapters 1-5 and many other places). If you sinned, even if it was only an accident, still you had to bring a sacrifice. Sacrifices are expensive. That money comes out of your pocket.

Pidyon ha-ben, the commandment to redeem your firstborn male child (*Shemos* 13:12,13, 34:19,20; *Bemidbar* 18:15-19). You have to pay the Kohen (priest) more hard-earned money to redeem your firstborn male.

Wait a second, Mr. Skeptic says. When it comes to spending money on your firstborn child, it's no big deal. It's only five coins. Besides, a person can have only one firstborn son in a lifetime, and it could be that a daughter would be born first, which would free him from the obligation of giving redemption money to the Kohen. Therefore, this law is no major ordeal.

Fine.

But, what happened when you owned many cattle and sheep? And, back then, almost everyone owned livestock. The law is that you had to bring every firstborn male animal up to a Kohen to be sacrificed (the meat then belonging to the Kohen). This could add up to a tremendous amount of money. Picture it for a moment. You had a big business dealing in livestock. Then,

---

29. Lending or borrowing with interest from a gentile is permissible.

the religion committee comes and tells you, "Every single first-born male from all your animals needs to be redeemed." Over a lifetime that can add up to a fortune.

Wait a second, I can hear the diehard skeptic say. With all these tithes and sacrifices going to the Kohen and Levite, perhaps they made all these laws for their benefit? Then let me ask you this — continuing with your logic that maybe the tribe of Levi wrote the Torah, would these Kohanim have written in the Torah a law which prohibits *terumah* (a certain amount of produce that had to go to a Kohen) that has become *tamei* (ritually defiled)? But that is the law. A Kohen was only permitted to eat *terumah* which had not been defiled, and most of their food came from *terumah*. Furthermore, there's something much more significant here. Their tribe was not given any portion in the land, and land meant power, especially in those days. Think about it, would you put yourself in such a precarious position where your main livelihood (the *matnas kehunah*) was dependent on the handouts of other people? What would happen if there was a little shortage, and what if you weren't the most popular Kohen or Levite? Then most people would not give you their *terumah* or *ma'aser* tithes, but would give it to a more popular Kohen or Levite. You'd eventually turn into a real pauper. Would you want to put yourself or your children into such a predicament? Of course not. Yet, the Kohen and Levite were not given a permanent share in the land.[30] They depended on the tithes of the people. And if the *terumah* became *tamei* the Kohen had to burn it. And don't think there weren't a lot of ways *terumah* could become *tamei*. There were. If the Kohanim had made up the Torah, you could be sure that they wouldn't have applied a law of *tu-*

---

30. Which is why the Kohanim were compensated by receiving *terumah*, and part of many of the *korbanos*. In addition, they didn't demand any payment for their services, so these "tips" were granted to them. Similarly, the Levites were given *ma'aser rishon*, because they too did not have a portion in the land, and in gratitude for their services in the Temple.

mah with regard to *terumah*. And even if they had applied the law of *tumah*, at least you would have expected them to make up some law which somehow would have enabled them to remove the defilement in an easy way to make the *terumah* permissible to eat again. But they didn't. In fact, the law is that you had to burn it if it became *tamei*!

And what if he ate *tamei terumah* once in a while? you say. Who would be the worse for it? But, no; it was classified as an *averah chamurah*, a serious sin (if a Kohen ate something forbidden for him to eat). Every bite of food he ate needed great care. No one gets away with anything. Not even the Kohen.[31]

We have only mentioned a few of the major expenditures inherent in Torah observance. There are still many more, like building a *sukkah*, buying a *lulav* and *esrog*, *tefillin* and *mezuzos*, keeping *shemittah*, traveling at least three times a year to Jerusalem, and so on — all those cost money. The Torah makes you pay the price, no matter who you are. If a human being wanted

---

31. There are many other reasons why it wouldn't make sense to say that people from the priestly tribe of Levi wrote the Torah. First, according to the Torah, the Kohanim are descendants of Leah, one of the four Matriarchs, who is clearly described as the less favored of Ya'akov's wives. Would human writers from the tribe of Levi write that fact, or even allow it to be put down in the Scripture? Furthermore, would they include the curse their father pronounced upon them at the time he blessed the other brothers (*Bereshis* 49:5–7)? And would they divulge that the pride of their tribe, Aharon, had a share in the making of the Golden Calf (*Shemos* 32:35)? Nor would they put in the Torah that originally the *bechorim*, the firstborn, were to do the services in the *Mishkan*, the sanctuary in the desert, and only after the *bechorim* sinned did the right to perform the Temple service transfer to the tribe of Levi, implying that they were only God's second choice (*Bemidbar*, Chapter 8). And would they allow it to be written that the two most prominent figures of their tribe, Moshe and Aharon, sinned to God (albeit, in a minuscule way) and therefore were denied entry into Eretz Yisrael? And why don't we find someone of the tribe of Levi taking over after Moshe? Yehoshua, who took over after Moshe, was from the tribe of Ephraim. For these reasons alone, it is against all logic to say that the Kohanim composed the Torah.

to create a religion to sell to the masses, he would not have created the Torah as we have it — as we have always had it and observed it for over 3,300 years.

DIVINE WISDOM

Let's now consider more internal evidence that the Torah is Divine. Let's analyze a few statements in the Torah which unnecessarily leaves itself open for easy refutation *if it had been written by humans.*

When the Torah classifies certain animals which are permissible to eat, it mentions that they must have two signs: they must chew their cud and they must have true cloven hooves (*Vayikra* 11:1-8; *Devarim* 14:4-8). Of those animals which are not kosher, the Torah mentions that only four have one of the two signs (while all other non-kosher animals are missing both signs). The camel, rabbit (*arneves*), and hare (*shafan*) chew their cud but don't have split hooves, while the pig has split hooves but does not chew its cud. And the Talmud (*Chullin* 59-60) explicitly states, based on a Scriptural citation, that these are the only four species which have only one of the two characteristics of the kosher animal.

And that's the way it is, even today — these are still the only species in the world which either only chew their cud or only have split hooves (but not both). That assertion may not strike you as particularly outstanding until you think about it a little. Was Moshe a zoologist? Did he travel the entire globe and examine every species on earth? Was he in Africa, Asia, America, Australia, or anywhere else studying the animal kingdom? Yet, no other animals in the entire world other than the four mentioned in the Torah have only one of the two signs which make an animal kosher.

How could a human writer back then unequivocally state that these four species are the only species of their kind? Whoever wrote the Torah must have known exactly what was going on in the entire world. Which human being could have known that? No human being would have taken the chance of writing such easily refutable "facts." Only the Creator of the animal kingdom could have written it.

Here's another statement that no human being would have had the audacity to write.

In *Devarim* 4:32–36 it says:

> You might inquire about times long past, going back to the time that God created man on earth, from one end of the heavens to the other. See if anything as great as this has ever happened, or if the like has ever been heard. Has any nation ever heard God speaking out of fire, as you have, and remained alive? Has God ever done miracles bringing one nation from the midst of another nation with such tremendous trials, signs and wonders, and war, and a mighty hand and outstretched arm, and terrifying phenomena, as God did for you in Egypt before your very eyes? You are the ones who have been shown, so that you will know that God is the Supreme Being, and there is none other besides Him. From Heaven, He let you hear His voice so as to discipline you, and on earth He showed you His great fire, and you heard His words from within the fire.

In these verses Moshe is explaining why Hashem is going to punish *Klal Yisrael* if they disobey the Torah laws, no matter what point in history it may be. Even if it happens at the "end of days" (even thousands of years later) (verse 30). Why? Because we should have known better then to follow the ways of the surrounding nations. Why is that? Because no nation or religion at any point in history will *ever* have any claims of open miracles done for them on a national level, nor will any nation have any claim to a revelation of God. Therefore, we as a nation are expected to be on a higher level and are expected to behave as the Torah requires of us, and not to fall down to the level of the neighboring gentiles. And that's why Hashem is so upset when we forget that we are the only Chosen Nation, that has the only real truth, the truth of the Torah.

Wow! What a bold statement! Who would have the *chutzpah* to proclaim "See if anything as great as this has ever happened, or if the like has been heard"? How could a human being living 3,300 years ago make such a statement? All it would take would be one world-domineering empire to perpetrate a big fraud, and the entire Torah would be undermined forever. And between the Roman Empire from where Christianity spread, and the Islamic Empire, from where Islam spread, there was plenty of opportunity for a world-dominant empire to make whatever claims it wanted without proving it's position. Yet, nowhere in world history, nowhere in all the writings of the Christians and the Moslems, has anything like the Exodus from Egypt or the Revelation at Mt. Sinai been claimed. All they have is our claims. But that's not our point here. Our point is as follows: which human would ever make such a risky prediction? 1) If it's all a lie, then just like you think you can get away with such a colossal lie, then who's to say that at no other time in history another person won't make up similar claims? 2) And even if the events that you claim are true, still, who are you that you are able to make such long-range predictions? How do you know that some jealous religion won't make up similar claims? Why explain the future punishments of our nation based on facts over which you don't have any control? Unless of course you do have control. If you're Hashem Who gave us the Torah, and you're Hashem Who controls history according to the way His Torah dictates, only then can such claims be made and actually be carried out.

For one more example of the above, please see Appendix F where it speaks about the Western Wall.

IMPERFECT LEADERS

Let's consider one more type of internal evidence for the Torah's authenticity.

If you are trying to sell a new religion, you would want to paint the most rosy picture possible of all your leaders. And indeed, you find that other religions rarely if ever criticize their founders. Their leaders are all great, holy saints — or God Himself incarnate — who never made any mistakes. Yet in the Torah, we find just the opposite. Something negative is said about every leader.

Let's start with Avraham. Although he is not sharply criticized, nevertheless, he is blemished simply by his being the progenitor of the infamous Yishmael (*Bereshis* 11:15). Had the Torah been written by human beings, they would not have made Yishmael the founding father's son. A nephew maybe. A first cousin perhaps. But to make one of the Jewish people's most persistent and vicious enemies the very son of its original forefather is a condemnation of someone very important. We're not proud of it, but the Torah is recording the truth, not just what some man-made committee would find acceptable to be included between its pages.

The same is true with Yitzchak. He gives birth to Esav, who is equated with evil itself (*Bereshis* 25:25). And if that's not enough, the Torah tells us that Yitzchak wanted to give his blessings to Esav. Does that speak favorably for the second of our three forefathers? No, it makes him appear unwise. And not only is Esav the child of our second forefather, but he is our third forefather's twin brother! Why would a man-made religion associate such people as Yishmael and Esav with the nuclear family of its founders (unless of course it was doing nothing more than recounting the truthful facts).

And think about Ya'akov. He had to run away from Esav (*Bereshis* 28:7). Not exactly the most complimentary thing to ascribe to a founding father. And where does he run to? To Lavan, a crook, where he has to spend twenty years of his life (*Bereshis* 29:13–28). And, then, to top it off the Torah tells us that he marries that crook's two daughters!

And the dark details of Ya'akov's life do not stop there. There is the incident with his daughter, Dinah. Is it a nice thing to relate that a daughter of one of the founding fathers was violated? That is a very degrading thing to write in the Torah. Why not just skip the whole incident?

And then Ya'akov's sons, the holy tribes of Israel, sell their brother Yosef. In fact, first they want to kill him (*Bereshis*, Chapter 34). Only afterward do they decide to "merely" sell him into slavery. The Torah does not gloss over those events.[32] Neither does it gloss over the incident between Tamar (the former daughter-in-law of Yehudah) and Yehudah, from whose union came Peretz, the ancestor of the Messiah (*Bereshis*, Chapter 37)!

Of course, even though the story with the brothers ends on a happy note, as soon as they die their descendants become slaves to the Egyptians. Is that a dignified beginning for the Chosen People? It could have been written that they remained in Egypt because they were very good workers, or they had businesses, or they were good for the economy, etc. No! Lowly slaves — the lowest of the low. That is a terrible disclosure to make about the beginning of a nation. But that's what the Torah says, because that's the way our nation started off — in Egypt, under the most degrading servitude.

And Moshe: who does the redeemer of our people marry? The daughter of a former idol worshiper. Couldn't he find someone from a more dignified family? And then later the Torah tells us clearly that because he sinned he was not allowed to enter the Holy Land (*Bemidbar* 20:12). What an embarrassing statement! Do you think Moshe wanted to write that down? It could have undermined his entire leadership. If they're trying to sell a religion, they would make sure not to write such things about their greatest leader.

Then we come to the Golden Calf. Why mention such an event? And if a committee of human beings was going to mention it, why mix in Aharon, the brother of Moshe, their great leader (*Shemos* 32:35)? But the Torah has no mercy: Aharon, the second in command — the future High Priest — is associated with creating the Golden Calf. (Even though we know that his

---

32. Of course, we know that the brothers thought they were justified, because they had reason to believe Yosef would be another Yishmael or Esav. Nevertheless, the whole story would have been left out entirely had human beings written it.

intentions were good, i.e., he wanted to stall for time, knowing that Moshe would arrive shortly, his name is still besmirched by simple association. Why does that have to be written?)

And what about David, king of Israel, from whom will come the Messiah? David wrote *Tehillim* (*Psalms*). Yet, the Scripture tells us about the episode with Batsheva (*Shmuel* II, Chapters 11, 12). (Of course, you have to learn that passage with the insights of the Sages, who assure us that "no sin was committed; anyone who says David sinned is making a mistake"(*Meseches Shabbos* 56). But why write it in the first place? No committee member would dream of writing such a story about our beloved King David.)

And there are so many other such stories in the *Prophets*. Why write those unseemly things so openly? Why besmirch and blacken the faces of our great leaders, our heroes?

No other nation does that with their leaders. Usually, it is just the opposite. There are obvious attempts to lie about the degrading truth. For instance, one will often find recorded in the history books of nations which opposed each other in war that they each won the same war! Or take George Washington; American schoolchildren are taught that he never told a lie. Of course, if you look in the real history books you find out that the man was riddled with major faults. And the same holds true for all the other "great leaders" of America on down to today. We find that the private and not-so-private lives of today's politicians are soiled with the lowest type of behavior. Yet, you rarely if ever find it mentioned in mainstream history books.

That is not the way of Jewish scriptural history. The Jewish people possess a vast written (and oral) history detailing our failures and defeats, individually and collectively. The reason why we could risk telling such "stories" about our leaders is simple: we know that the Torah was given by God. True, if you're trying to make up a religion, you want to make everything sound nice and rosy. But if you are not making one up — but rather what you have is God giving human beings a Scripture that they can learn from — then the object is to provide real-life lessons.

Authors of a man-made religion have to fear that such a forthright approach will turn people away. However, God was not afraid that His people were not going to accept His Torah given at Mt. Sinai. He did not have to sell anything. His intention was to write down the pertinent stories that would convey important lessons.

Now, we are not going to explain each of the different lessons of the above accounts, though there are many; but one of the most obvious, general lessons that can be derived from all the shortcomings of the Torah's founders and leaders is that no matter how great you are, you have to watch your step. Our Torah's role models were human beings, like us. Through their shortcomings (albeit microscopic shortcomings compared to ours) we see how they dealt with trials, tribulations and even failure. We are supposed to learn from their good points, and we are supposed to learn to avoid repeating their mistakes. The word "Torah" means to teach. The Torah is a book of teaching. It is not a book of flowery fairytales related in order to try and sell us a religion. God had no problem telling the truth.

Until now, we've presented several types of arguments showing the truth of our Torah based mostly on internal evidence found in the actual text of the Torah. Let's now shift our focus and consider evidence from external sources, namely, archaeology.

ARCHAEOLOGY

Over a century ago, a new breed of "scholar" came into existence: the Bible critic. These were originally non-Jews, and later Jews, who had a stake in the attempt to disprove the Bible. (Among the early Jewish Bible critics were Reform or assimilated Jews who had already cast off their observance of Torah law. In order to create a rationale for their behavior, they set out to find ways of discrediting the Torah.) Without any real bona fide proof, they would make statements like: "The stories concerning Avraham, Yitzchak, Ya'akov, the brothers, and Egypt, etc., cannot be true. Probably at a much later date, maybe during the times of Ezra, those stories were made up."

How do we respond to their claims? The response today is very simple, surprisingly simple.[33]

Back then, when the Bible critics first made their claims, no one had any real archaeological proof one way or another. That was in the mid- to late 1800's. However, by the early 1900's, archaeological evidence started mounting. All the different discoveries showed that the stories in the Torah were accurate, down to the most minute cultural details — details that the later generations, during which the Torah was supposedly written couldn't have known, since the Biblical stories took place at a much earlier time, a time when the culture was completely different from "theirs." (Whoever the supposed "theirs" is.)[34]

For instance, if the Torah said such and such event happened at a certain time and place, archaeologists eventually dug up evidence for it. If the Torah said such and such people in such and such locale had such and such customs, archaeology eventually confirmed it.

Virtually all contemporary Bible scholars no longer side with the conclusions of the early Bible critics. Except for a few real "diehards," they have retracted their claims. They all now agree that the evidence stands overwhelmingly against the Bible critics

---

33. For a quick background to the "strike first, try and prove it later" approach of the original "enlightened" Bible critics, it is essential to read *The Road Back*, by M. Schiller, pp. 83-103 (Jerusalem: Feldheim Publishers, 2001).

34. There is a very interesting book called *The Gold of Exodus: The Discovery of the True Mount Sinai*, by Howard Blum (New York: Simon and Schuster, 1998). The people in this non-fiction book actually followed the Torah's narrative of the Exodus of the Jews from Egypt, through their early travels in the desert, culminating at Mt. Sinai. Along the way they discovered the springs and palm trees of Elim (*Shemos* 15:27), the springs of Marah (*Shemos* 15:22,23), twelve pillars (*Shemos* 24:4), and what many now believe to be the real Mt. Sinai.

and their assertions. And, thus, nowadays most of them trust the Torah to be historically true and accurate even where no evidence has yet been found.

Of course, I would not expect you to take my word for it, so let me begin by quoting one of the most respected and well-known scholars of ancient history, W. F. Albright. He writes in his book, *From the Stone Age to Christianity*:[35]

> It is not our intention here to dwell on the history of the Patriarchal Age in Palestine. So many corroborations of details have been discovered in recent years that most competent scholars have given up the old critical theory, according to which the stories of the Patriarchs are mostly retrojections from the time of the Dual Monarchy...[which means that they were supposedly made up at a later time].

Also from W. F. Albright:[36]

> Hebrew national tradition excels all others in its clear picture of tribal and family origins. In Egypt and Babylonia, in Assyria, in Phoenicia, in Greece and Rome, we look in vain for anything comparable. There is nothing like it in the tradition of the Germanic peoples. Neither India nor China can produce anything similar. In contrast with these other peoples, the Israelites preserved an unusually clear picture of simple beginnings, of complex migrations, and of extreme vicissitudes [problems], which plunged them from their favored status under Joseph, to bitter oppression after his death.

> Until recently, it was the fashion among Biblical historians to treat the patriarchal sages of Genesis as though they were artificial creations of Israelite scribes of the divided monarchy or tales told by imaginative [storytellers] around Israelite campfires during the centuries following their occupation of the country.... [However], archaeological discoveries since 1925 have changed all this.

---

35. Baltimore: Johns Hopkins Press, 1940.
36. *The Jews*, Vol. I, The Biblical Period, Philadelphia: Jewish Publication Society of America, 1963.

> Aside from a few diehards among older scholars, there is scarcely
> a single Biblical historian who has not been impressed by the
> rapid accumulation of data supporting the substantial historicity
> of patriarchal tradition....

In other words, the archaeological evidence totally exposed
the early Bible critics as irresponsible scholars, even though they
were regarded as the eminent intellectuals of their day. The evidence is so massive and complex, we cannot begin to review it
all here. Consider, though, some of the following.

To begin with, we know that over the course of centuries cultures and customs change drastically. We can't know precisely
how things were done in America or in Europe a thousand years
ago. Yet wherever archaeologists find evidence of ancient Biblical history they find that all the geographical, cultural, and historical details in the Torah are accurate in the most uncanny way.
For instance, Dr. Y. Aharoni writes:[37]

> Recent archaeological discoveries have decisively changed the en-
> tire approach of Bible critics. They now appreciate the Torah as a
> historical document of the highest caliber. The approach of the
> Bible critics has been drastically altered, because parallel docu-
> ments have been found which describe the very same events told
> in the Biblical narrative from the perspective of the Egyptians, the
> Syrians, or the ancient Canaanites. ...We are familiar [now] with
> the customs and the laws that are described in the Biblical narra-
> tives, as well as the names of the people and places which are
> mentioned (all from archaeological discoveries). All of these are
> compatible solely with the period of Biblical history under con-
> sideration. No author or editors could have put together or in-
> vented these stories hundreds of years after they happened. No
> serious Bible scholar remains who can argue with the fact [of]
> these historical events.

One of the most important archaeological finds in this vein is

---

37. *Canaanite Israel during the Period of Israeli Occupation*, published by the
Israel Defense Forces, 1959, pp. 2–3.

known as the Nuzi tablets.

> These tablets shed light on the lives and customs of the Hurians, and are of importance for Biblical studies, particularly for the patriarchal period. ...A study of the Nuzi tablets sheds light on the archaic nature of the society, reflected in narratives about the Patriarchs, and confirms [a simple point:] the accuracy of the early traditions embodied in these narratives.[38]

Thus, for instance, the Torah tells us that Avraham complained to God:

> "What will You give me, seeing that I am childless, and Eliezer, a member of my household, is going to inherit what is mine?"

> God responded to him, "No. This servant of yours will not inherit you. Rather, an actual child of yours will take over." (BERESHIS 15:2-4)

"The Nuzi tablets show that it was a well-established custom for childless persons to adopt a stranger, even a slave, as a son."[39]

The Torah states that if a woman could not have a child, she would give her husband a concubine, someone else to bear children for her. The children, in turn, were considered as her own. That is why Sarah gave Hagar, her maidservant, to Avraham for a wife (*Bereshis* 16:2, 3). Rachel, too, seeing that she was childless, gave her handmaid Bilhah to her husband Ya'akov and said: "I will consider it as if I had the son" (*Bereshis* 30:3). So too, "in Nuzi, marriage contracts obliged the wife [that] if [she went] childless, [she would have] to provide her husband with a substitute."[40]

It is revealed in the Nuzi text that the socio-legal dealings of the chapter of Eliezer's journey to find a wife for Yitzchak is identical with the societal customs of Mesopotamia at the time.

---

38. *Encyclopedia Judaica*, Vol. IX, p. 1290.
39. N.M. Sarna, *Understanding Genesis*, Schocken Books, 1966, pp. 122–23.
40. *A History of Israel.*

The marriage customs described in the Nuzi documents show the brother of the bride taking the place of the father, just as in the Torah's account where Lavan plays a central role in arranging the marriage of Rivkah, his sister. In the Nuzi marriage documents, called the "Sister Documents," a clause is found wherein the young girl announces her willingness to accept a certain group.[41] In the Torah it says:

> Let us call the young girl and ask her.
> They called Rivkah and said to her, "Will you go with this person?"
> And she said, "I will go." (BERESHIS 24:57, 58)

Until the Nuzi findings, scholars scoffed at that account, claiming that ancient society never would have given a young girl any right to refuse. However, archaeology proved the Torah right again. You had to officially get her consent, just as was found in the Nuzi contracts. That was the custom. Archaeological finds like this clearly show how the Torah's description of customs in the ancient world is accurate down to the most intimate details. It could not have been made up at a much later date, as the original critics conjectured so arrogantly, since no one could have known the details of their customs at a later date.[42] (See *Permission to Receive*, pp. 90–94, for more evidence of the truthfulness of the Patriarchal era.)

One of the most famous Biblical accounts thought to be sheer fantasy by the Bible critics was the story of Noach and the flood. Over the decades, however, evidence from across the globe came to lend support to the Torah account.[43] For instance, high on mountains in Michigan, in Vermont, and near Montreal, whale

---

41. *Biblical World Encyclopedia* (Revivim Publishers, 1982), p. 152.
42. We find John Bright, in *A History of the Jews* (pp. 77–79), also using the Nuzi tablets to corroborate all the early Patriarchal events down to the most minute detail.
43. Much of what I will bring can be found in *Sing You Righteous* (#122), by Rabbi Avigdor Miller, *zt"l*.

skeletons were found. In Alabama, farmers complained about the abundance of whale bones which covered their fields. In Georgia, walrus bones were found. It is clear that at one point in history, the American continent was under the waters of the sea. The great number of deep sea fish fossils lying on top of mountain ranges only makes sense when we understand that at one time the waters of the world rose and deposited fish from the deep sea onto the top of these mountains. And something even stranger was found, on high hills, at a number of different places over the globe. Great masses of bones of competitive animals, such as deer and wolves, were found lying together. I don't have to tell you that deer and wolves don't usually get along. Yet, they're lying together. More than that, the bones show no signs of being gnawed or chewed at. It makes no sense, unless one puts two and two together and realizes that only something like a flood could have caused them to flee to high ground, where in their state of terror they were busier saving themselves from drowning, than to be concerned about eating or being eaten.

Furthermore, there are inscriptions all over the world about the flood. In 1853, during excavations at ancient Ninveh, tablets on which was inscribed the now-famous Gilgamesh epic were found. The pagan gods there are depicted as assembling to pass judgment on a wicked mankind. One righteous man was chosen for deliverance and commanded to erect a ship in which to rescue his kin and every sort of living creature. A great deluge followed which erased all mankind and all animals and fowl. Interestingly, this Gilgamesh epic describes that pitch was used for smearing to waterproof this boat; and that the craft had a window; and that a dove was sent out and came back; which is exactly as the Torah describes it (*Bereshis*, Chapter 6).

At Nipor, a tablet inscribed in Sumerian which also describes a flood was discovered. It relates how the hero was informed beforehand of its coming, how he erected a craft, and how after the flood he gave offerings to God and was blessed. Similar records are found elsewhere, proving that the only fantasy was the theories of the "intellectuals" who rejected the Torah's account of

Noach without any evidence to the contrary whatsoever.[44]

Another incredible archaeological find in support of the Torah is the Ipuwer Papyrus. Archaeologists discovered in Egypt an entire book which describes cataclysmic events similar to the Ten Plagues. For instance, in Papyrus 2:10 it says: "The river is blood." In the same chapter it says: "Plague is throughout the land, blood is everywhere. Men shrink from tasting...and thirst after water." It's apparently describing the plague of blood.

Next, the plague of pestilence (*dever*) seems to be described in Papyrus 5:5: "All animals, their hearts weep, cattle moan...."

Also the plague of hailfire (*barad*) is seemingly described in Papyrus 2:10: "Gates, columns, and walls are consumed by fire...."

The plague of locusts: "...No fruit, nor herbs are found. Hunger" (Papyrus 6:1). "Grain has perished on every side" (Papyrus 6:3).

Finally, it says in the document: "He who places his brother in the ground is everywhere...It is groaning that is throughout the land mingled with lamentations." This certainly seems to be referring to the slaying of the firstborn.

And the Ipuwer Papyrus is dated in the same general era as when the Torah says the plagues would have happened. The archaeologists write of it:[45]

> The papyrus is a script of lamentations, a description of ruin and horror. It is a record of some natural catastrophe, followed by a tremendous social upheaval, and, in the description of this catastrophe, we recognize many details of the disturbances that ac-

---

44. The information here is taken from the books *Ages in Chaos* and *World in Collision*, both written by Immanuel Valikovsky, Abacus Publications. Also in *Permission to Receive*, pp. 88–90, much more evidence is brought to show the truth behind the account of the flood.
45. From the introduction to "*Admonitions of an Egyptian Sage – from a Heiratic Papyrus in Leiden*," by Alan H. Gardner, M.A. Oxford, Leipzig:. J.C. Hinrich Buchhandlung, 1909, pp. 8–18. Cited in *Ages in Chaos*, pp. 42–57.

companied the Exodus, as narrated in the Scriptures. And we don't have any recorded history of any such other problem in the history of Egypt.

(See *Permission to Receive*, pp. 98–108, for much more evidence supporting the narratives of the era of the Jews during their stay in Egypt.)

In conclusion, let me quote another renowned historian, Will Durant:[46]

> Each passing year adds to our store of knowledge and provides us with more and more documents, inscriptions, monuments, and excavations which confirm the Bible's historical accuracy. ...Science is now in a position to state categorically that the Bible is factual till proven otherwise.

That last line is worth repeating: "Science is now in a position to state categorically that the Bible is factual till proven otherwise." There are many archaeologists and historians who make similar statements, and there are many more pieces of evidence we can bring. However, the point has been made well enough. With regard to the theory which Bible critics (Wellhausen's theory) wished to claim; that there is evidence that the Bible was written by different authors because of some deviations in the style of writing from one place to the other, these are ideas that have also been disproven by many later scholars, with Drs. Isaac Kilkawada and Arthur Quinn, professors at the University of California (Berkley), being among those who recently wrote (in 1989) about this theory: "Its formation may well have represented the dawn of a new day for Bible scholarship, but days have their dawns and their dusks."[47]

Without archaeology, we had all the proofs necessary to

---

46. Will Durant, *The Story of Civilization*, Vol. I, New York: Simon and Schuster, 1950.

47. Isaac Kilkawada and Arthur Quinn, *Before Abraham Was: A Provocative Challenge to the Documentary Hypothesis*, San Francisco: Ignatius Press, 1989, p.13.

know that the Torah is authentic. Archaeological evidence, however, answers the skeptic from his own sources. Only the real diehards refuse to submit to the obvious conclusion: the Torah is authentic beyond a reasonable doubt.

3

―――― The ――――
World to Come

ETERNAL EXISTENCE

WE'VE COME A LONG WAY. We've strengthened our faith in the existence of God and our belief in the Divine origin of the Torah. However, there's another major principle of belief that we must discuss, namely, that everyone possesses a soul which, after one's death, is destined to "experience" the afterlife (commonly referred to as *Olam ha-ba*, the "World to Come"), i.e., the place where the soul will receive its just reward and/or punishment based on its performance in carrying out the will of Hashem as dictated by His Torah, while it was down here in this world.

Belief in the World to Come is one of the main tenets of Judaism. It's therefore very important to be absolutely convinced of its existence. It's also a great motivator for performing good deeds, as well as a strong deterrent from doing sins. Of course, chances are you probably already have a certain amount of belief in an afterlife; after all, every primary work of the Sages, from the Talmud to the Midrash, speaks of it matter-of-factly over and over again. However, we were put into this world to gain for ourselves the greatest share possible in *Olam ha-ba* (*Avos*, Chapter 4, *mishnayos* 21,22). Consequently, the more concrete our belief in *Olam ha-ba* is, the more careful we will be with our observance of the Torah and its laws, which in turn will ultimately entitle us to a greater share in *Olam ha-ba*. If we find ourselves trying to do whatever we can to increase our material acquisitions, though they are transient, then surely we should do whatever we can to maximize our eternal acquisitions. Therefore, let's see how we can increase and fortify our faith in *Olam ha-ba*.

BESSIE THE COW — A LIFE OF BLISS

Some of our greatest sages found it worthwhile and important to prove the existence of *Olam ha-ba* through means of pure logic. (Later in this chapter we will also focus on some of the Scriptural sources for the ideas of afterlife, immortality, and the soul.) The most recent sage, the Steipler Gaon (Rabbi Yaakov Yisroel Kanievsky, zt"l, 1899–1985), in his *Chayei Olam* (Chapters 2–13), writes at great length about this. Obviously he felt it was an important endeavor.[1] Since faith can often be strengthened through sound reasoning, I've taken the liberty to synthesize some of the best rational arguments for the existence of a World to Come into what I call the "Bessie the Cow" argument. To understand this argument properly we must first bear in mind two simple principles:

- Everything God does is purposeful
- Everything God does is good and kind (i.e., an expression of *kindliness*)

Concerning the first principle, in Chapter 1 we discussed how everything in the world is inherently purposeful. There is no detail — from the trigger hairs on a Venus' flytrap to the human brain — which is not purposeful. We saw how all the details found in a complex entity interact with one another in the most wondrous ways, showing how all that God does is pur-

---

1. Rabbi A. Miller, zt"l, also writes at length on this topic in *Rejoice O Youth*, pp. 97–116.

poseful. The intricate designs that are found in nature, down to the microscopic level, point to the Infinite Intelligence of a Great Designer.

Concerning the second principle, we have to understand that not only does this world point to the Infinite Intelligence of God, but it also points to the great kindliness, or *chesed*, of the Creator. *Olam chesed yibaneh*, "The world is built by *chesed*" (*Tehillim* 89:3). Just to cite one example, consider the many different types of food there are. There are many kinds of grains, meat products, and dairy products. There's a tremendous variety of fruits and vegetables, all having different tastes and colors. If you don't like green peppers, you can find red peppers. If you don't like peppers, perhaps you like oranges. And if you don't like oranges, there are nectarines. If you don't like nectarines, maybe you like plums. You don't like plums either? Fine, but maybe you like cherries or apples? You don't like every kind of apple? But you probably can find one type of apple that you enjoy among the Cortland apples, or Macintosh apples, or Red Delicious apples, or green Granny Smith apples. There's something for everybody's taste.

And we can't forget to mention how we live in such a beautiful world. There's the particular beauty of the winter and there's the unique beauty of the summer; and there are the distinctive beauties of fall and spring. There are the breathtaking sunrises and sunsets. There are the waves of the ocean, and there are the lakes and flowing rivers. There are the beautiful trees blossoming at the beginning of spring — and the delicious fragrance of green grass sprouting upon rolling hills, and all those magnificently colored flowers. And of course, there's the beautiful blue sky.

There's no doubt about it, it's a gorgeous world. God made it that way on purpose. He could have made the world plain and dreary. He could have substituted our delicious food for a single multi-vitamin (and not even a chewable vitamin, but a vitamin that you have to swallow whole). But, no. He created luscious fruits and vegetables in an array of beautiful colors amidst a world that inspires artists to the greatest heights. He made a beautiful, varied world filled with so much color and fragrance and taste, etc. — all for our pleasure.

That's called *chesed*, kindness. It's a world brimming with the Creator's *chesed* and purposefulness, wherever we turn.

That is, "wherever we turn" until we get to the zenith of creation: the human being. The human being, who is on top of the ecology ladder, the one who is utilizing this planet the most, the one for whom the Torah was written, is the only creature who is totally out of whack. He has tendencies and instincts which seem purposeless and even detrimental to his existence. I never really appreciated this until one day, my rebbe in the Yeshivah of Staten Island, Rabbi Gershon Weiss, *shlita*, challenged us with a very intriguing question: "Who do you think is happier, you or Bessie the Cow?" After he explained to us what he meant, there was no doubt — Bessie had us beat hands down. Let me explain.

Built into creation is the fact that every single species, whether it be a cow, bee, spider, fish, bird, etc., has it's own particular set of instincts which are custom-made to ensure its well-being and survival. For example, the spider has an instinct to spin the most complicated web. Bees are flying around looking for pollen and gathering nectar. All the creatures in the world instinctively do what they were programmed to do, and they live "happily ever after."

Except for human beings. Humans are plagued with instincts that unless their real purpose is understood, not only make people unhappy, *but actually come into conflict* with their most basic instinct, which is the instinct for survival. We will examine different human traits, instincts, and needs, and you will see what we mean. We will start by examining our inherent trait of jealousy. How many human lives have been ruined, how many people have died, how many have been killed, and how many wars have been fought all because of human jealousy? Do cows experience jealousy? It's highly doubtful. If one cow is living in a fancy barn, does his less ritzy cow-friend feel deprived? Of course not. He also has a barn. He just lays down on some grass and everything is fine. He's happy. You give him a little grass, a little water, and that's all he needs. But humans — forget it. Jealousy drives us humans crazy.

Even though your house is fine — it's got its roof, its heat, its air conditioner, and everything else the average human being needs these days — since your friend down the block has a much fancier house, with marble steps no less, it eats you up. All of sudden you feel the need to make more money for "much needed" home improvements. Consequently, even though you have to work overtime, sometimes to the point that it may endanger your health, the jealousy is so real that you are willing to make the sacrifice. Am I going to be without marble? Am I going to be without such a fancy house? (And I won't even begin to describe all the fancy cars in his friend's driveway.) It's called keeping up with the Joneses. Everyone feels it.

And if it's not your neighbor's house, then you're jealous of someone in your office who's more successful than you. And if you think you're "above" jealousy, think again. Yes, you. Think back to your yeshivah (school) days — or perhaps you are still in yeshivah now. You don't feel jealous, right? Sure. You're a nice yeshivah boy, minding your own business. Then, what about that other guy in your class — the one everyone's always asking their questions to and trying to see if he has any extra time to learn with them? Did you notice your mind trying to undercut his arguments? Did you notice your urge to tell others how this guy is really not as smart as they think? Did you ever wonder why you just don't happen to like this guy too much? It's called jealousy. And all of us are prone to it.

Yes, people get ulcers because of jealousy. People die because of jealousy. They overwork so much that they ruin their health. It's called the rat race, a never-ending rat race. And if one day you do catch up with "the rat," all of a sudden you turn the corner, and lo and behold, there you see an even bigger house of somebody else you know. Now you'll have to add a porch in the back of your house and a whole new floor.

It's very similar regarding our desire for honor. Honor is not so much a matter of jealousy — wanting what the other person has — but it is more a matter of trying to possess a certain status for its own sake. You want a fancy house, and even an expensive car, even if no one else that you know has one. Why? Not because of jealousy, but because you want people to talk about you. It will show others your "true worth." Of course, you know money doesn't grow on trees, so you will have to work hard, days and nights probably, to satisfy your need for honor. But it's worth it, even though it could cause you all types of health problems and perhaps even kill you. Nevertheless, it's worth it. Honor.

Do you find cows running around looking for any type of honor? Do they want a prominent seat in the synagogue, fancy clothes, a million-dollar barn? Cows don't know what honor means. You give a cow some grass and it's one hundred percent happy. But humans will even commit murder or suicide if they feel they were, or will soon be dishonored. No cow is going to kill another because of a little insult to its honor.

And consider human passions and lusts. Animals are not driven mad by lusts and desires. They breed during certain seasons and that's it. When the mating season is over, they're not interested anymore. But human beings are plagued with lusts all the time. It's a 365-day-a-year season. Lust literally kills people. People are contracting all types of diseases because they can't control their lusts. But even if they never contract any terrible diseases, the constant necessity to overcome one's passions causes all humans much distress.[2] Many people who had tre-

---

2. Those who live according to the Torah are much happier in this respect (and in many other respects). The Jew marries with the full acceptance that the wife that he married was preordained by God, and therefore he accepts that all other women are clearly off limits now, and transgressing in this area would bring the severest of penalties. Therefore, under normal circumstances, the average Jew isn't looking for trouble. So he commits himself to the wife he chose and just keeps his eyes and mind off other women, which enables him to live with great tranquility.

mendous potential for greatness never reached it, because in their youth they got swept away by their passions which completely distracted them from pursuing more noble and rewarding accomplishments. It's a powerful instinct which drives people crazy. People have murdered those who have gotten in their way of fulfilling their lusts. People have committed suicide because of lustful relationships that broke up. Why do we need such strong instincts? And the desire for other physical pleasures can also cause problems. People overeat, which is very unhealthy. Smoking, drinking, drugs, etc., all come to trouble and problems. We'd be better off being Bessie.

But we're not finished. We come now to another human shortcoming: getting along with one other. *Shalom*, peace. So much depends on getting along with others. Every relationship is a challenge. Whether it's a mean boss. Or fellow employees who are very difficult to get along with. Sometimes it's parents. Sometimes it's children who are difficult. Grandparents. Brothers and sisters. Our whole life is surrounded daily with people with whom we have to get along, and it's usually not that simple.

Shalom can even be a problem for yeshivah students, a population educated in good character traits, who all are sharing, more or less, the same goals in life. And still you find that many have a hard time getting along as roommates in a dormitory. This guy wants the light on. That guy wants the light off. This guy wants the air conditioner on. That guy wants the air conditioner off. This one wants the heat on. That one wants the heat off. Sometimes it seems as if all their good character traits are ready to go right out the window.

And what about marriage? Women, as you've probably noticed, are very different from men. And vice versa. Men tend to talk about things like their careers, cars, sports, and making money. Women in general tend to talk about raising children, clothing, food, and recipes. Yet, men and women have to get along in marriage. (And they usually have the same squabbles as the above roommates.) Why couldn't God have made life much simpler and created humans with extremely fine character traits, and with identical, or at least very similar needs and interests, so that everyone could live in harmony, "happily ever after"?

Now, let's look at Bessie.

Cows generally get along wonderfully with one another. They don't mock or denigrate each other. They're not cynical. They don't embarrass each other. And they aren't driven by a desire for honor. Or have problems with jealousy. Or have character problems. Or display arrogance. Cows get along with everyone. They're not such complicated creatures as we humans are. "Just give me my little patch of grass and I'm happy," is their motto.

People, on the other hand, have problems with mothers, fathers, brothers, sisters, in-laws — mothers-in-law, fathers-in-law, brothers-in-law, and sisters-in-law. There are so many different types of people to get along with, but lucky for cows, they don't have that problem.

And another thing: Cows don't commit suicide.

But humans are plagued with so many problems that in the past few decades psychology has become a major profession. There are more people going to psychologists than ever before. And there are also more people committing suicide than ever before. People are unhappy.

Humans are also possessed with a never-ending quest to have more and more money and possessions — and not just to obtain honor through them, or out of jealousy, but there's simply a drive to acquire. When it comes to money, a person just never has enough. "He who has 100 wants 200" (*Midrash Rabbah, Koheles* 1:34, 3:12). There's something in us that always wants more. "No man dies with even half of his desires fulfilled" (Ibid.). What is it in human beings that makes them so money-hungry? In the long run, it's terrible for us. It's stressful. A roller coaster stock market. Heavy competition. Overworking. Worshiping the holy dollar. It's rough.

Cows, you ask? Cows don't work for a living. All a cow needs is grass. It's not hard to get grass — the grass grows by itself. Other animals? There are leaves on trees, and berries on

bushes. They don't have to plant anything. All the food an animal needs is readily available. They don't need any clothing either. They were created with lots of fat, and warm fur. Even if
it's freezing outside, they're warm. It's amazing. There's not a
single animal in the world that needs any clothing. Whatever fur
or skin it has is always sufficient. (When you see poodles wearing sweaters, remember it's completely unnecessary. A poodle
doesn't need a sweater! It's just that the poodle's owner wants to
get a sweater for her poodle. It looks cute.)

However, we find that humans must go through quite a lot
just to acquire their basic necessities. Not only is clothing a hassle to come by, but even obtaining our most fundamental necessities of life, like food, is a major hassle. It takes such an effort
until you finally get a little wheat or corn to grow. So much
work. So much time. So much effort must be expended until we
can put a simple piece of bread into our mouths.

And then there's the problem of shelter. Animals have natural shelters. Humans have to spend so much time and money,
making, buying, or renting a proper shelter.

And raising children — such a difficult, expensive, time-
consuming job which lasts for years and years. A baby animal,
by contrast, is already out on its own after a few months — some
in even less than a few months — some even in a day, in a minute, or even in a second. A calf in just a short time goes out and
starts to eat grass. What else does it have to do? Yet, humans
have to raise children for so many years. Why? Why should we
have that struggle? Why is it necessary?

And sicknesses. Humans are extremely frail and constantly
subject to all types of sicknesses. Animals suffer from far fewer
ailments when left alone in their natural habitat. Humans, who
in so many ways are superior to all animals, are also in many
ways frailer than animals. Why is this so?

And another question: Why does a human being need such
tremendous mental capacity? I mean, as the saying goes, "Ignorance is bliss." If you don't know too much, fewer things bother
you. And don't we see people who are very simple and some-

times even slightly deficient in their mental capacities, who are happier than most others? So why did God endow us with such great and seemingly excessive mental capacities? It seems unnecessary. We can get along fine or even better without it.

And one more point. Free will. Animals never truly change. They have their set of instincts and they live their lives without change. But human beings can change drastically overnight. This afternoon he was an evil person. Then something happened in his life and all of a sudden he turned over a new leaf. Why do we need to have such a vast ability to change? Is free will necessary for our *physical* preservation? Absolutely not. Humanity could also have been governed by unchanging instincts, without opportunity for free will, and we probably would have been much better off. Most human anguish and pain, suffered because of wars that have been fought, have been due to the misuse of one's free will for evil objectives. So what good is it?

In summary, most human beings are working very hard, and many are suffering and/or unhappy a great portion of their lives. Either you're struggling to make ends meet or worried about losing what you already have. There are moments of jealousy and moments of desperation. There's the desiring of that which cannot be acquired, and the disappointment over that which finally is acquired. There's the endless pursuit of honor and the inevitable feeling that one never receives the honor he deserves. There's the difficulty of dealing morally with our passions. There are difficult relationships with peers, neighbors, friends, spouses, and children. And finally, if one has weathered all of the above, there is sickness, and the infirmities of old age, and ultimately death. By now, I think you should be pretty convinced that "Bessie the Cow" is much better off than we are.

What has God wrought? Why such a difficult, roller-coaster life with its unceasing ups and downs? Why should we have been given drives that are detrimental for our physical preservation? No animals have such a phenomenon.

So why *did* God create humans this way? Humans — the apex, the acme, the zenith of the universe, the purpose of all creation — and there God goofs?! Has God, the consistent Doer of every type of *chesed* and compassion toward all creatures, forgotten us?! Animals, birds, and insects were all created with everything they need. Yet, we humans have all of these seemingly harmful needs, desires, aspirations, and instincts. What happened? Was it all a big mistake? A cruel joke?

The basic answer is, "Yes" — if we make the mistake of thinking that a person lives *only for this world*. Then it truly *doesn't* make any sense. However, in reality, as we shall see, the whole makeup of humans points to the fact that they were *not* created for this world, that is, for this world alone. Hashem obviously never goofs, nor does He play cruel jokes. If we'll just study all of the above human frailties closely, we will come to the obvious conclusion that, as usual, God has designed everything perfectly, and more so, we will see that there must be a greater world that God has created us for. We will come to realize that this world is only a preparation for the eternal World to Come. Ultimately, we have been endowed with all of these needs, desires, and complex character traits, etc., for one reason; because we were put in this world to be tested by God in various ways. Passing these tests, perfecting our character, and purifying our souls through a lifetime of spiritual pursuits will enable us to merit the enormous, eternal pleasures the worthy soul will receive by meriting to be together with God in the World to Come. The more spiritually inclined we make ourselves in this world by passing these tests, the closer we'll get to God in the World to Come. To be worthy of true eternal bliss, it surely pays to have instincts and drives that although can be detrimental to ones physical well-being when used incorrectly, can be used properly to acquire true spiritual gains — the real reason why these instincts were created.

The question then is as follows: Precisely how do all those unique human "frailties," such as jealousy, desires, honor, etc., prepare us for the future world? Let's take each "frailty" one by one, and we'll begin to understand.

PREPARING FOR OLAM HA-BA

Jealousy. True jealousy can be very detrimental to our physical well-being when used for material pursuits. However, if we understand that we were created to accomplish in the spiritual realm, in order to make ourselves worthy of the great bliss of being with God in the World to Come, then jealousy can be very beneficial. This can be understood in two ways.

First of all, jealousy can be used to spur us on toward spiritual self-improvement, and that's obviously good. If one is jealous of a friend who is advancing in his knowledge of Torah, or of a friend who is very active in charitable organizations, and the jealous person thereby overcomes his laziness and starts to learn more himself, or he starts to become more involved in charities, then he is utilizing jealousy in a positive way. So, too, when one sees a righteous person and he decides to try and be like him, he too is utilizing jealousy in a proper fashion.

A second benefit of jealousy is that it sets us up to all the tests that jealousy affords us. Will a person cheat, steal, or slander his competitor because he is jealous over his competitor's success? When a person overcomes powerful feelings of jealousy toward his fellow Jew he is making himself worthy of great reward (*Shemos* 20:14; *Devarim* 5:18). God definitely had His good reasons for bestowing jealousy upon us. Surely it wasn't for the negative physical effects that it can have on us, but rather for the possible spiritual benefits that it can cause us. And that only makes sense when we admit to the existence of the World to Come.[3]

Honor. Honor can also be a great help in our preparation for

---

3. If one thinks that jealously is for the advancement of technology, then we must ask if it is really such an advancement. The fact is that the world was a much happier one (or certainly not as stressed and neurotic) when people had less "gadgets." People lived a quiet tranquil life. Even today, country people live a much more relaxed life than busy city dwellers, who are always on the run, never standing still a minute to enjoy life to its fullest.

the World to Come, when it is used as an incentive for one's spiritual progress. A person may want to be a righteous person or a renowned scholar because of the honor it will bestow him. People sometimes give large donations to worthy causes when they know that they will be honored for it. (Of course it is better to do things strictly for the sake of Heaven, but until we reach that level, honor is a valid and even necessary incentive.[4] As our Sages tell us, it's all right to begin our service to God on a lower level, since it will usually lead to a higher level of service once you get used to serving Him.) And so, the desire for honor can also help people achieve important spiritual accomplishments.

Honor also helps prepare us for the World to Come by serving as a major test. Will a person who is well-honored turn haughty? Will he yell at anyone who doesn't fulfill his every wish and desire? Will the rich person still pray to God for continued success, and will he thank God for all that He has bestowed upon him, or will he attribute his success and honor to his own wisdom and hard work? Will he give charity in proportion to his wealth? If he loses his honor, in whatever way, will he rebel against God? Honor is good when we realize that it's a drive set up by God as a test that we must utilize for the spiritual gains that it can afford us, which is just one more way of making ourselves worthy of *Olam ha-ba*.

Desires, passions, *ta'avah*. The fact that we aren't given any rest from our desires can only be understood if we realize that we were put in this world to make ourselves worthy of the World to Come. Life is short, and therefore, in order to utilize it to its fullest we need to be constantly tested. And so we are. A cow has its short breeding season (and still there are plenty of cows even though we keep eating them), but humans have no seasons. But why must we be subjected to such constant "torture"? You want to know why? It's because we were put in this world to be tested, each and every day, all year round. Anytime

---

4. See *Michtav Me'Eliyahu*, *ma'amer* on *Mi-toch she'lo lishmah ba lishmah*.

we overcome our animal instincts, and give precedence to the spiritual side of us, we are improving ourselves and making ourselves holy, thereby making ourselves more and more worthy to be with God in the World to Come.

Of course, this is true of all desires, even the desire to eat food. We are being tested to see if we will compromise our standard of *kashrus*. We are also being tested to see if we will damage the bodies that God gave us, by either overeating, or by eating unhealthy foods, etc. All of these desires were planted in us to constantly challenge us, thereby enabling us to spiritually improve ourselves in order to be worthy of more and more in *Olam ha-ba*. One can also gain in his spirituality by practicing different levels of abstinence from any of the different types of physical pleasures available to him in this world, thereby making himself a holy being which will surely make him worthy of closeness to God in the World to Come.

And now, let's consider *middos*, character traits. Every minute is another test of our character. Are you going to yell and get angry whenever you feel like it? Are you going to talk to others arrogantly? Are you going to gossip? Are you going to make fun of people? Are you nice to people? Are you a role model for them? Are you trying to help them when you can? Are you cruel to people? We are continually surrounded by tests of character. Every person you bump into is another test. These tests are tailor-made to enable us to improve ourselves in order to earn eternal reward in *Olam ha-ba*.

The desire for wealth is also meant to be a test. Supporting a family isn't easy and it's also filled with many tests. Will you cheat or steal in order to get what you need for your family? Will you violate the Torah prohibition of taking interest? Will you violate any other of the intricate laws of business? Will this rat race bring you to work more than really necessary, instead of spending more time in the pursuit of spiritual endeavors? Will we be satisfied with our basic necessities of food, clothing, and shelter, or will we overdo things and spend too much time trying to amass wealth so that we can have delicacies to eat, fancy clothing, expensive cars, extravagant vacations, and a huge mansion? These are lifelong tests.

Raising children. Raising children is a major test. Will you raise them with the proper spiritual values? (In other words, will you let your children destroy their souls by allowing them to become exposed to the pollution of the TV, VCR, Internet, etc.?) Will you yourself, in your own home, set a good example of how a Jew must act? Will you give your children a proper Jewish education by sending them to appropriate religious schools? These are all tests that only humans have, and only humans need, because only humans are in this world to be tested to make themselves, and their children, worthy of *Olam ha-ba*.

Sickness. This is only beneficial if we understand our purpose in life. Sicknesses provide us with many different tests. Will you accept the fact that God has made you sick (realizing that obviously He has a good reason for what He has done), or will you turn against God in anger? During the illness, will you push yourself and still try to pursue the service of God to the best of your ability, or will you be lazy and use the sickness as an excuse to slacken off? Will you put your whole trust in the doctor, or will you realize that the doctor is only an agent of God (and therefore your trust must be in God and your prayers must go out to God)? And most important, will you utilize your illness to repent for past bad deeds, or will you continue to hold onto your bad ways? Once again we are faced with tests, tests, and more tests.

But cows, on the other hand, who don't have a soul, and don't get *Olam ha-ba*, don't need to be tested to see how they will raise their calves, and they don't need the test of sickness. Nor do they have tests of jealousy, honor, and other *middos* and desires — because they don't need them. Therefore, God created them with their set of built-in instincts which ensure them an "easy" life, with a minimal amount of problems.

Fantastic mental capacity. Why is it necessary to have such huge mental potential? (I say potential, since, according to experts, most humans don't even use a tenth of their mental capacity.) We know that "ignorance is bliss." It's simply not necessary to be so smart. All you need is a good set of instincts, just like a cow, bee, or ant, and you'll manage just fine. A human's mental capacity is sort of similar to a small child wearing an adult's overcoat and hat. It's obviously not for him. To the contrary, it's an extra heavy burden that he doesn't need for his physical survival.

However, if we understand that the purpose of human life is to recognize our Creator, and to properly serve Him, and if we know that we have to learn to love and fear God simultaneously, then we can easily understand why we need a huge mental capacity. It's not easy at all to properly comprehend God's Torah and to be able to meticulously follow all of the laws and ethical teachings found in the Torah, something which is surely necessary if we are looking forward to being close with God in the World to Come. For such matters a large mental capacity is certainly necessary.

Which leads us to free will.

Why do we need free will? No other creature in the world has free will. All creatures have pre-programmed sets of instincts which keep them within certain bounds of behavior. They never change. Humans, however, have the amazing capacity to change all their different character traits from good to bad, or vice versa, whenever they wish. A human has the ability to always change his way of life in the most drastic of ways, for good or for bad. But wouldn't it have been much better for society if we all had been pre-programmed to be good? Why give us free will to be bad, really bad?

The answer by now should be obvious! We are here to be tested, to choose good over bad, so that we can earn a place with God in the World to Come, true eternal bliss. If we were pre-programmed robots, then we wouldn't be deserving of any reward, just like a cow isn't deserving of a reward in the World to Come, since it hasn't done anything to deserve it. Therefore, God has given us free will to earn our *Olam ha-ba*.[5]

Thus, the Bessie quandary finally makes sense. God made everything perfect, especially humans — and especially when it comes to the unique, seemingly negative human character traits such as jealousy, honor, etc. This world is not an end unto itself. Everything is tied into the fact that a human being was put into this world to use every opportunity possible to prepare himself for eternal life with God, the Source of all good, in the World to Come. This world just serves as a corridor, a hallway, to a tremendous banquet room where we will reap the benefits of having led a righteous life, where we will enjoy for eternity the splendor of God's presence. This knowledge gives purpose and

---

5. This answers the famous question of why God didn't put us all straight into *Olam ha-ba*? The answer is that truthfully, that's where our soul actually came from before it came down to this world. But our souls were "unhappy" since they were just getting handouts, and nobody really feels good about a handout, no matter how big it is. These souls want to be more Godly. How do you become more Godly? You try to be like God (and actually a soul is *in a certain sense* a part of God [see *Bereshis* 1:27, 2:7, 5:1, as brought in many of the holy works of our rabbis]). Just like God is self-sufficient, so too the soul wants to be self-sufficient and earn its own "living," so to speak. Thus, God, Who loves to bestow good, wants to bestow the ultimate good, which is that we earn through our own merits, the perfection necessary that will enable our souls to be as close as possible to God in the World to Come — which is the ultimate bliss that a soul can experience. Consequently, God gave each person free will to earn on his own his portion in the World to Come. God sets up many tests of righteousness throughout one's life, tests which when passed are the source of one's perfection. Of course, with opportunity always comes some risk, and this is no exception. We must be careful while we are in this world not to distance ourselves from God by failing the tests presented to us, thereby defiling our souls, sometimes to the point where God will not accept us anymore in His presence. Of course, one should never despair since God always, at any time in a person's life, accepts sincere repentance.

great meaning to an otherwise pretty purposeless world.[6]

Of course, living a life pursuing spiritual endeavors does not mean that a person is allowed to forget that he is a physical being. And that, too, is a test. Watching our health is a test. Going to sleep on time is also a test. Believing in the World to Come does not mean that we can neglect our physical necessities. However, the point is that we must make sure that our physical needs are not *the main focus* of our lives. We must be keenly focused on utilizing all the tests that life offers us, in order to properly prepare ourselves for *Olam ha-ba*, the far more important world, the world where if we deserve it, we will bask eternally in the splendor of the "light of God." (See the *Chovos Ha-Levavos* in the chapter on *bitachon*, where he states that our ultimate purpose is to bask in the "light of God." He brings verses to back it up from *Yeshayahu* 58:8, *Daniel* 12:3, and *Iyov* 33:30; and there are many other verses that espouse such a concept.)

Every minute in this world is another opportunity knocking. That's what God wants. We are down here for 70 years or so, and every minute, in fact every second, can be utilized to help prepare ourselves for the World to Come. And so, you can stop feeling jealous of Bessie, and be happy you're a human, and even happier that you're an eternal Jew! (Of course, under certain circumstances a gentile, also, can receive a share in the World to Come.)

---

6. As a "side benefit" of keeping the Torah, one is treated with the most balanced, nutritious diet for optimum living. The Torah, which was made by the Creator of mankind, was made with mankind in mind. The Torah is a perfectly balanced plan for living, optimally blending the physical and spiritual needs of humans, and thereby providing a true Torah Jew with the greatest potential to live a harmonious and content life.

Living as a Torah-observant Jew gives one myriad opportunities to turn all of our mundane actions into constant, eternal, Godly actions, making us suitable to be worthy of the World to Come. (See *Shulchan Aruch*, *Orach Chayim*, Chapter 231.) What can be a more fulfilling and meaningful life than that?

WHEN BAD THINGS HAPPEN — MORE EVIDENCE THAT THERE'S A WORLD TO COME

Knowing that God is intimately involved with every little thing that occurs in this world, how can we reconcile the fact that we live in a world of seemingly chaotic justice, a world in which we seem to see *tzaddik v'ra lo, rasha v'tov lo* — "a righteous person has bad happen to him; and an evil person has good happen to him"? This question is one of life's greatest puzzles, a question that has occupied the minds of the greatest thinkers in history.

Now, of course, we could eliminate half the question by pointing out that not everyone that we think is a righteous person is indeed a righteous person. Similarly, not everyone that we think is an evil person is actually an evil person. If we would know the truth, then we would discover that outer appearances are often not as they seem.

And we could minimize the problem even further, because not everything that looks bad is actually bad. Just because this righteous person doesn't have a Lincoln Towncar or a Lexus doesn't mean things are going badly for him. He's quite happy with his jalopy. I mean, it moves, doesn't it? And if he's lucky, the car may even have a working air conditioner in it. Moreover, at least he has a house. So he doesn't have a fancy house, and maybe he's just renting an apartment, but at least he has a roof over his head and perhaps he even has one or two air conditioners in his apartment as well. And I'm sure he has heat in the winter. So, thank God, everything is fine. Vacations? So he doesn't go to Florida. Who says going to Florida is so good anyway? He doesn't need it. So what's so bad?

And the same, in reverse, goes for the evil person. Not all his "good" is really "so good." Many wealthy people commit suicide, get divorced, or live pretty miserable lives despite the "good." They don't hang their dirty laundry out for all of us to see, but it's there. They can have plenty of problems, problems directly related to their health and wealth, despite what it may seem to the outsider.

Nevertheless, after all is said and done, it's fair to assume that there are times when a righteous person suffers. Similarly, many times you see an evil person really enjoying good times. And thus, we are left with our puzzle of how to understand God's justice.

Here again, if we view the grave as the "end of the line" then we'll never understand anything; we'll just keep questioning God. However, our questions will begin to clear up once we understand that this world is directly connected to the reward and punishment of the World to Come. There are two important premises to make in order to understand the matter properly:

- A person can "eat up" some, or even all, of his future reward (*Olam ha-ba*) that was set aside for him, while he is still in this world;[7] and,
- A person can be spared the suffering of punishment in the next world (*Gehinnom*), due to his sins, through the difficulties and hardships endured during his lifetime in this world[8]

This entire concept is brought out in Psalm 92. David begins this psalm by speaking of the importance of thanking and singing to God for the kindness which He continually does for us. (We elaborated on some of the *chesed* and kindness of God earlier in this chapter.) David is in awe of the grandiosity and complexity of his Creator's world, with all its wisdom and beauty. In fact, he was so awe-inspired with God's kindness and wisdom, it's no wonder that when David came to an area which seemed to contradict this *chesed*, he stopped to comment on it. Which is why Psalm 92 abruptly changes its tone right in middle of the psalm.

---

7. See *Devarim* 7:10; *Tehillim* 92; *Berachos* 55b (See Rashi: *l'adam tov marin lo chalom ra, l'adam ra marin lo chalom tov*); *Shabbos* 32a; *Midrash Bereshis Rabbah, Lech Lecha* 44:4.

8. *Berachos* 5a; *Kiddushin* 40b; *Pesikta Zitrasa, Mishpatim* 21:27; *Mechilta, Yisro* 20:20; *Tosefta, Yisro* 16; *Tanna d'Vei Eliyahu Zuta*, Chapter 2; *Eliyahu Rabbah*, Chapter 18; and in many other places.

All of a sudden, in the middle of expressing, "I'll sing about the works of Your hands," David stops his praise and says: "When the wicked bloom (flourish) like grass and all the doers of sin blossom — it's so that they can be destroyed for all eternity."

What is this change of pace all about? Why did David change the topic?

In actuality, David was addressing the classic question: "Why do good people suffer and the wicked prosper?" It bothered him, too. David saw a world filled with an infinite amount of his Creator's *chesed* and wisdom, and yet sticking out like a sore thumb is this phenomenon of injustice in human affairs. And David, who knows that Hashem is behind everything which transpires, was therefore bothered as to why God tolerates, or better yet, why God sets up situations of *tzaddik v'ra lo*, and *rasha v'tov lo*. Therefore, without even enunciating this self-understood question, he immediately answered it: "When [we see] the wicked bloom (flourish) like grass and all the doers of sin blossom — it's so that they can be destroyed for all eternity."

In other words, David is saying that these wicked people whom you see living it up, obviously did, and most likely still presently are doing, some good deeds. Therefore, they must get some reward for their good deeds.[9] However, God doesn't want to admit people who devote their lives to evil into *Olam ha-ba*. So what does He do? He "pays them up" in this world by giving them an abundance of "good" and success.[10] And it's fair too, since they aren't interested in getting *Olam ha-ba*; this is the world that *really* counts to these people, so that's where they get

---

9. "God doesn't hold back the reward of any creature." *Bava Kamma* 38b, *Nazir* 23b, *Pesachim* 118a.

10. We don't mean to imply that anyone who is rich is automatically to be considered a bad person. There can be many other reasons why God would give a person wealth and good fortune. For instance, it could be that it was sent as a test to see if affluence would divert him from the Torah way of life, or it could be that God gave him wealth since God knows that he is a good person who will use the money for charitable purposes, etc.

their reward. God lets them "blossom" — lets them rise to the top — only so that they can be destroyed for all eternity. This is the greatest punishment possible. Their loss of *Olam ha-ba*.

Now, regarding the question of why bad things happen to the righteous, David continues: "[Don't worry.] The righteous will flourish like a date palm, like a cedar in Lebanon he will grow tall.... He will still be fruitful in old age; vigorous and fresh they will be."

David is telling us that although the righteous man may not be "rolling in dough" now, nevertheless, he enjoys life in a very meaningful, kosher way; for instance, by developing into a respected Torah scholar who reaps the fruits of his labors by seeing his own success, and the success of his children and disciples. "They are fruitful even in old age" means in a literal sense that they will lead their congregations to great heights even in their old age, and in a figurative sense it means that the spiritual investments which they make in themselves and others while they are young will pay off in their old age.

Of course, none of this "good" takes away from his reward in *Olam ha-ba*. On the contrary, he is being rewarded in this world with the fruits of his righteous labors, but they are only considered the "interest" of his reward. A righteous person feels great happiness throughout his life in the knowledge that he has lived his life as dictated in God's Torah, thereby gaining for himself a "large share" of reward in *Olam ha-ba*.

However, if we do see a righteous person deeply suffering in this world, it's for his greatest benefit. It's said in the name of the Chafetz Chaim that "in the World to Come, when we see all the benefits that our suffering has brought us, we will actually be upset that God didn't cause us to suffer more while we were still alive." Sins, so to speak, stain our soul. Suffering in this world removes some, or even all of the stains of our sins, thereby sparing us much, or even all, possible suffering in *Gehinnom* — suffering which is much worse than any of the suffering found in this world — which we may otherwise have had to undergo. Only this cleansing can assure that a basically righteous person will be able to have a close and strong connection to Hashem in *Olam ha-ba*, because God doesn't let impure souls come close to Him in the World to Come. Therefore, the righteous person knows that any suffering he may experience is not cause to complain against Hashem.[11] In fact, if the righteous person were on a high enough spiritual plateau, he would even thank God for the sufferings brought upon him. (See *Berachos*, Chapter 9, *mishnah* 5.)

David finishes this chapter by telling us: "To declare that God is just, my Rock in Whom there is no wrong."

Just as we see His wisdom in all of creation, so too does He run His world with the greatest wisdom and justice. But this wisdom and justice can only be understood if we know that there's a much more important existence than the life of this world: the eternal bliss of being with God in *Olam ha-ba*. Then the questions of "*tzaddik v'ra lo*," etc., fall away.

However, if there is no *Olam ha-ba*, then the entire world makes no sense. Nothing makes less sense than believing that an All-Merciful God would let a chaotic world exist, because that is the exact opposite of kindness. Nothing could be crueler than for Hashem to let this world run chaotically by itself, where the results are such that many times things go good for wicked people and bad for righteous people. Only with the knowledge that there's a World to Come do the deeds of God start to make sense. Of course, we can't expect to understand God, but there's nothing wrong with using our God-given minds to try to understand, based on Torah concepts, a little bit of God's ways.

In conclusion, we see that the only way to understand at least a little of this world which is being run by God, Who is just, merciful, and kind (*Tehillim* 145 and many other verses throughout

---

11. See *Chovos Ha-Levavos, Sha'ar Ha-Bitachon*, Chapter 3, for other reasons why God sometimes causes misfortune for a righteous person. See also *The Informed Soul*, by Rabbi David Gottlieb, Artscroll/Mesorah Publications, pp. 127–156, for an in-depth discussion of this topic.

Scriptures),[12] is to come to the realization that the main purpose of our lives is not for this world, but for *Olam ha-ba.*

THE SOUL AND AFTERLIFE IN THE SCRIPTURES

We've presented a couple of rational arguments for the existence of *Olam ha-ba.* For the Torah Jew, though, belief in the World to Come (as well as all the other tenets) ultimately has to be found in the Torah itself. It's surprising, therefore, to find that the Written Torah, from *Bereshis* (Genesis) to *Devarim* (Deuteronomy), as well as throughout the writings of the Prophets, is relatively obscure about the topic of the afterlife and the immortality of the soul. In fact, its obscurity is glaring. When the Torah talks about reward and punishment, it almost invariably speaks in terms of earthly rewards and punishments, and not of rewards and punishments in the World to Come. The author of the classic *sefer Chovos Ha-Levavos* (in the section called *Sha'ar Ha-Bitachon*) asks why this is so, and he provides us with quite a few answers, two of which I will discuss.

First, as you may know, there are two Torahs, the Written Torah and the Oral Torah. And in a certain sense, the more impor-

---

12. Of course, this isn't a contradiction to free will. It's just saying that free will is limited. For example, if Mr. A truly intends to steal money from another person, Mr. B, and God doesn't want Mr. B to lose the money, God manipulates the situation and causes something to happen which foils Mr. A's planned robbery. Now with regard to punishment, Mr. A is held responsible in Heaven for a robbery, since had God not intervened, Mr. A would have carried out his planned theft. (See *Kiddushin* 40a, and Rabbenu Yonah, in his *Sha'arei Teshuvah*, First Gate #5, for an exception to that rule.) Therefore, free will doesn't mean that anyone can just go and murder or steal, God forbid, if God doesn't will it. Everything is under the Divine and just guidance of God. Because the world is under God's control, free will is often confined to our determined thoughts — which we are responsible for — be them good or bad thoughts, although we are not always permitted by God to actually carry them out. (See *Chovos Ha-Levavos, Sha'ar Avodas Elokim*, Chapter 8.)

tant of the two is the Oral Torah.[13] Of course, it's the two together that comprise the will of God, but we have to understand
that the Written Torah is to the Oral Torah what short notes on
an index card are to the actual speech of a lecturer. The notes are
only the briefest reminders of a much greater amount of knowledge which can conceivably take hours and hours for the lecturer
to deliver. So, too, the Written Laws are just the "notes" to the
Oral Law; they're just the tip of the iceberg.[14] If you want to understand the full and detailed meaning of the commandments
(for example, how to keep Shabbos, how to make a kosher pair
of *tefillin*, how to make a *sukkah*, etc.) you have to turn primarily
to the Oral Torah.[15] (See Appendix A for further discussion).
Similarly, the details pertaining to *Olam ha-ba* are reserved for
discussion in the Oral Torah. In the Oral Torah (the Midrash and
the Talmud) the subject of the eternal soul, and in particular, the
subject of reward and punishment in the World to Come, are
discussed at length. Thus, in essence, the afterlife is indicated in
our Torah — in the "main" Torah, the Oral Torah.

Another answer given by the author of the *Chovos Ha-Levavos*
is that the Written Torah is addressed to human beings — human beings of flesh and blood. The Torah is not an abstract, eso-
teric guide intended for the few; but a pragmatic handbook for
the many. Therefore, when the Torah wishes to provide a re-

---

13. Rabbi Yochanan said, "God made a covenant with Israel only because
of the Oral Torah."
14. See Appendix A for a more detailed discussion.
15. Two basic reasons why the understanding of the Written Torah is con-
tingent upon thorough knowledge of the Oral Torah are: (1) the transmission of Torah wisdom isn't just a matter of book knowledge; it's first and
foremost a teacher-student relationship, not only to ensure proper understanding of the laws being taught, but also so that the student will have a
proper role model to develop his character in the Torah way. (2) So that the
real meaning of the Torah would be the exclusive inheritance of the Jewish
people alone; if gentiles want to know its true interpretation, they have to
rely on the oral traditions of the Jewish people.

ward-and-punishment incentive, it speaks to the average person in the language he can relate to best: physical reward and physical punishment right now *in this world,* not flowery, vague, futuristic reward and punishment in another world. Moreover, it would be next to impossible to relate information about the true reward and punishment in the next world. Could we really expect to understand and appreciate it? Can we really understand the experience of the soul basking in the presence of God's glory, while we are still trapped within the confines of the finite body? Therefore, the Torah avoided entering into essentially moot and useless discussions and descriptions about a world that would be too difficult to truly comprehend.[16]

Whatever the reason for the Written Torah's relative deemphasis of the afterlife, all Torah authorities agree that belief in the afterlife (as well as the immortality of the soul) is a basic tenet of Judaism. Moreover, although it may not be emphasized enough or systematically presented in the Written Torah, we still will show how the basic idea *is* embedded in the Torah's text. First, we will see where the Torah tells us that we have a soul,

---

16. See *Sha'ar Ha-Bitachon* in *Chovos Ha-Levavos* for other answers; and see the *Keli Yakar* on *Vayikra* 26:12 for even more reasons. The *Keli Yakar* asks that while we can understand why the Torah did not get into detailed descriptions of the World to Come, why didn't it at least push the point a little more, at least in general terms? One of his answers is as follows: One of the Torah's objectives is to uproot the heresy of the nations who say that the world is not run by God. Consequently, the Torah is interested in making direct connections between our observance of the Torah and reward and punishment in this world, in order to show how God is in control of the world. If the Torah would focus mostly on reward and punishment in the World to Come, the nations would say that this is because there is no God who is running the world in accordance with our deeds; therefore it has to put off those rewards and punishments to a world which can't be verified. Thus, the Torah promises rewards that can be verified. Rabbi A. Miller, *zt"l,* (in his *Rejoice O Youth,* p. 215, paragraphs 452–454) adds to this point by explaining that the Torah didn't want to get into a "My World to Come is better than yours" argument, which would be futile. It wanted to stick to promises of this world, which are usually verifiable.

then we will show how we can recognize through real-life experiences that we have a soul, and lastly we will bring Torah sources which support the existence of an afterlife — the place where our soul goes after the body it was in has expired.

THE SOUL IN SCRIPTURES

Despite that fact that the Written Torah does not formulate a detailed doctrine of the makeup of a soul, in several places it unmistakably presents the basic principle that there is a soul.

In *Bereshis* (2:7) we are told how the human being was created with two opposing forces within him, the material and the spiritual: "Then God formed man from the dust of the ground [i.e., material] and breathed into man's nostrils the soul of life; thus man became a living being."

Note that instead of the verse saying, "...and God *placed* into man a living soul," it says that God *breathed* into man a living soul. This implies a transference of sorts; just as one who blows air transfers air from within himself into something else, so too God transferred "something" from within Himself into the first human. The verse is not merely stating that God gave us the ability to breath, be alive, and function in a physical sense, but the verse is stressing that God transferred to man "so to speak" a part of Himself, i.e., an actual spiritual entity, a soul.[17]

In many places in the Torah, a major reference to the existence of a spiritual soul is through the punishment called *kares*. In numerous verses, the Torah uses expressions such as *v'nichrasah ha-nefesh*, "and the soul will be cut off."[18] The Torah

---

17. As the verse in *Mishlei* 20:27 states, "The light of God [is] the soul of man."

18. See *Bereshis* 17:14; *Shemos* 12:15, 19; 30:30, 38; 31:14; *Vayikra* 7:20, 21, 25, 27; 17:49; 19:9; 23:29; *Bemidbar* 9:13; 15:30, 31; 19:13, 20.

is clearly indicating to us that we have a soul which can be "cut off." We will discuss this in greater detail a little further on.

Another reference to the soul is in *Bereshis* 1:27: "God created man in His image (*b'tzalmo*); in the image of God He created him."

It also says (*Bereshis* 5:1): "In the day that God created man, in the likeness (*b'dimus*) of God He made him."

There are numerous ways to understand what it means to be made in God's "image" and "likeness," but the verses above clearly indicate that there is something of the Divine in human beings. Maimonides (*Guide for the Perplexed*) explains these two verses as follows: "in His image" refers to the ability of humans to be able to differentiate between right and wrong. "In the likeness of God" means that the human was given special intellectual capacity to perceive, distinguish, observe, discern, and understand all that is taking place around him. These two abilities (the ability to distinguish between right and wrong, as well as the ability for advanced intellectual thought) certainly can be classified as abilities of the soul. Being made in "God's image" and "likeness" means that we were given eternal, sublime, and heavenly qualities commonly associated with a soul.

Let me note here that these are only a few examples of the verses which teach us of the existence of a soul. We have not yet discussed the verses supporting the existence of an afterlife, which obviously assumes the existence of a soul, i.e., the spiritual part of us that lives on after death. It should be clear though, just from these few examples, that the Written Torah does espouse the existence of a spiritual soul in humans.

REAL-LIFE SOUL EXPERIENCE

In addition to all of the verses which tell us of the soul's existence, it's possible to verify the existence of a sublime, spiritual soul in humans by contemplating different human feelings, attitudes, emotions, and behaviors — in a word, through human life experiences. Now, none of the following pieces of evidence, if they were to stand alone on their own feet, would necessarily be enough evidence to support the existence of the soul; however, after putting together *all* of the pieces of evidence that we will present, we will have a very strong case going for us.

For instance, we see that when one does an extraordinarily good deed he feels very good about it. After one has finished an intense prayer, or after one has overcome a desire to sin — even if he just held himself back from saying a slightly derogatory statement about somebody else — one still feels very good deep down inside himself. The question is why? Why should a body, made up of only flesh and blood, feel good about a non-physical accomplishment? Moreover, these feelings can be experienced even by someone who is not particularly sensitive to his spiritual side. What else but the spiritual soul can explain these good feelings that are felt in even the most spiritually insensitive people?

Looking at the other side of the coin, we must ask ourselves, why does a person who did a bad deed feel guilt? What is guilt? Where do such feelings come from? Someone might answer that it comes from the human conscience. But what is the conscience? Where did the "conscience" come from? And if he says we feel guilty because "society" beat into us a sense of right and wrong, then we ask, who started that society? Was it not people who were told by earlier people, who were told by earlier people, etc., what right and wrong are? So, from where did those original people get their conscience? The real answer is, from their soul. The soul is naturally endowed with Divine qualities; the soul is the origin of the unique human sense of what's right and what's wrong.

This also explains an amazing phenomenon. We find that mankind is constantly seeking happiness, and yet no matter how much material wealth and success they may have already achieved, they are still unhappy. Just read the diaries of the most successful stars of Hollywood and you will see that behind all their laughter, fun, fame, and success lies a sad and dejected person. And why is it that even youth who come from affluent homes are so unhappy, to the extent that there is a record amount of drug abuse and suicide attempts among them? Why doesn't all their material success and pleasure bring their "physical bodies" the happiness which they seek? The answer to this phenomenon lies only by understanding a very fundamental point — the point that there are two basic parts in every human, the physical and the spiritual. We are like Siamese twins that must be fed. If you offer them food that only one of the twins likes, then as a whole unit they won't be happy, because the needs of one of the twins have been neglected. Similarly, we can only be happy if the soul within us is "also given to eat." Only by putting some spiritual meaning and accomplishment into one's life, will that half of us, our soul, be placated. Only by achieving some true meaning in one's life will a person feel that badly needed "inner contentment." It's the feeding of the hungry soul that brings us to that "inner contentment," which is really the "happiness" that mankind seeks. Materialism alone cannot bring this happiness. Only when the proper doses of spiritualism are *mixed* with the proper doses of materialism can we expect to achieve true happiness. (Living according to the prescribed way of the Torah gives us the proper doses of each.) Let's face it, there are many more happy, yet poor, spiritual people, than there are rich, happy, non-spiritual people. It's all in the soul.

There are other ways to perceive the existence of the soul. For instance, how can we explain the powerful longing and sublime feelings experienced when listening to inspirational music, or when observing the beauty of the sun setting, or while viewing a majestic mountain range in the distance? How can we explain how all of a sudden we are sometimes unexplainably aroused to ask ourselves, "What I am doing with my life?" or "Am I leading a purposeful life?" or "When will I change?" What arouses those sudden thoughts of introspection and spiritual longing? Certainly it's not our physical side of us that brings us to such thoughts. What else could it really be, but our soul? Somehow, the soul becomes stimulated by the stirring music; somehow it is awakened by coming in touch with God's beautiful world, or by experiencing something out of the ordinary. These yearnings and feelings emanate from one's soul.

Yet another way to come to a rational understanding that humans possess a soul is hearing stories about how depraved, corrupt, and even vicious criminals, all of a sudden experience moments of true regret — moments of regret that many times lead to a complete turn around of their corrupt behavior. These feelings can't really be said to come from societal training or even from their conscience. These are people that have long ago "killed" their conscience. Rather, it makes sense to say that it emanates from the soul, since the soul has innate, eternal, good qualities that can never be destroyed. As much as the hardened criminal's innate good qualities have been covered up until then, they still can always unexpectantly burst to the surface. No part of his physical makeup caused him to make such a dramatic change in his way of life. If a person actually turns over a new leaf and starts living a consistently moral life, what else can really account for such a turnaround, but his soul?

And only the power of the soul can explain the following phenomenon: Nowhere in nature do we find a creature other than the human being which has a power in it that works in direct opposition to its instincts for pleasure-seeking and for survival. Where does this power come from? We find individuals deeply immersed in a materialistic, pleasure-seeking lifestyle. Suddenly, this person follows through on a yearning to become spiritual. What gives this person the strength to sacrifice his physical pleasures for a higher ideal or principle if not the soul, which intuitively knows the value of spiritual endeavors? It's the soul, the Divine part of the human, which gives humans the power of free will (*bechirah*) to overcome the physical urges and instincts of the body, and choose a more spiritual way in life. How else could there be people willing to forfeit their comforts, and their livelihoods and sometimes even their very lives for what they perceive as a higher good? What force can convince a person to forfeit his whole physical being, if not the powerful Godly soul? What force can get someone to make incredible physical sacrifices for the simple sake of abstract ideas? People will risk their lives to rescue a drowning person, or will go back into a house on fire to try to save someone. Some pursue with all their physical being, to the point of physical exhaustion, acts of kindness and charity. Man is the only creature capable of consciously acting against the interest of his body and material well-being. Such actions can only be empowered by an independent force which can rule over the whims, desires, and instincts of the physical body — and that power comes from the soul.

This also explains the phenomenon that we find that people are ready to give up their physical needs and desires just to be able to attain some status in the eyes of their fellowman. Humans want honor. But what *is* honor? Honor is an intangible, spiritual "thing," so what part of our bodies is ready to forego its physical needs for the sake of honor? You may answer that the honor and status gives one a good feeling about himself — it boosts his self-esteem. That in itself needs some thought. If we are but physical "accidents," completely void of any elements of spirituality, then what part of our physical bodies needs to feel self-esteem? Animals live quite well without any need to feel self-esteem. However, humans desire honor because they have an inherent, subconscious awareness that they possess great potential, and they strive to reach that potential greatness. These are feelings which emanate from the soul, for the benefit of the soul, which it attains when it reaches the status of a high-level spiritual performer.

This also explains the phenomenon that people are ready to spend much time, effort, and money, and are prepared to suffer various forms of physical deprivation, for the sake of attaining "righteous justice." In a large number of cases, however, by the time the justice is carried out, it will not really accomplish anything. Yet, there is a deep desire to carry out justice, and there is a deep satisfaction felt when justice is finally carried out. (When a murderer is found guilty and he receives punishment, the family feels good that justice is being done, even though it won't help in any way to get back their loved one. Similarly, people risked their lives trying to find Nazi war criminals just for the sake of bringing about "righteous justice.") Why should a physical body give up its physical needs and desires just to be able to carry out that "righteous vengeance?" Understanding that we have a soul which emanates from the source of all righteousness and justice, we can understand how it yearns deeply to see that righteous justice is carried out, even if it means giving up on some physical needs of the body in which it resides.

Another window into the existence of soul is the inborn feeling of embarrassment that we humans possess. If we are nothing more than intelligent animals, why should we be embarrassed to stand naked or to be seen performing any of our bodily functions? To think that these feelings arise only because we were trained this way is a weak argument. The question is, why does society train their offspring in this way? Why did the first societies try to cover up? This is another hint that we have a soul which makes us realize that our physical functions are the animalistic part of ourselves; and therefore it's the soul that is making us feel embarrassed by these functions.

What about the desire for self-perpetuation? Where does that come from? It's a universal human longing to want a child. The average person wants to leave some continuation of himself when he departs from this world. Childless couples will often seek to adopt a child although it will mean undergoing the hardships of raising a child, and all the expenses that go along with it. Many times it's for the purpose of self-perpetuation. If you leave a child behind, you feel that you're still somewhat alive, that in a certain way you're still around. People will continue to remember you. The question is, who cares if people remember you if you're dead? We often find that many people about to leave this world will arrange to have their money donated to some good cause. Some will have buildings built just to have their name put on it, which gives the dying person some feeling of continuance. Sometimes we find that a selfish, wealthy miser assigns a large portion of his will to the self-perpetuation of his name rather than leaving an inheritance to his family. He is expressing this irrational need to be remembered after death by erecting a mausoleum or an extravagant monument with his name engraved on it. The question is, why? What is this drive for posthumous glory? The person himself is dead and won't feel the glory, so why "waste" his money? The answer is that it's not the glory that he seeks. These feelings emanate from the soul. He won't get any glory, and he knows it. Spiritual, eternal entities (the soul) want to achieve spiritual, eternal accomplishments. Why, you ask? Since the soul intuitively knows that it comes from an eternal source, and it also knows that it will eventually return to its eternal source and remain eternal, it instinctively wants to achieve eternal accomplishments that will continue to benefit it in the World to Come. (Just as there is a concept that a son can bring merit to a parent by doing good deeds even after the parent has passed away [see *Sanhedrin* 104a], so too, good deeds that one has done while still alive and that have an effect extending even beyond his lifetime, can continue to bring reward to the doer even after his death.) Therefore, we see that the human need for perpetuation, in whatever form, is an expression of the eternal soul.

It's also interesting to note that people have a strong desire to live long. Of course, younger and even older people who are healthy will obviously want to continue to live long. But how can we understand why sick, old people desire to keep living? Again, these feelings seem to emanate from the soul. Since the soul subconsciously knows that it is eternal, while it's still in this world it desires to stay in its present state eternally. And it may be that since the soul knows the tremendous value of every second of life, it wishes to cling to life as long as possible. These are not feelings of the body, but of the soul.

Dreams are additional evidence that we have a soul, and that there is an afterlife. They even show current connections between the living of this world and the dead of the next world. For instance, in the book *All for the Best*, by Ruchoma Shain (Feldheim Publishers, 1995), in the chapter entitled "Highlights to Heaven" (pp. 179-192), she brings a number of amazing and uncanny dreams that inexplicably show how dead souls come to living souls with certain particular messages and missions that they request be carried out on their behalf, that were clearly impossible for anyone else to have known about. Being that these are verified stories that Ruchoma Shain heard firsthand, it gives us additional evidence that we have a soul that lives on into the next world.

Finally, if you attend any funeral where a eulogy is delivered, chances are that the speaker will attempt to find some spiritually redeeming quality in the deceased — even if the deceased was not exactly a spiritual person! The eulogizer doesn't say, "This person was so great, after all he had a Rolls Royce, a yacht, a private plane, three summer homes, etc." Why not? Since people realize that once a person is lying there helplessly, ready to be put into the ground, all his material accomplishments cease to matter. What really counts are his spiritual accomplishments, and the eulogizer digs as deep as he can, to find (or make up) some hidden virtue that the deceased had. This universal phenomenon indicates that all people, deep down, realize that what really matters is the spirit. Where does that realization come from, if not from the inner voice of the human soul? Looking at all of the above, it becomes pretty convincing that there's more to the human body than meets the eye.[19]

SCRIPTURAL REFERENCES TO THE WORLD TO COME

Now that we have provided some of the evidence for the existence of a soul, we turn back to the topic of the World to Come. As we said, although the Written Torah does not make the World to Come a central dogma or supply extensive descriptions of the afterlife, it is filled with verses which point to its existence.

19. Some of the thoughts brought in these pages are from the book *Gesher Ha-Chayim: The Bridge of Life* (Y.M. Tuchachinsky), Moznaim Publishers Corp.; and from *Return to the Source – Selected Articles on Judaism and Teshuvah*, from an article entitled "Life after Death and the World to Come," Feldheim Publishers, pp. 130–141.

Rabbi Avigdor Miller (*Rejoice O Youth*, pp. 70,71) cites over twenty such verses, and in the *sefer Gesher Ha-Chayim*, Chapter 6, there are many more. Let's present a sampling.

The death of Avraham (*Bereshis* 25:8), Yitzchak (*Bereshis* 35:29), Ya'akov (*Bereshis* 49:33), Yishmael (*Bereshis* 25:17), Aharon (*Bemidbar* 20:24) and Moshe (*Bemidbar* 27:13; *Devarim* 32:50) are described with the conspicuous phrase, "...and he was gathered to his people." In each of these circumstances it is obvious that the phrase must pertain to the afterlife. For instance, Avraham was the first of his line to be buried in the Cave of Machpelah. Therefore, the phrase "gathered to his people" cannot be talking about his family buried in that cemetery. It must refer to the afterlife.[20] Aharon and Moshe were buried alone and still it says that each was "gathered to his people." Obviously, then, all of these verses indicate that after death the souls of these people joined the souls of their fathers and other righteous ancestors in the World to Come.

There are many more sources.[21] For instance, the wicked sorcerer Bilaam states: "...let me die the death of the righteous and let my end be like his" (*Bemidbar* 23:10). Obviously, Bilaam saw no advantage of burial in a Jewish cemetery. Rather he is expressing his awareness of the exalted place a righteous person has in the World to Come. God is recording the words of Bilaam to show us how basic a doctrine the World to Come was, even to the gentiles.

The existence of an afterlife is so self-understood in the Torah that it even prohibits contacting the spirits of the dead (*Vayikra* 19:31, 20:6, 27; *Devarim* 18:10–12). If the Torah doesn't espouse the existence of an afterlife, why would it prohibit contact with

---

20. Ya'akov died in Egypt and yet it says at the time of his death, "he was gathered to his people," long before he was actually buried in the Cave of Machpelah.

21. Much of the following can also be found in the *sefer Nishmas Chayim* (Chapters 3–9, first section), by Menasheh Ben Israel, published in 1654 and recently republished by Saphrograph Corp., NY.

dead spirits?

Perhaps the most convincing evidence for the existence of an afterlife is the concept of *kares*, being "cut off," which was briefly mentioned above.

"...An uncircumcised male who does not circumcise the flesh of his foreskin — that soul shall be cut off from his people; he has broken My covenant" (*Bereshis* 17:14). What does "the soul shall be 'cut off'" mean? First, we have to understand that the punishment mentioned in the above passage refers to the uncircumcised child. He is transgressing a positive commandment of the Torah (the need to have himself circumcised) each day of his life that he is not circumcised. However, as long as he eventually circumcises himself anytime before he dies, then his soul will not be cut off; only if he dies without ever circumcising himself will his soul be cut off. The question, then, is: If the punishment of being "cut off" does not apply until he dies, then from what is his soul being "cut off?" He's dead already!! Obviously, then, it cannot mean that his soul is merely cut off from physical life — it must mean that it's cut off from what all the other souls of his people are receiving — it means he is "cut off" from the World to Come.[22]

There are several other places where the Written Torah talks about the punishment of *kares*. Our Sages explain that in most instances the punishment refers to the soul losing its connection to the afterlife (although in some instances it simply means that a person will die young).[23] And as the Ramban (Nachmanides) points out, if being "cut off" is the result of a serious transgression, then we see that the soul's natural state is to be "connected" to its Godly source, and thereby is naturally connected to God in the afterlife. This demonstrates that the Torah believes in the ex-

---

22. See Rambam, *Mishnah Torah*, Laws of Circumcision, Chapter 1.
23. *Sifra, Toras Kohanim*; see Ramban's commentary on *Vayikra* 18:29, which explains this in detail.

istence of a soul which is naturally destined for continued existence in the World to Come.

One last point. We find that Avraham was concerned about
where he would bury Sarah (*Bereshis*, Chapter 23). We also find
how Ya'akov apologized to Yosef for not having buried his
mother Rachel in the Cave of Machpelah.[24] We see that Ya'akov
himself was extremely concerned about making sure that after
his death he should eventually be taken from Egypt and be buried in the Cave of Machpelah.[25] Yosef also made his family
swear that when they left Egypt they would be sure to bring his
bones to the Holy Land.[26] Now who cares where one is buried, if
death is the end of everything? And if you say they were concerned about being in the Land of Israel, then we must ask, why?
If there's no such thing as a soul, which will eventually be resurrected, why did they want to be in Israel? If there's no soul that
lives on after death, then who cares where one is buried? Obviously we see that it's important, for whatever reason, for a soul
to be buried near righteous people, and in Israel. (See also *Melachim* II 13:21.) But for the body itself, it makes absolutely no difference where one is buried, nor does it make a difference if one
gets buried at all.

Moving from the *Five Books of Moses* to the *Prophets*, we find
in the book of *Shmuel* (I, 28:19) that the spirit of Shmuel the
prophet — who previously had died — was conjured up by a
medium to speak to King Shaul. Shmuel, as a spirit, told the despondent king that because of his sin, "you and your sons [who
were about to accompany him to battle the Philistines] will be
with me tomorrow." This verse clearly states that Shaul and his
sons would perish the next day in battle, which they did, and
then join Shmuel in the World to Come. (This is not the place to
discuss the permissibility of contacting dead spirits.) It also has

---

24. *Bereshis* 48:7; see Rashi who brings *Midrash Rabbah* to make this point.
25. Ibid. 47:29–31, 49:29–32.
26. Ibid. 50:22.

Shmuel complaining to Shaul for having disturbed him by bringing him up. These verses clearly show the existence of a soul,
and the existence of an afterlife.

In *Shmuel* II (12:23), we read of how King David had a sickly
newborn child. After much fasting and praying by King David,
the baby died, upon which David returned to normal life, stating, "Can I cause him to return any more? I am going to him;
he's not returning to me." Now, if there's no World to Come,
what consolation was there in the fact that David would some
day also die? Obviously, David was consoling himself that eventually he would meet his son in the World to Come.

In *Koheles* (3:20–21) we have a direct reference to an afterlife:

> Everything is going to one place. We all come from the earth and
> we all return to the earth. [However] who knows [and under-
> stands the] spirit of mankind which goes up [to the heavens] as
> opposed to the spirit of an animal which goes down below into
> the earth.

Similarly, it says in 12:7: "...the dust will return to the ground
as it was [in its original state] and the spirit will return to God
Who gave it." We see from here that the spirit does not die with
the death of the body. It returns to Heaven, to God, Who sent it
down here in the first place.

It is clear, even from the limited sample of verses presented
here, that the Written Torah, although reticent to elaborate on the
exact nature of the afterlife and to state dogmas concerning it,
definitely promotes the idea of there being a soul which goes to,
what we refer to as, the World to Come.

THE TWINS

As a final note, let me relate a parable to help us understand the
idea of a world beyond this one, a world which we can't see.[27]

---

27. Taken from *Gesher Ha-Chayim*, by Y.M. Tuchachinsky.

Imagine twin brothers squeezed together inside their mother's womb. One is pessimistic, since he bases his conclusions strictly on what he sees and feels, while the other is optimistic and believes that eventually they will live in a better situation. These two brothers constantly argue back and forth whether a better situation could possibly be awaiting them beyond their presently cramped quarters.

The first brother argues, "What better situation could there be? What you see is what you get. This is it, nothing's ever going to change."

His twin replies, "That can't be. There's got to be a better situation. It can't be that we were created just to bounce around this dark cramped place. There must be a bigger and better situation awaiting us."

And so they argue back and forth for quite some time. One day, all of sudden, the optimistic brother gets swept away. The remaining twin, terribly distraught, bemoans, "Brother, don't leave me, don't leave me all alone in here. Oh, it's too late. I told you this was going to happen. Now you are gone forever."

Meanwhile, on the outside a newborn baby cries. And people shout, "*Mazel tov!*" Another child has entered this world, leaving his previous, relatively insignificant existence for a much more glorious life.

The lesson is obvious. If we only relate to, and believe in what our eyes see, then we are no wiser than the pessimistic brother, the brother who just couldn't envision a different situation. How wrong he was! What a surprise he will get when it's his chance to be born. So, too, and even more so, will be the difference between the world we are experiencing now, and the awesomely delightful, spiritual experiences which await those who with foresight prepared themselves — i.e. their souls — to be worthy of life in *Olam ha-ba*.

(This parable really should be understood in a much deeper way. We know that the conditions of a fetus in the mother's womb are the very opposite of the conditions necessary for the existence of a live human being after birth. The fetus lives under water, without any air to breathe. The lungs of a fetus are in a collapsed state, and its blood bypasses its lungs, and takes a strange route through a special hole in its heart. Yet, miracle of miracles, at the moment of birth, perfectly timed inversions take place. The lungs immediately expand to take in its first breath of air. The special hole in its heart closes up, forcing blood through the lungs as well. A complete metamorphosis takes place in seconds, and body systems barely resemble anything of their previous state of existence. These amazing, beneficial changes take place in this world, and in the same physical body. One can only imagine the great, beneficial changes that will take place when our existence transfers from this physical world, in our physical bodies, to a spiritual world, void of any physical impediments, with only our spiritual souls close to God in the World to Come.)

Death has dominion only over the body. The soul, since it is made of the spirit, isn't bound by any of the laws of matter, so it continues to exist even after death, and it returns to its Maker.

Note: As to the nature of the *spiritual* enjoyment that the soul will experience by being close to the source of all enjoyment, God Himself, it is beyond the scope of such a book to explain. However, I'd like to make one point. We see that the main physical pleasures of this world (eating, music, etc.) are pleasures that we haven't done anything to earn. They were made by God strictly as bait — a worm on a hook — to ensure the continued existence of the human race. (They are also around to test us, but that's not up for discussion now.) So let's think a moment; if pleasures which we did nothing to earn are so good, then what infinitely greater pleasures — spiritual pleasures which have no limits — await those who sanctify their lives by living their lives doing the will of Hashem as dictated to us in His Torah. And don't moan when we say that there's only going to be spiritual pleasures in the World to Come, because let's not forget that at death, we leave our physical bodies behind us in the grave. There's nothing to feel bad about; since there are no physical pleasures in heaven anyway, you won't be missing anything. And that's to our benefit, since physical pleasures are only temporary, as opposed to the eternal bliss that Hashem has waiting for those who were close to Him in their lifetime and did His will.

4

What Are the
SEVEN WONDERS
—— of ——
JEWISH HISTORY?

WE ARE CALLED THE CHOSEN PEOPLE (*Shemos* 4:22;[1] *Vayikra* 20:24;[2] *Devarim* 4:37,38,[3] 7:6,7,[4] 10:15,[5] 14:1,2[6]). Furthermore, God calls Himself the special God of Israel over 100 times in the Scriptures.[7] But, aside from the above verses, are you convinced that the Jewish people are really so special? Do you feel it in your bones? By studying the "seven wonders of Jewish history" we

---

1. "...My son, My firstborn is Israel."
2. "...I am Hashem your God Who has set you apart from the peoples.... And you shall be holy to Me, for I God am holy, and have separated you from the nations that you should be Mine."
3. "And because I have loved your fathers and have chosen his [their] children after them..."
4. "Because you are a Holy Nation to Hashem your God, it is you that Hashem your God has chosen to be His treasured nation from all the other nations on the face of the earth."
5. "Only in your fathers did God delight, to love them, He chose their seed after them, even you, above all peoples, as it is this day."
6. "You are the children of Hashem your God..."
7. In a Random House 1985 dictionary, under the word Israel, one of the translations is as follows: "a group considered as God's chosen people."

will see more evidence to the truth of the Torah itself, we will be convinced that there's Divine Providence, and we'll feel more than ever that the Jewish people are God's Chosen People. The seven unique aspects of Jewish history that teach us this are:

1. The eternal and chosen status of the Jewish people
2. Their function as a "light unto the nations"
3. Their unique relationship with the Land of Israel
4. Their predicted capacity for spiritual rejuvenation (*te-shuvah*)
5. Their predicted survival, despite their exile and world-wide dispersion
6. Their predicted survival, despite persistent, vehement anti-Semitism
7. Their predicted survival, despite minority status wherever they settled in exile

The material in this chapter is adapted from a highly recommended presentation called "The Seven Wonders of Jewish History," offered through the Discovery Seminar of Aish HaTorah.[8] The "seven wonders" highlight several important points. First, the fact that our history was predicted in the Torah long before it ever occurred is further evidence to the Divine origin of the Torah. This point will be elaborated upon later in this chapter. Second, the nature of the predictions, as we will explain toward the end of this chapter, demonstrates that history has been controlled by God in order for all these predictions to come true (this topic is the thrust of the following chapter). Third, the "seven wonders" prove beyond a reasonable doubt that the Jewish people are unique, and indeed the Chosen People of God.

Before we begin I want to first deal with some natural skepti-

---

8. Those familiar with this Aish HaTorah presentation will notice that we changed the order of the seven wonders. This was done for various reasons; however, we have essentially kept the full thrust of the lecture intact. I thank them for permission to use their material for this book.

cism which may be creeping around in our minds. The little skeptic in each of us might be thinking, "Of course, these predictions of the Prophets look impressive now, but maybe they were written after the events actually took place. Who knows, maybe writers later doctored up some of the prophesies."

In response to that, one should know that there is a famous Greek translation of the Torah called the Septuagint, written in the year 3515 (245 B.C.E.), 313 years before the Romans destroyed the Second Temple (which was in the year 3828), and *all of the prophesies that we've discussed refer to the time period after the destruction of the Second Temple.* Therefore, even if we had wanted to doctor up the prophesies, we couldn't have, because a translation had been in the hands of the gentiles long before. That's an important point to keep in mind. All of the distant prophesies predicting exile to the four corners of the world, the miraculous return of the Jewish people to their land, etc., could not have been doctored up. A copy of our Torah has all along been in the hands of those who have sought to detract, denigrate, and annihilate us. They would never be quiet about any doctoring up of the Scriptures that would be in our favor. And so, read on, and marvel at the wonders of Jewish history.

1. THE ETERNAL NATION

Some of us may take for granted how unique these seven wonders really are. For instance, we may think that since we are still around as a people today, then it must be normal to survive thousands of years of exile and persecution. Consequently, when we read in the Torah how the Jewish people are going to be an eternal nation we are not particularly impressed. Big deal. But that is mistaken thinking, as we shall soon see.

The Jewish nation is the eternal nation. Our eternity began with God's promise to Avraham (*Bereshis* 17:7): "And I will establish my covenant (*bris*) between Me and you and your descendants after you throughout their generations, an eternal covenant, to be to you a God and to all your children after you."

This blessing of eternity was then passed on to Yitzchak, as God later told Avraham (*Bereshis* 21:12): "Through Yitzchak your descendants will be called." This, of course, excluded Yishmael from the blessing of eternity. Yitzchak, in turn, passed the blessing onto Ya'akov, to the exclusion of Esav, when he told Ya'akov (*Bereshis* 28:3, 4): "...[God] will grant Avraham's blessing to you and your descendants, so that you will take over the land which God gave to Avraham..."

Avraham's blessing is the eternal covenant. It's a covenant referred to again and again throughout Scriptural history. For instance, *Yeshayahu* (54:10) prophesies: "For the mountains may move and the hills may be shaken, but My kindness shall never move from you, and My covenant of peace shall never be shaken, says God Who has compassion."

And in *Malachi* (3:6): "Just as I am God and I do not change, so too you, the children of Ya'akov, shall never be wiped out."

A person might still argue: What if the Jewish people become undeserving? Will God still uphold His end of the covenant? In response, we turn to the following (*Vayikra* 26:44,45): "And yet, even so, while they are still in the land of their enemies, I will not reject or spurn them, lest I break my covenant with them by destroying them."

In *Yirmeyahu* 5:18: "But even in those days [when because of their sins punishments will be brought on the Jewish people], declares God, I will not make a complete destruction [of you]."

The Jewish people, Avraham's heirs, may have to go through exile and persecution, but God promises He will never destroy them. Why not? Because of the covenant He made with Avraham. They are going to be eternal, no matter what. The Torah thus clearly testifies that the Jewish people are chosen to be the eternal nation.

Besides our Torah, there's much outside evidence which backs up this claim. First, the hatred of the gentiles is one indicator. Why should it bother the gentiles that we claim to be the Chosen Nation? If it was a totally preposterous claim then would it bother them? Obviously, their hatred has deep roots of jealousy since deep down they really know that we are the Chosen Nation.

Another outside indicator is the fact that some of the most educated and articulate gentiles of recent history have written flowery compliments about us. Compliments that we would never dare to write about ourselves, they have written. Here, then, is an appropriate place to cite the famous article of Mark Twain, entitled "Concerning the Jews."[9]

> If the statistics are right, the Jews constitute but one percent of the human race. It suggests a nebulous dim puff of stardust lost in the blaze of the Milky Way. Properly, the Jew ought hardly to be heard of; but he is heard of, has always been heard of. He is as prominent on the planet as any other people, and his commercial importance is extravagantly out of proportion to the smallness of his bulk. His contributions to the world's list of great names in literature, science, art, music, finance, medicine, and abstruse learning, are also way out of proportion to the weakness of his numbers. He has made a marvelous fight in this world, in all the ages; and has done it with his hands tied behind him. He could be vain of himself and be excused for it. The Egyptian, the Babylonian, and the Persian rose, filled the planet with sound and splendor, and then faded to dream stuff and passed away; the Greek and the Roman followed, and made a vast noise, and they are gone; other peoples have sprung up and held their torch high for a time, but it burned out, and they sit in twilight now, or have vanished. The Jew saw them all, beat them all, and is now what he always was, exhibiting no decadence, no infirmities of age, no weakening of his parts, no slowing of his energies, no dulling of his alert and aggressive mind. All things are mortal, but the Jew; all other forces pass, but he remains. What is the secret of his immortality?

Who should ever have heard of Jews? That's a good question. Do you know how many tribal nations there are in Africa that

---

9. The article first appeared in *Harper's* magazine, in 1899. See also *The Complete Essays of Mark Twain* (New York: Doubleday, 1963).

you and I never heard of? There were, and are, innumerable peoples in Africa, Asia, the Far East, the Near East, North America, South America, etc. whom you have never heard of, and you will never hear of. Yet these little people, this tiny Jewish nation — between ten and fourteen million of us — are always in the news, making waves, influencing society.

It is said that the modern world has been shaped by four major thinkers: Marx in politics, Freud in psychology, Einstein in science, and Darwin in evolution. And, as Rabbi Motty Berger, who many times delivers the "Seven Wonders" seminar for Aish HaTorah, likes to say, "Three out of the four were Jews...and the fourth (Darwin) was wrong."

Despite their paltry numbers (about .2% of the world's population today), Mark Twain remarks, Jews are always amply represented in commerce, banking, business, literature, science, art, music, finance, medicine, and abstruse learning. (Of course, Twain was only aware of the achievements of secular Jews. He made his statement without knowing of the unsurpassed genius and accomplishments of the likes of Rashi, Rambam, Ramban, Abarbanel, Rabbi Yosef Karo, the Maharal, the Ba'al Shem Tov, the Vilna Gaon and so on.)

Twain remarks that if a Jew was to be haughty (vain) no one could blame him. The greatest, most prestigious nations and empires were eventually wiped off the face of the map. They're gone, but the Jew is still around. We should be proud to be Jews. We should feel, "Wow, imagine that, we're still around. We truly are the Eternal People."

Mark Twain was not the only well-known and respected non-Jew who recognized the greatness of the Jew. Leo Tolstoy, considered by many as the greatest novelist ever, authored an article entitled "What is a Jew?"

> What is a Jew? This question is not as odd as it seems. Let us see what kind of peculiar creature the Jew is, whom all the rulers and all the nations have, together and separately, abused and molested, oppressed and persecuted, trampled and butchered, burned and hanged, and in spite of all this, is yet alive. What is a

Jew, who has never allowed himself to be led astray by all the earthly possessions which his oppressors and persecutors constantly offered him, in order that he should change his faith and forsake his own Jewish religion?

At the end of the article, he concludes:

> The Jew is the emblem of eternity. He whom neither slaughter nor torture of thousands of years could destroy, he whom neither fire nor sword nor inquisition was able to wipe off the face of the earth, he who was the first to produce the oracles of God, he who has been for so long the guardian of prophesy and who transmitted it to the rest of the world — such a nation cannot be destroyed. The Jew is as everlasting as is eternity itself.[10]

Twain and Tolstoy were dead by the early 1900's. One can only wonder what they would have written about Jewish eternity after the persecutions and pogroms in Czarist Russia. What would they have said after World War I and the Holocaust? What would they have said after all the wars in the Land of Israel, the 1948 war, the '56 war, the '67 war, the '73 war, and the Gulf War? And what would they say after learning how 70 years of living under oppressive Communist rule in Russia could not squelch the Jew and his spirit?

That's the eternity of the Jew. There are other examples, but the point is made. All agree that the Jews are the eternal nation.

2. A LIGHT UNTO THE NATIONS

The second wonder of Jewish history is a concept already familiar to many, namely that the Jewish people will be a light to the nations, which basically means that they will have a very positive impact on all civilization. And we will see below that even the gentiles agree that no nation in history has had such a favorable impact on the world as the Jewish people. But let's first see

---

10. From *The Jewish World*, London, 1908.

some verses predicting this phenomenon long before it happened.

In *Yeshayahu* (42:6) we have the famous verse: "I, God, have called you in righteousness, and will hold your hand and watch you. I will establish you as a covenant of the people, for a light to the nations."

Another verse in *Yeshayahu* (60:2,3): "Behold, darkness will cover the land, and a thick darkness to the nations, but God will shine upon you [the Jewish people], and His glory shall be seen upon you. And the nations will go by your light, and the kings by your radiant illumination."

As famous as the "light to the nations" prophesy is, it was really the echo of a much earlier prophesy, a prophesy said to none other than Avraham (*Bereshis* 12:2,3): "And I [God] will make you a great nation, and I will bless you, and I will make your name great, and you will be a blessing. Those who bless you, I will bless; and those who curse you, I will curse. And they will be blessed by you, all the families of the land."

This was reiterated a short while later (*Bereshis* 22:18): "All the nations of the world shall be blessed through your children, because you, Avraham, have listened to Me."

This reiteration extends the original promise. It tells us that not only through Avraham will the world be blessed, but even through his children, the Jewish people, "the whole world" will be blessed.

Few people realize how literally true it is that whoever has blessed the Jewish people have themselves been blessed. One gentile to recognize this was Professor Huston Smith, author of *The Religions of Man*,[11] a book considered by the general populace as a classic in its field. He writes:

> There is a striking point that runs through Jewish history as a whole. Western civilization was born in the Middle East, and the Jews were at its crossroads. In the heyday of Rome, the Jews were

---

11. New York: HarperCollins, 1989.

close to the Empire's center. When power shifted eastward, the Jewish center was in Babylon; when it skipped to Spain, there again were the Jews. When in the Middle Ages the center of civilization moved into Central Europe, the Jews were waiting for it in Germany and Poland. The rise of the United States to the leading world power found Judaism focused there. And now, today, when the pendulum seems to be swinging back toward the Old World and the East rises to renewed importance, there again are the Jews in Israel...

His words provide testimony for the Torah's claim that God had promised Avraham, "Those who bless you, I will bless; and those that curse you, I will curse." Wherever civilization reached an apex, the Jewish people were to be found.

Professor Smith does not directly mention it, but the opposite is also true: Whenever a particular civilization turned distinctively ugly toward the Jews it lost its dominance not long thereafter. Thus, when Jewish persecution in the Roman Empire reached new heights (which not accidentally coincided with the Empire's official conversion to Christianity), Rome, began its irreversible slide away from history's center stage. The same pattern repeated itself in Babylonia (the Occident), where Jews were first shown relative tolerance. Then, by approximately the year 1000 C.E., persecution made Jewish life unbearable in Babylonia, which again coincided with the beginning of that civilization's disappearance in world events. From Babylonia, the center of Jewish life and scholarship shifted to the Iberian Peninsula (Spain), where the Spanish Moors welcomed Jewish business and intellectual activity. Not coincidentally did Spain then rise to the forefront of world leadership for a couple of centuries, until it too began progressive persecutions of the Jews, culminating in the infamous Spanish Inquisition and final expulsion of the Jewish population in 1492. Jews then resettled into other various parts of Europe, while Spain, in less than a century, fell ignobly from civilization's leading power to a corrupt, decaying has-been. Not surprisingly, with Jews scattered throughout the European continent, Europe then came to dominate world civilization, until World War II and the Holocaust. And now the United States. "Those who bless you, I will bless; and those who curse you, I will curse." Truly, the world's fate has been intimately intertwined with ours, for better or for worse.

Of course, most gentiles will not admit that. On the other hand, let me now quote from some very well-known gentiles who felt compelled to agree that the Jews have always been a blessing and a light to the nations. I start with a letter from John Adams, the second president of the United States of America. He wrote the following in response to someone arguing that Jews should not be given equal rights:[12]

> In spite of Bolingbrook and Voltaire [both of whom wrote anti-Semitic diatribes], I will insist that the Hebrews have done more to civilize men than any other nation. If I were an atheist and believed in blind eternal fate, I should still believe that fate had ordained the Jews to be the most essential instrument for civilizing the nations....to propagate to all mankind the doctrine of a supreme, intelligent, wise, almighty, sovereign of the universe, which I believe to be the greatest essential principle of all morality, and consequently, of all civilization....
>
> How is it possible that this old fellow should represent the Hebrews in such contemptible light? They are the most glorious nation that ever inhabited this earth. The Romans and their empire were but a bauble in comparison of the Jews. They have given religion to three quarters of the globe, and have influenced the affairs of mankind more, and more happily, than any other nation, ancient or modern.

On the same topic, Leo Tolstoy wrote (I quote from the same article cited earlier, "What Is a Jew?"):

> The Jew is that sacred being who has brought down from heaven the everlasting fire and has illumined with it the entire world. He

---

12. From a letter to F. A. Vanderkempt (1808), Pennsylvania Historical Society.

is the religious source, spring and fountain out of which all the rest of the peoples have drawn their beliefs and their religions.

Now let us turn to Paul Johnson (a Roman Catholic), the present-day historian who authored *A History of the Jews*. Writing in the epilogue to his book he states:

> To [the Jews] we owe the idea of...the sanctity of life...of individual conscience...and so, of social responsibility; of peace as an abstract ideal and love as the foundation of justice, and many other items which constitute the basic moral furniture of the human mind. Without the Jews, it [the world] might have been a much emptier place. Above all, the Jews taught us how to rationalize the unknown. The result was monotheism, and the three great religions which profess it. It is almost beyond our capacity to imagine how the world would have fared if the Jews had never emerged.

Toward the end of his epilogue, Johnson writes: "The Jewish society was appointed to be a pilot project for the entire human race." Thus, in very mystical overtones for an historian, he says that, looking back objectively over history, one has to conclude that the Jewish people were "appointed" to show everyone the way to live up to a higher standard. I wonder who "appointed" them?

Certainly with regard to religious and spiritual aspects, Jews have been the greatest light to the nations, but as we said before, even in secular ways — Marx, Freud, Einstein, in business, finance, and medicine, etc. — the Jews have contributed in the largest way. That is a unique characteristic of the Jewish people. No other people, among all those who have ever lived on the earth, can make the same claim. We have truly been a "light to the nations." (Whatever good may be coming from the "other" religions — as the above three writers have written — it was the Jews and their Torah that supplied the main values and teachings that those religions espouse.)

3. HOLY PEOPLE, HOLY LAND

The next prophesy concerns the interdependency between the People of Israel and their land. The basic dynamic working behind this prophesy is as follows: As long as the Jews are in the Land of Israel, the land will be very fertile; it will be "a land flowing with milk and honey." However, as soon as the Jewish people leave the land, or are expelled from the land, the land is going to become desolate and inhospitable to all others who try to reside there.

Obviously, no scientist could ever begin to explain how a plot of land could grow and flourish only for one particular people to the exclusion of all others. But that, as we shall see, is exactly what has happened. First, let us show that it was predicted.

As is well-known, the Land of Israel was once a very fertile land (*Devarim* 8:7–10):

> God will bring you to a good land, a land with flowing streams and springs gushing out in the valley and the mountains. It is a land of wheat, barley, grapes, figs and pomegranates, a land of oil, olives and honey dates. It is a land where you shall not eat your bread in rations, you will not lack anything; a land whose stones are iron and from whose mountains you will quarry copper. And when you eat and are satiated, you shall then bless God for the good land that He is giving you.

The symbol of the land's fertility is captured in the famous "milk and honey" description (*Shemos* 3:9): "I've come down to rescue them from Egypt, and to take them up from this land to a good and spacious land, to a land that is flowing with milk and honey."

Even though the Land of Israel was "a land flowing with milk and honey," the Torah predicted long ago that should the Jewish people be exiled from their land, then it will became desolate, so desolate that no other nation would be able to permanently settle there. There are several verses which make that prediction. First (*Vayikra* 26:32,33):

I will devastate the land, and your enemies who dwell in it will be desolate. You, I will scatter among the nations, at the point of My drawn sword, and your land will be completely desolate, and your cities will be in ruins.

Similarly the Torah states (*Devarim* 29:21,22):

In later generations your descendants will rise up after you, as well as any gentile who gets up from a different land, and will see the tremendous calamities that came to the land, and all the ills with which God has smitten this land. All its soil will be nothing but sulfur and salt, a burnt out and devastated waste. Unsown and unfruitful, it won't even grow any grass. It will look like Sedom and Amorah, Admah and Tzevoyim, which God overthrew with His fury and His wrath.

And then we have in *Yirmeyahu* (9:10): "I will turn Yerushalayim into a heap of ruins, a haunt of jackals. I will make the cities of Yehudah into a desolation without inhabitants."

The prophet *Yechezkel* (33:28,29), too, made similar predictions: "I will make the land a desolate waste, and its proud strength will cease, and the mountains of the Land of Israel will be desolate; no one will cross them. And you will know that I am God, when I make this land a complete desolate waste."

Consider for a moment the context of these prophesies. One can only imagine the great dismay, and almost disbelief, of the people who first heard them. The prophet's warning of exile is unbelievable enough, but they are also told that when they will be exiled, their fertile land will become, and remain, desolate.

"Look how great this land is," they must have said. "Even if it is true that we deserve to be exiled, how is it possible that the land will become permanently desolate? Won't our conquerors, or some other neighboring country, revitalize our land? Do you really expect us to believe that this fertile land will stop growing?"

No one living at the time of Yirmeyahu and Yechezkel would have been able to logically understand how their land could suddenly turn desolate, and continue to remain so, as long as it stayed in foreign hands. The unlikelihood of this prophesy is further amplified when we take into consideration the fact that the Land of Israel is located at the intersection of three continents: Asia, Europe, and Africa. It's situated at the center of the Fertile Crescent. During the 2,000 years that Israel was exiled from its land, numerous empires conquered the territory, and countless wars were fought for its possession. And, yet, astonishingly, no conqueror succeeded in permanently annexing the land to its own borders, in settling the land, or in causing the desolate waste to blossom. Exactly as predicted, the land became desolate, despite all the odds, and it remained desolate.

To get a feeling of how desolate it was, consider the words of Mark Twain who visited the Land of Israel in 1867 and wrote the following: [13]

> We traversed some miles of desolate country whose soil is rich enough, but is given wholly to weeds — a silent, mournful expanse.... A desolation is here that not even imagination can grace with the pomp of life and action. We reached Tabor safely... We never saw a human being on the whole route. We pressed on toward the goal of our crusade, renowned Jerusalem. The further we went, the hotter the sun got and the more rocky and bare, repulsive and dreary, the landscape became... There was hardly a tree or a shrub anywhere. Even the olive and the cactus, those fast friends of a worthless soil, had almost deserted the country. No landscape exists that is more tiresome to the eye than that which bounds the approaches to Jerusalem.
>
> Jerusalem is mournful, dreary and lifeless. I would not desire to live here. It is a hopeless, dreary, heartbroken, land.... Palestine sits in sackcloth and ashes. Over it broods the spell of a curse that has withered its fields and fettered its energies.... Palestine is desolate and unlovely. And why should it be otherwise? Can the curse of the Deity beautify a land? Palestine is no more of this

---

13. Mark Twain, *The Innocents Abroad or the New Pilgrim's Progress*, Vol. II, New York: Harper and Brothers, 1922, pp. 216–359.

workday world. It is sacred to poetry and tradition. It is a dream-land.

Many times different nations tried to take over the land and settle there. In fact, Jerusalem was overrun numerous times, but not one of her conquerors was able to remain. The land never grew for them. Who would have honestly given credence to the prediction that the land would be desolate after the Jewish people were exiled from it? Only now, in the perspective of history, is it really possible to feel the proper awe attached to that prophesy.

Professor Sir John William Dosson perhaps said it best when he wrote:[14]

> Until today (1888), no people has succeeded in establishing national dominion in the Land of Israel. No national unity, in the spirit of nationalism, has acquired any hold there. The mixed multitude of itinerant tribes that managed to settle there did so on lease, as temporary residents. It seems that they await the return of the permanent residents of the land.

This leads us to the other half of this wonder of Jewish history, namely, the prophesy that the Jewish people will eventually return to the Land of Israel, and with their return will be the miraculous physical rejuvenation of the desolate lands: "And Hashem, your God, will return your captured ones (*shevusecha*), and He will have compassion upon you, and He will gather you in from all the nations that God scattered you there" (*Devarim* 30:3–5).

The word *shevusecha* refers to someone who is in captivity. It sounds strange. Were we ever in captivity? Yes. Sometimes entire countries literally become prisons. Take, for instance, the Russian Jews of our century. Only recently were they able to start leaving Russia. Jews in Syria were in captivity; they have

---

14. Professor Sir John William Dosson, *Modern Science in Bible Lands*, London: Harper and Brothers, 1889, pp. 449–450.

only recently been allowed out. Jews in Iran were in captivity; they had to be smuggled out. Many went to the Land of Israel, and soon hopefully all of us will end up in the Land of Israel. This is the "return of the captured ones."

The return is also predicted in the words of the prophets. For instance, *Yirmeyahu* (33:10,11) writes:

> So says God, in this place that you say is deserted and without people — there are no animals in the cities of Yehudah and the streets of Yerushalayim which are now deserted — there will yet be heard [in this place] the voice of rejoicing, the voice of happiness, the voice of the bridegroom, the voice of the bride, the voice proclaiming, "Praise to God of Hosts, for good is God, forever is His kindness."

And then a very important verse in *Yechezkel* (36:8–11):

> And you, O mountains of Israel, you shall shoot forth your branches, and you shall bear your fruit to My nation Israel, because their return is close at hand. For, behold, I am with you and I shall return to you; then you shall be tilled and sown...And there will come a lot of men and animals; they will increase and multiply, and I will return you there as in your former times. And I will make you even more bountiful than it used to be. And you will know that I'm God...

In a famous Talmudic passage on this verse, our Sages teach (*Sanhedrin* 98a): "And so said Rabbi Abba, 'There can be no more manifest sign of the end of exile than this. As it says: And you, O mountains of Israel, you shall shoot forth your branches, and you shall bear your fruit to My nation Israel, because their return is close at hand.'"

On this passage, Rashi, who lived some 900 years ago, commented: "When the Land of Israel will yield its produce in superabundance, this will signal the approach of the end of the exile."

And the Maharsha, over 400 years ago, commented on this passage: "As long as Israel does not dwell on its land, the land does not give of her produce as she is accustomed. When she will begin to reflourish, however, and give of her fruits in abundance, this is a clear sign that the end, the time of redemption, is approaching, when all of Israel will return to their land."

The Discovery Seminar concludes: "Perhaps it may be inferred that the land, by giving of its fruits again, is preparing for the arrival of an entire nation. We ourselves are witness to the fact that in less than one generation Israel has undergone an unbelievable transformation from a desolate wasteland into a green and blossoming land. The Land of Israel responds only to her own children in preparation for the full return." Amazing! Who could have predicted such a phenomenon?

4. SPIRITUAL AWAKENING

The fourth wonder concerns the prophesy that a *Teshuvah* Movement would start. It amazingly predicted that people who have strayed off the beaten path of Torah Judaism will sincerely "return" to the ways of their forefathers, towards the end of their stay in exile (*Devarim* 30:1,2):

> It will happen when all these things take place, the blessings and the curses, which I have given before you, that you will take it to heart wherever you are, in whichever nation or land you're in, where I, God, scattered you and pushed you away. And you will return to Hashem your God, and start listening to His words, in everything that I command you today, you and your children, with all your mind and all your soul.

Another passage (*Devarim* 4:29,31) predicts:

> And you will begin to seek Hashem your God, and you will find Him when you seek Him with all your mind and heart. And when you're under stress, and all these words that I said, the blessings and the curses, find you, at the end of days, then you will return to Hashem, your God, and you will listen to Him. He is compassionate; He will not fail you, and will not let you perish. And He will not forget the covenant with your fathers, that He swore to them.

One of the most famous prophesies of this type is found in *Amos* (8:11,12): "Behold, days are coming, says God, when I will send a famine in the land. Not a famine for bread, nor a thirst for water, but for hearing the words of God."

And in *Hoshea* (3:4,5): "The children of Israel will remain for many days without king, prince, sacrifices . . . But afterwards, the children of Israel will return and they will search out Hashem, their God. And they will also search out David, their king, and they'll come trembling to God and to His goodness at the End of Days."

Of course, today, we know of the *ba'al teshuvah* movement, where many Jews from all walks of life have been seeking out God, and returning to true Torah Judaism. It's amazing, since just a generation ago people were predicting the absolute end of Torah-observant Judaism. But in the past two decades, tens of thousands of Jews have become Torah observant, and the numbers keep increasing every year. Each *ba'al teshuvah* exerts an influence on his whole family, and then they have an influence on other families, and so on. Related to this phenomenon, the prophet Malachi (in 3:22–24) predicts: "Behold, I will send to you Eliyahu HaNavi (Elijah the Prophet). And he will return the heart of the fathers to the children, and the hearts of the children to their fathers."

As Rashi explains the verse, "the hearts of the fathers" will be returned to genuine observance of the Torah "*through* the children." In other words, it will be the children who will teach the parents. Just two centuries ago, how could Jews have understood this verse? How could the children turn the hearts of their parents back to Torah observance? The parents were all observant, and so were the children, for that matter! But, today, we see firsthand how this verse is absolutely accurate. Many of our youth are turning to God, and then these youth go on to have an influence on their parents.

The prediction of a large scale *teshuvah* movement makes sense to the rational mind from our perspective today, when unfortunately most of the Jewish world is estranged from the Torah and its teachings. However, it was not always so. For centuries and centuries Jewish tradition was observed by all of Jewry. Therefore, we should take notice that the prediction of massive Jewish renewal and rejuvenation was a highly unlikely scenario — especially a prediction of children turning back his or her parents to Hashem. Yet, that is precisely what was predicted, and that's precisely what is presently taking place among many of the Jewish people.

5. EXILE

The fifth, sixth, and seventh "Wonders of Jewish History" all regard prophesies which predict negative situations occurring to our nation. First we will simply cite the verses where they are predicted and then, after outlining all three categories, we will discuss the truly wondrous nature of these prophesies.

To begin, the fifth wonder is the prophesy that the Jewish people will be sent into exile, dispersed to many different lands. This is first clearly prophesied in *Vayikra* (26:33): "You, I will scatter among the nations, at the point of My drawn sword, and your land will be completely desolate, and your cities will be in ruins."

Another well-known verse is in *Devarim* (4:26,27): "I call Heaven and Earth as witnesses for you today, that you will be cut off quickly from the land that you're crossing the Jordan to acquire. You will not remain there long, for you'll be wiped out. God will scatter you amongst the nations, and you'll be few in number, among the nations where God will lead you there."

Another (*Devarim* 28:63,64): "God will scatter you among all the peoples, from one end of the earth to the other. And you'll serve idols of wood and stone, that neither you nor your fathers have known."

This prophesy of exile is reiterated in the words of the Prophets as well (*Yechezkel* 22:15): "I will scatter you among the nations and disperse you among foreign lands."

There are numerous other verses concerning this. However, as I said, my purpose now is simply to present some of the sources, and later we will deal with their implications.

6. ANTI-SEMITISM

The sixth wonder is the prophesy that Jews will be confronted with anti-Semitism, perhaps not directly, and not all the time, but at the very least it means that a Jew will have cause to be nervous about his situation among the gentiles. Even when the gentile is not thinking about us, we think he is thinking about us. The concept of anti-Semitism — and the feeling that there is anti-Semitism even though there may not be — is an aspect of our history predicted long ago. For instance, we have the following passage (*Vayikra* 26:36–39):

> And those who survive the enemies, I shall bring a fear and faintness of heart in the land of their enemies; the leaves which rustle behind them chase them away. And they will run as if someone is running after them with a sword. They'll fall down and hurt themselves, but there was no one chasing them. And one is going to stumble over the other, as if running away from a sword, but there was no one chasing them. And you will not be able to stand up against your foes. You will perish among the nations, and the land of the enemy shall consume you; and those that are left from that they will decay because of their sins in the land of their enemies, and also, if they are still holding on to the sins of their fathers, they will be destroyed.

So we see that there is going to be a lot of fear and suffering while we're among the gentiles. We are always going to think that they are chasing after us. Even when it was just some leaves rustling, we will be so self-conscious and nervous, that the rustling of leaves will send us running. And, we will be consumed, and killed, among the nations.

Then we have this verse (*Devarim* 28:65–67):

> And among those nations you shall find no respite, and there will

be no rest for your foot, and God will give you a trembling heart and wasted eyes and a dismayed spirit. You will live in constant suspense and stand in dread of day and night, never sure of your existence. In the morning you will say, "Last night was better than this morning" [as Rashi explains, you thought that last night was bad; now when you see what is going on in the morning, you will wish it was yesterday], and in that following evening you will say, "Would that it would be the morning" [the previous morning, since things keep getting worse and worse].

And then (*Devarim* 28:37): "And you will be *l'shamah, l'mashal v'li-shninah* in all the nations where I'll lead you."

L'shamah has different translations. Onkelos says *litzudo*, which means "confused." You will be confused; you will despair. Others say that it means astonishment. Whoever will see their dreadful fate will be astonished.

L'mashal means you'll be a laughing stock or you'll be a byword. Rashi explains *l'mashal* to mean that when misfortune befalls someone, people will say, "That guy, he's suffering like a Jew."

V'li-shninah is similar to *l'mashal*, meaning mockery or a byword. The bottom line is that people will make fun of the Jews while they are in exile.

We see from these few verses that long ago it was prophesied that anti-Semitism, sometimes mild and sometimes virulent, will be a fact of Jewish life in exile.

7. FEW IN NUMBER

The last prophesy is that the Jewish people will be few in number (while in exile) *and despite that they will survive*. Thus, we have the explicit verse mentioned earlier (*Devarim* 4:27): "God will scatter you among the nations, and you will remain few in number, among the nations, where God will lead you there."

Likewise (*Devarim* 28:62): "And you shall remain few in number, even though you could have been as numerous as the stars in the heavens. [Why will you be a small number?] Because you didn't listen to the voice of Hashem, your God."

We see that the Jewish people were told long ago that when they would be sent into exile because of their sins, they would become, and remain, few in number.

We will get back to the significance of these last three prophesies shortly.

BEYOND THE ABILITY OF HUMANS TO PREDICT

We have now gone through the seven wonders of Jewish history, at least superficially. As we said before, the verses quoted above for each "wonder" were only a sampling of the many possible verses which could have been brought for each of the seven categories. Our goal now is to show that a human being would never have written these prophesies the way they were written. These predictions only made sense to predict if they were dictated by God to His true prophets; only God could have manipulated history in such a way that all these prophesies actually have occurred.

However, a natural skepticism might exist concerning the predictability of the seven wonders. A skeptic might say, "It's an impressive set of predictions, but nevertheless they were just flukes, or lucky guesses. Maybe they just prophesied based on some common sense assumptions and certain laws of history that they had observed among other nations. After all, they had seen and learned of other nations — how they managed, how they existed, and how they passed from existence. So they took a couple of lucky guesses and made predictions according to certain recurring patterns of history."

However, that reasoning is easily refuted because of two basic points. First of all, there had been no nation with a similar history upon which the prophets could base their predictions. As we indicated above, Jewish history is unique. There is no precedent for it.

A second reason why the prophesies could not have been

lucky guesses is because they are mutually exclusive of each other. In other words, they contradict each other: If I predict X is going to happen, then it makes no sense to predict Y is going to happen since the occurrence of Y under normal circumstances would cancel out the possibility of X occurring. This is an important point to understand, so let me elaborate.

Let's start with the prophesy that the Jewish people will be eternal. That's a nice prophesy. I imagine that other societies, religions, and countries predicted the same for themselves. However, none of them, I dare say, ever predicted simultaneously that they would endure circumstances over the centuries which would virtually guarantee that they would be wiped out! Yet, that is what the Torah does when it prophesies that the Jewish people will be exiled to the four corners of the world, face unmatched anti-Semitism, and always hold a minority status.

The dispersion of the Jewish people over the entire face of the globe is a unique phenomenon in the annals of history. Usually, when a nation conquers another land, it keeps the original inhabitants in the land and uses them as slaves or as a source of revenue through the collection of high taxes. Of course, in history there have been cases where other nations were exiled, but never has one nation ever been exiled over such a wide area and for so long a time as the Jewish people. Our exile is a unique phenomenon. And that alone makes the Torah's prediction extraordinary. However, what truly shows that the prophesy comes from a Divine source is that the same Torah that predicted a harsh exile also states that the Jewish people will be the eternal people! To the rational mind, how could the two ever go hand in hand? Exile is the surest way to guarantee that a people are not going to be eternal. Historically speaking, when a nation is exiled to a foreign land, what usually happens is a kind of national "survival of the fittest." The exiled people get swallowed up by the stronger culture, either forcibly by conquest or over time by the attraction to dominant cultural influences. In either case, the absorbed culture loses its identity, dropping its individualism, and adopts the identity of the surrounding culture. Nevertheless, even though the Torah predicted that the Jewish people would be sent into exile and remain few in number, still it predicts that they will maintain their identity as the eternal Jewish people. That's against all logic!

Furthermore, what makes the prediction even more extraordinary is that the Torah promises that the exiled Jews will have to face frightening anti-Semitism, another factor that should have led to our getting lost amongst the nations. We do not have to be reminded of how true that prediction has been. In Europe, for hundreds of years, Jews were persecuted because they were different. They didn't accept Christianity, wouldn't intermarry, and wouldn't integrate. And that led to persecution. That is the concept of "the dislike of the unlike." If someone is openly "unlike" you, you naturally "dislike" him. A natural consequence of "the dislike of the unlike" is a swing, by the unliked minority, to the other side, i.e., assimilation, since no one likes to be disliked. As we said before, the results are that the conquered or exiled minority becomes absorbed by the dominant culture and loses their distinct identity.

In fact, the "dislike of the unlike" was a prominent feature in recent Jewish history. It is not surprising that there were segments of our people who decided it was best to assimilate. And yet the incredible thing is, contrary to what the normal laws of society should be, even open acceptance of the gentile's ways did not eliminate anti-Semitism. In fact, it made it worse. As we know, many of the German Jews, from the early 1800's until the 1930's, wanted nothing more than to adopt the ways of their German countrymen. They even "out-Germaned the Germans." The German Jews reasoned that they were hated because for hundreds of years they didn't want to be like the gentiles. Our ancestors were stubborn, the "enlightened" nineteenth century German Jew reasoned. "We will be different," they said. "We are ready to marry their daughters, attend their universities, and even convert and attend their churches — then they will accept us."

Unfortunately, contrary to what normal logic should expect,

that is not what happened. The German Jews, except for a small minority, assimilated, but ultimately they were not accepted. Instead, a new and different type of anti-Semitism arose, one that was even worse than any before. The German gentile reasoned: "The Jews are trying to be like us. They are taking over our jobs, our government, and marrying our women." And so the Germans started getting paranoid. The result: Nazi Germany, the Holocaust.

The Jew who assimilated was just as much a victim of anti-Semitism as the religious Jew who was massacred in the marketplace by a gentile mob. Both were victims of anti-Semitism, just as the Torah predicted. You're either going to be wiped out through persecution or through assimilation. In either scenario you're going to get swallowed up like every other nation in history that experienced the "dislike of the unlike." And yet the same Torah declares that the Jews are the eternal people! Our Torah tells us that despite being persecuted in exile, we will always exist as a distinct eternal people. It doesn't make sense. They're contradictory predictions. It's contrary to all the rules of history.

And then, to top it all off, the Torah foretells that while in the lands of exile the Jewish people will be "few in number." That greatly compounds the improbability of the promise of eternity. According to statistics there should be many, many more Jews in the world today.[15] We are a very old people, dating back to antiquity. Two thousand years ago we had roughly the same amount of people as the Chinese. Today, there are over one billion Chinese. Yet, we Jews are very few, numbering approximately fifteen million. Of course, the persecutions and servitude,

---

15. In the times of the Roman Empire, there were about six million Jews. About two million were killed during the hundred-year revolt against Rome (33–136 C.E.), leaving about four million. According to the Malthusian population growth doctrine, Jews should today number in the hundreds of millions.

the forced conversions, and the eager assimilationists all contributed to the stunting of our numbers. Fine. We can understand that. However, the question is: How could the Torah predict that we would be so few in number and *yet know that we won't be wiped out*? The strongest nations and empires have been wiped off the face of the earth. And here, the Jewish people, who are dispersed all over the globe, hated, and very small in number, will never be wiped out. Who, but the Overseer of life and history, would have put these two prophesies together in the same Torah?

And, to top it off, we have the amazingly accurate prediction that the Jewish people will be a light to the nations. This prophesy totally contradicts everything else that has been prophesied. Think about it. Earlier I cited letters from some of the greatest, most respected and intelligent gentiles the world has known, who acknowledged the unsurpassed positive impact that the Jews have had on world civilization. If that is so, then how can the prophet predict that we'll also be few in number? Who is going to listen to such an insignificant, tiny nation? And if we are looked up to, then won't others want to join our ranks? And still the Torah says we are going to be small in numbers. And not only that, but we are going to be hated. We're going to be *l'shamah, l'mashal v'li-shninah,* as we explained above. One usually doesn't learn from people one hates. Yet, the Torah predicts that we will be a light to the nations. The world, at least a tremendous portion of it, will follow our lead — the lead of this despised little nation, scattered all over the world. It doesn't make sense to make such a wild prediction.

Unless, of course, it's God telling it to his prophets.

A university professor or a political strategist can try to predict the future based on what's relatively predictable. But how could a human being know things that are so unpredictable? Why would someone dream of making such predictions? Predictions that contradict one another. Do we need any greater proof that all these prophesies about the future of the Jewish people were dictated by God to His true prophets?

Let's not stop here, though. Consider the prediction that as long as the Jewish people dwell in the Land of Israel the land is going to be fruitful and lush, yet as soon as the Jews are gone the land will become desolate. As you know, in the olden days there were no airplanes. People from that region traveled by ship or caravan between the continents of Asia, Europe and Africa — and the crossroads between the three continents was the Land of Israel. What a strategically situated land. And everyone knew how plush the land was. Finally, after 850 years in the land we were exiled. Peoples of all types, from many different countries, settled there over the years, and yet the land didn't grow for them. For 2,000 years the land was pretty much a desolate desert.

Who could have predicted that? How could anyone "predict" such an unnatural occurrence? And then to "predict" that as soon as the Jewish people return to their land it will become fertile again — what human being could have foretold that? Why should the fruit trees of the land begin blossoming again? Because the Jews are coming? Does that make sense? Scientifically, why should someone predict something so unlikely to happen, and so easily refutable, unless God Who controls the world told him to?

And, last but not least, let's recall the wonder of the Jewish *Teshuvah* Movement. Today, it seems so matter of fact because we are witness to it firsthand. But who would have dreamed even 200 years ago (let alone 2,000 years ago) that it would turn out this way? Everyone back then who read these prophesies must have been wondering, "What is this business of returning to God? Everyone is religious today. (Until 200 years ago all Jews were basically observant.) Who needs to do *teshuvah*?" Let alone who would have dreamed of a situation that will have children bringing their parents back to the fold?

Even the Jews of a hundred years ago...fifty years ago...twenty-five years ago, who unfortunately saw the need for a *Teshuvah* Movement, would never have imagined how quickly and dramatically it would have taken hold. Judaism was almost dead. Ben Gurion, it's well known, did not make a big fuss over forcing yeshivah students to join the army because he was sure that in twenty years there would be no more religious Jews left. Then, starting in the 1960's — especially after the Six Day War and the Yom Kippur War — there began a great movement of secular Jews turning back to their roots.

These seven predictions are unique. Now, if it would just happen to be a unique history, without having been predicted, one could conclude that although the Jewish people have an unusual history, it nevertheless was simply a fluke. And even having been predicted, had the predictions been based on normal historical processes, then perhaps one could have concluded that the Jewish prophets took an educated guess. But our history is unique *and* the prophesies are not based on normal historical processes; the predictions are not based on any previously established rules of history, so the prophets couldn't have taken just an "educated guess." Thus, both points — our unique history, together with its accurate prediction — make it very hard for a person not to believe that there must be a God, Who gave us His Torah, Who also dictated His words to His prophets telling them what the future of the Jewish people will be — and there must be a God Who is running this world based on those prophesies. In an objective court of law, this argument would stand as evidence beyond a reasonable doubt.

DIVINE GUIDANCE
—— Throughout ——
JEWISH HISTORY

BY NOW, YOU SHOULD REALLY believe, beyond a reasonable doubt, in the existence of God, in the Divine origin of the Torah, in the World to Come, in the uniqueness of the Jewish people, and in the truth of the Prophets. You are now a certified believer. You can turn on the automatic pilot and glide to your destiny in life, right? After all, what more is there to believe in?

Unfortunately, while these few chapters may be enough to qualify you for a degree in basic belief, there is still some way to go before you will earn your "Ph.D." (And even then, life is an ongoing learning process through which one may deepen his belief). This is because we have not really gone into one of the most important cornerstones of our belief, belief in *hashgachah pratis*.

The common English translation of *hashgachah pratis* is "Divine Providence." ("Divine," of course, refers to God. And "Providence" means "to manage" or "to oversee.") Literally translated, the word *hashgachah* means to "oversee," while the word *pratis* means "particular" or "individual." *Hashgachah pratis*, then, is the concept that God watches and oversees every single particular of our lives, great and small alike. Of course, it's impossible for us with our puny, finite minds to fathom how

God can take care of the countless trillions of events going on simultaneously on this planet. Yet, to say that He is incapable of anything less, is to confine Him to our human expectations. God cannot be confined. He can do anything, despite the fact that it is beyond our comprehension to figure out how He can do it. Obviously, we shouldn't be thinking that we can understand the greatness of God. However, in order to help us comprehend a tiny drop of His capabilities, God specifically went "out of His way" to create a vast universe. God made planet Earth just a speck of dust in comparison to the universe as a whole. But why? So that when we look at a particle of dust in the palm of our hand, we come to realize that it's so easy to watch over. And that it's the same idea with regard to God's ability to run our "tiny" world. To God, planet Earth is no more difficult to oversee than a speck of dust. God made our planet just a small speck in a vast universe in order to teach us that this planet, which to us is so huge, is nothing at all for Him to watch over and have full control of — that's *hashgachah pratis*.

Another possible reason why God created such a vast universe is to help us generate in ourselves at least a little precious feeling of *yiras Shamayim*, "fear of Heaven." God thought it worthwhile to create the most mind-bogging colossal universe, even if only one person would gain by it a little more respect for his Creator. *Elokim asah she-yiru milfanav*, "God made this [tremendous universe] so that we should fear Him" (*Koheles* 3:14). Every single heavenly body is worthwhile if just one person thinks to himself and says, "Wow, I better be careful. Look Who I'm starting up with — a real, powerful Creator. I'd better watch my step." Sometimes when you hear a little thunder and see a little lightning you also get that feeling of fear and respect for God's power. For that feeling alone, the Talmud tells us that thunder and lightning were worthwhile for God to create (*Berachos* 59a). The enormity of the universe is to teach us that nothing is too vast for God. Not a single event which occurs, happens without it being overseen by God. Nothing escapes God's attention — not the object on the floor that you stubbed your little toe on, nor the grandiose plans of world leaders. All is under His scrutiny and control, every minute. And now we present more evidence that God was, and still is, pulling all the strings of history and of our private lives.

JEWISH HISTORY: HASHGACHAH PRATIS IN ACTION

A world-famous, nineteenth-century Emperor of Russia, once asked a Church official for proof that God existed.

"The Jewish people," the clergyman answered.

What he meant was that our survival alone is the greatest miracle, the greatest proof of a living God. As we showed in the last chapter, Jewish survival defies all the rules of history.

However, that was, and is, only possible because the Creator of the Universe personally oversees all the everyday affairs of the Jewish people. It follows, then, that one of the best ways to see *hashgachah pratis* in action is through the study of Jewish history. So, let's embark on a quick tour of some of the more well-known highlights of our history, in order to see clearly the Divine hand in all that has transpired to our people.[1]

It is obvious to all who read the Torah that one of its purposes is to teach us (among other important lessons) that God is especially involved with this little portion of humanity called the Jewish people. He is constantly guiding us to our ultimate destiny. Biblical history, as recorded in the twenty-four books of the *Tanach*, is all one long chain of open *hashgachah pratis*. But even when Biblical history ends shortly after the destruction of the First *Beis Ha-Mikdash* (Temple) and the exile of the Jewish people, still we see that *hashgachah pratis* is very much in operation, albeit in different ways. True, the era of open national miracles ended, but the era of "natural, hidden" national miracles began. Let us

---

1. Many of the ideas written here were taken from *Permission to Believe*, by Lawrence Kelemen (Jerusalem: Targum/Feldheim Publishers, pp. 174–182).

begin our historical lesson from this point in history.

After the Persians conquered Babylonia (and inherited their empire and all the Jews who dwelled therein), the wicked Haman arose. That should really have been the end of the Jews, since all the Jews of the world were under Persian rule at the time. However, the miracle of Purim occurred. Purim marks the official turning point in Jewish national history where God stopped performing open miracles for us and started running our affairs with hidden miracles. God saved His people through political intrigue rather than the "old-fashioned" way of open intervention which overturned the laws of nature. Nevertheless, it is the same *hashgachah pratis,* the same manipulation of events, that ensures that this nation of Jews never quite gets lost.

Shortly after the downfall of Haman, King Cyrus of Persia allowed the Jews to return to their land after seventy years of exile, to rebuild the Second Temple. Just those seventy years alone constitute a miracle of survival. The Jews, like so many other peoples driven from their homeland, should have been swallowed up by their host culture. They should have assimilated and eventually faded out of existence, as we explained in the previous chapter. However, they managed to maintain their distinct identity. That cannot be explained by the normal rules of history — only *hashgachah pratis* can account for it.

Then, in the Second Temple era we have *hashgachah pratis* operating behind the miracle of Chanukah. And the Jewish people really needed the boost of a Chanukah miracle to let them know that despite all the troubles they were having at that time with the Greeks and the Hellenist (i.e., assimilated) Jews, God was still with them. However, the good times didn't last long. After the trouble from the Greeks died down, trouble with the Romans arose. With the Romans came the end of whatever independence our nation had left, culminating in the tragedy to top all tragedies — the destruction of the Second Temple. By all odds, the end of the Jewish people should not have been far off. But the Jews, who were exiled from their land a second time, defied history again and endured.

No, the rough times weren't over by any means. There was the Bar Kochba revolt, the destruction of Betar, the persecution by the Roman Caesars, and the rise of Christianity bringing its heightened brand of persecution and anti-Semitism. Then, as if the Church-instigated persecution for the ensuing seven centuries were not enough, the Christians decided to initiate the Crusades. Although officially a campaign to fight the Moslems, the Crusades brought in its wake new waves of horrific massacres of the Jewish populace of Europe. And there was not one Crusade, but several which sporadically took place during the next two and a half centuries (1095–1348). Some of the most somber and heart-wrenching *kinos* (lamentations) that we say on Tishah b'Av, our national day of mourning, refer to the atrocities perpetrated against our people at that time.

Of course, the Christians did not need the Crusades for an excuse to kill Jews. In the mid-1300's the infamous Black Plague, a disease which killed millions of people, ensued. Notwithstanding the fact that Jews, as well as Christians, died because of it, the plague was blamed on the Jews, who were slaughtered with impunity once again. Towards the end of the 1300's the equally infamous Spanish Inquisition began. In the name of Christian "love," many Jews were coerced into converting, or were simply tortured and burned at the stake. For a good century, the Inquisition continued until finally the entire Jewish population was given the alternative of either conversion or expulsion. So, on Tishah b'Av 1492 (as Columbus set sail for America), hundreds of thousands of Jews were simply thrown out of Christian Spain to face inhospitable elements, pirates, starvation, disease, and ultimately death. (Even in the midst of this darkness, there was a little light. With Columbus' discovery of America, God was already "pulling the strings" to set up a safer haven for the Jews of Europe.)

The 1500's were no picnic either, but in 1648, rebelling Cossacks went wild. For almost two years, a period known as "*Tach v'Tat*" (1648–1649), they killed Jews across Eastern Europe with a ferocity and barbarity not previously encountered (which is hard to believe). Luckily, the Cossacks were only armed with simple weapons, such as swords and the like. Had they had modern weaponry, they would probably have approached the Nazis for sheer butchery.

Then, in the late 1700's came the *Haskalah* ("Enlightenment") Movement. This movement consisted of Jews who wanted to assimilate to avoid persecution. They concentrated on secularizing themselves as much as possible, and they dropped most, if not all, of their religious practices. It started when after centuries of being treated at best as second-class citizens, the Jews in European countries were finally given some liberties for the first time. However, the Enlightenment led to new problems, which in many ways surpassed the problems of the physical persecution that the Jews had known until then. It was from the Enlightenment that the Reform movement began. This caused a split among the Jewish people, and a defection from our ranks that still plagues us to this day. And contrary to what they had hoped, the Enlightenment did not solve the problem of anti-Semitism, not even for those who had assimilated. Thus, in the late 1800's, the Dreyfus Affair in France rocked the Enlightened Jewish establishment. A Jewish officer of the French army was falsely accused of treason. All of a sudden, the "Enlightened" gentiles, with whom the Enlightened Jews were so enamored, bared their fangs and showed that they could turn into a barbaric horde no less than the religious Christian of pre-Enlightenment Europe. The Dreyfus Affair was a rude awakening for Jews who thought that imitating the gentiles' ways was an antidote to anti-Semitism.

The "unenlightened" religious Jews of Eastern Europe were never so naive as to believe that assimilation would eliminate anti-Semitism. However, even they were not prepared for the intensified persecutions and pogroms of the 1880's and onward. (In fact, it was the pogroms and events of the 1880's which triggered the first waves of Eastern European Jews to emigrate to America.) Then, if times weren't hard enough, in 1914 World War I broke out in Europe. Called the "war to end all wars," it coincided with new pogroms unleashed by the Czars in Russia in 1915. In the aftermath, hundreds of thousands of Jews were either dead or reduced to a level of poverty so great that European Jewry never recovered. Of course, in comparison to World War II, Jewish suffering during the "war to end all wars" sounds like nothing. However, we will save our discussion of the Holocaust for later.

Most of these persecutions happened to the Ashkenazic Jews in Europe. Generally speaking, Sephardic Jews were not treated as badly in the Arab lands — however, that is not saying much. There were times when groups fueled by Islamic fanaticism decimated Jewish communities.[2] And even when the situation was relatively stable, still the Koran stipulated that Jews must be treated as second-class citizens. Of course, shortly after the turn of the twentieth century, life for Jews in Arab lands began to really deteriorate. By 1948, government-sponsored persecution of Sephardic Jews began in earnest and many were simply kicked out of the lands in which their families had dwelled for centuries.

Why have I listed a brief account of these horror stories and persecutions? To drive home the improbability of our survival. Which other people in the history of civilization has had their blood spilled as much as ours, and yet survived to tell about it? Not one. No other people has even come close. Anyone who thinks about it objectively has to realize that there is only one explanation for our survival: *hashgachah pratis*. God has been watching over us, despite the persecutions. (Of course, one may ask, if God has been watching over us, then how could all of these terrible events have happened in the first place? That is a question to which we will return later in this chapter.) Through all the persecutions, we still survived, which was only possible through His protection. This is the only logical way to under-

---

2. Maimonides, for instance, had to permanently leave his native Spain because of such a group.

stand our history.

Of course, the post-World War II era has had clear *hashgachah pratis* too. Ask yourselves: After such a long, bloody history, and especially after a Holocaust, what were the chances that the Jewish people would not only survive *but rebuild*; and not only rebuild, but rebuild at the same time a population of Arabs, outnumbering them more than a hundred to one, were at their throats? What were the chances? The Arabs hate the Jews. And we are talking about a hatred that knows no bounds, a hatred that defies all common sense. And yet we prevailed. Think about it. What were the chances? Let me elaborate on this point by dwelling on some recent history.

In 1948, the day the State of Israel was declared,[3] five fully armed mechanized Arab armies attacked the scattered, woefully unarmed, quarreling remnant of Jews, living in the Land of Israel. The Arab leaders proclaimed: "This will be a war of extermination, a momentous massacre." Nevertheless, against all odds, the ragtag army, which contained many Holocaust survivors, won.

In 1956, Egyptian leader Gamel Abdul Nasser cut off Israeli access to the Suez Canal and the Gulf of Aqaba. He then signed military pacts with Saudi Arabia and Yemen, and formed a unified military command with Jordan and Syria. The Jews did not wait, however. They launched a preemptive strike and to everyone's surprise quickly took the Egyptian outposts of Rafa, el-Arish, the Gaza strip, the coast of the Suez Canal, the Gulf of Aqaba, and Sharm el-Sheik. And all that was in just over a week until a cease-fire was imposed.

War came again in 1967. The same Egyptian leader, Gamel Abdul Nasser, moved 100,000 troops into the Sinai desert. He ordered United Nations "peacekeeping" units out of the area.

---

3. Incidentally, the return of the Jews to our homeland this century, marks the first time in human history that a nation which had been exiled from its land twice, returned again to establish a state a third time.

Incredibly, they complied. Several days later, he signed a military pact with King Hussein of Jordan. The same day, Iraqi forces took positions on the Israeli-Jordanian border.

On June 5, the Israeli army again launched a preemptive strike. In a single day, it destroyed the entire Egyptian air force. Jordan and Syria both declared war. In six days, Israel defeated all three armies. Each army was many times the size of its own. To this day, experts cannot adequately explain the 1967 victory. Of course they are at a loss for explanations, because they only look for natural causes and effects. They do not understand that everything in Jewish history comes down to one cause: God's protection through *hashgachah pratis*. But let's continue.

The Yom Kippur War, in 1973, was in many ways a greater victory than the victory in 1967. Egypt and Syria successfully launched a surprise attack while most of the Jews were praying during their holiest day of the year. This time the enemy penetrated the Israeli lines. Totally unprepared, Israel seemed doomed. Writers in foreign newspapers wrote of the "end of Israel," and of the "upcoming holocaust." Even Israeli leaders were publicly despondent and expected the worst.

Nevertheless, the Jews "somehow" overcame and conquered. And no one could say that it was the superior Israeli army this time. They had been caught by complete surprise. They were at the mercy of their enemies. The only thing that saved them those first crucial days were events that were nothing short of miraculous — in a word (actually two): *hashgachah pratis*.

Just to illustrate the kind of *hashgachah pratis* we are talking about, let me mention the well-known story involving the Syrian general in charge of driving his column of tanks straight into the heart of Israel. He found he had an open road into Tel Aviv — literally, an open road — yet mysteriously he called a halt to his unopposed column of tanks and troops. That hesitation gave the Israelis valuable time which eventually led to the Israeli victory, and a court-martial for the Syrian general. At his trial he was asked to explain his decision.

"It can't be this easy, I thought to myself," he said. "They must be waiting. We must be going straight into an ambush. The Israelis are going to attack us on both sides." So he stopped.

That general's decision made no sense. Their attack was a total surprise. Why, then, did he stop? Because no one was there to oppose him. Idiot! Of course, no one was there — you surprised them! That's the whole idea of a *surprise* attack! It's Yom Kippur! The Jews are praying! That's why no one was there!

But he stopped anyway. He was afraid of an ambush. Go explain this rationally.

I'll explain it. It's called the *yad Hashem*, the "hand of God." The verse says, "The heart of the king and his ministers (i.e., even his generals) are in the (*yad*) hand of God" (*Mishlei* 21:1). *Yad Hashem, hashgachah pratis.* Call it what you like, but we Jews would not be here today if there was not Someone above watching over us at every turn.

It took only eighteen days for the Israeli army to fully recover and re-establish Israel's borders. The world was rightfully amazed. Although the casualties were many, the Jewish people remained, against outrageous odds.

Most recently, the *yad Hashem* was evident in 1991 in the defeat of Saddam Hussein, a modern-day Haman intent on annihilating the Jews, whose surrender — "coincidence of coincidences" — happened on Purim. Saddam had built the world's fourth largest army. There was the United States, Russia, China, and then Saddam's Iraqi army.[4]

But, even though this modern-day Haman was smart enough to build the fourth largest army in the world, he was guided by God to make a real unexplainable "dumb" move. He attacked tiny Kuwait a little too early, despite warnings from the United

---

4. It's well-known that he was on the verge of creating an atomic bomb. He already possessed chemical weapons, and he even had used them against Iranian soldiers and civilians during the 1980's. A nuclear warhead though, is much more powerful than any chemical warhead, and Saddam would have had one by that time if Israel hadn't bombed Iraq's nuclear reactor ten years earlier. But that's a different story of *hashgachah pratis*.

States that he shouldn't. What an idiotic maneuver! Wait a couple years, Saddam, and you will have nuclear power! Had he had nuclear power, the United States would have been much more cautious in their dealings with Iraq. But no. He can't wait to go into Kuwait. He has to attack before he is capable of nuclear engagement. "The heart of the king and his ministers is in the hand of God." *Yad Hashem*.

On the other hand, some observers wanted to argue that perhaps his decision to conquer Kuwait was not so thoughtless. Perhaps he thought that no one would really care too much. Sure they would rant and rave. But no one, he calculated, would risk their lives for little Kuwait. Actually, if that was his thinking, then he was not thinking so irrationally. How many weak countries have been overrun by stronger powers while the rest of the world stood by silently? Too many to count.

Consequently, Saddam went into Kuwait.

However, the world was up in arms. He had miscalculated, and miscalculated badly. Kuwait was one of the richest oil nations in the entire Middle East. If you hit Kuwait, you hit the good old Western pocketbook, and that is asking for real trouble. Still, Saddam did not think anyone would care too much.

He was mistaken.

Everyone lined up against him. And they meant it. Even Russia, who was an ally of Iraq, abandoned him. And that was another very important piece of the puzzle in the *hashgachah pratis* that decided the outcome of the Gulf War. As the events in Kuwait first unfolded, Russia was on the verge of collapse. Seventy years of Soviet Communism was coming to an end. When Saddam went into Kuwait, the Soviets, long-time friends of Saddam, were all of a sudden too preoccupied with their own problems. As a result, America was allowed to do what it wanted without worrying about starting a conflict with the Soviet Union. *Yad Hashem*.

What did Saddam decide to do? Virtually the entire civilized world was lined up against him ready to fight. There was nothing left to do but back down, right? Wrong.

Saddam decided to blame the Jews. Make the Jews give the Palestinians autonomy (i.e., let the Arabs have a section in Israel to be ruled completely by the Arabs) and Iraq will back out of Kuwait, he declared.[5] And Saddam threatened that if anyone started up with him, he would destroy Israel with his Scud missiles.

During this time, a sizeable army was being put together, and for the first time ever, the Arabs joined and formed a coalition with the Americans and Europeans in possible combat against their own Arab brothers. Israel however, wasn't allowed to join this coalition. The Arabs wouldn't hear of letting Jews kill other Arabs. They said, "Sorry, no Jews allowed. If the Jews join in, we break up the party." So the Jews were not allowed to fight. Israel was in a quandary, however, because they wanted to destroy the Scuds, but if they would attack Iraq, the entire coalition threatened to break up. Consequently, America and the rest of the coalition promised to fight for Israel. And remember, who is part of this coalition? America, the West...and the Arabs! Can you imagine it!? Saudi Arabia, who financed the PLO, and Syria, the haven for terrorists, sided in essence with Israel. Saddam threatens the Jews, and our sworn enemies, the Arabs, decide to fight for us! Result: no Jewish blood is spilled. The Arabs helped to protect the Jews.

Who can understand it? Not one bullet was fired by Israel. And the Israelis were ready for a fight. Believe me, they really wanted one. But, no. They were prevailed upon by America to

---

5. The American President, George Bush, said many times that he would not accept Saddam's attempt to transfer blame for the war over to the Israelis. Bush even made famous the term "No linkage" which meant that he would not listen to any discussion of a "link" between the demand that Saddam withdraw from Kuwait and the issue of Palestinian autonomy (meaning that the Palestinians, too, should have their own state). What happened right after the war? "Linkage!" All of a sudden everyone was in a uproar against Israel that they had to do something about the Palestinian situation.

stay away. Everyone else was ready and anxious to do the dirty work for them.

Of course, Israel was not going to get off so easily. Saddam wanted to draw the Israelis into a fight to cause the coalition to break up. Therefore, he launched Scud missiles into densely populated civilian centers, in particular Tel Aviv, which he promised to destroy. All told, Saddam fired thirty-nine Scud missiles into Israel.

Now, during the Iran-Iraq war in the 1980's, many Scud missiles were launched. On the average, dozens of people were killed (not to mention many more injured) from a single missile attack. Saddam Hussein fired thirty-nine Scuds toward Israel with only one direct fatality. Many just completely missed and went off course. *Hashgachah pratis.*

In the end, the brunt of the "Mother of all Wars," as Saddam had called it before it took place, lasted all of four days. In that time the Iraqi army was thoroughly routed, reduced from the world's fourth largest army to a fourth-rate power. Approximate losses from the four days of fighting totaled more than 100,000 Iraqi soldiers, as compared to 100 or so for the entire coalition.[6] And, to top everything, the Iraqis finally surrendered on none other than the day of Purim, the day which celebrates the downfall of Haman. "Behold, the Guardian of Israel neither slumbers nor sleeps" (*Tehillim* 121:4).

Our history is one long chain of *hashgachah pratis.* And, now, looking back upon more than 2,000 years of exile, it is no exaggeration to say that the hidden miracles of the past two millennia are equal to, and perhaps even surpass, the open miracles of the Biblical era. In fact, that is what Rabbi Ya'akov Emden wrote in the introduction to his prayer book (*Siddur Beis Ya'akov*):

Whoever delves into the uniqueness of our status in the world, a

---

6. "And five of you shall chase a hundred, and a hundred of you shall chase 10,000, and your enemies shall fall before you by the sword" (*Vayikra* 26:8).

nation in exile, an abandoned sheep, and after all that has afflicted us, the tribulations and events of thousands of years [must come to the following conclusion]. As my soul lives, I declare that when I reflect upon these wonders, they strike me as greater than all the miracles and wonders which God performed for our forefathers in Egypt and in the desert, and in the Land of Israel. And the longer the exile persists, the more the miracle is verified...

And if that was true 200 years ago in the time of Rabbi Ya'akov Emdem, it is incalculably more true today. Our existence in exile has been one long miracle. Only a closed mind would fail to see the *hashgachah pratis* — the *yad Hashem* — in Jewish history. Its presence is evident beyond a reasonable doubt.

Even secular writers have noticed this. Paul Johnson (the non-Jewish historian mentioned in the previous chapter), formerly a writer for the New York Times, recorded the following thoughts while touring Israel:[7]

> When one visits Hebron today he asks himself, "Where are all those peoples which once held the place? Where are the Canaanites? Where are the Edomites? Where are the ancient Hellenes and the Romans, the Byzantine, the Franks, the Mamelukes, and the Ottomans?" They have vanished into time. Irrevocably. But the Jews are still in Hebron. All the great Pharaohs who sought to wipe out the Jews throughout their history are themselves gone. But the Jew remains and thrives. All peoples pass in and out of existence, but the Jew defies history.

Professor Nicholas Berdayev, Russian historian, writes in *The Meaning of History*:

> Their destiny [i.e., the destiny of the Jewish people] is too imbued with the metaphysical to be explained in either material or positive historical terms.

> I remember how the materialist interpretation of history, when I

---

7. *A History of the Jews* cited in *Permission to Believe*, pp. 82–83.

attempted in my youth to verify it by applying it to the destinies of [other] peoples, broke down in the case of the Jews, where destiny seemed absolutely inexplicable from the materialistic standpoint. And, indeed, according to the materialistic and positivist criterion, this people ought long ago to have perished.

The attempt to explain Jewish survival in secular terms is futile and bound to end up at a dead end. Some will claim we survived because we were rich, others claim it's because we were poor. Some will credit it to the fact that we were pacifists, others claim that we were militant. Some point out that we were concentrated, others point out that we were scattered. The secular historian is baffled. How have the Jews survived?

It's hard for an objective person to avoid the conclusion that God exists, and watches over the Jewish people.

WHEN BAD THINGS HAPPEN TO THE JEWISH PEOPLE (MAKING SOME SENSE OF THE HOLOCAUST)

However, we come to a very serious question. If God truly watches over us, then why have we suffered so much? After all, what other people has had so much of its blood shed? Does God show special concern for us or not? To answer that question thoroughly would take us far beyond the scope of this book. However, the question is too obvious to ignore completely. In a similar vein come questions about the Holocaust. However, before attempting to comment about the Holocaust, we must mention that there are many rabbis who feel that the Holocaust is a topic that shouldn't be discussed. Their reasoning comes from their keen realization that we humans are completely inadequate when it comes to trying to understand God, for we are absolutely incapable of understanding Him, and therefore, it's sheer audacity to even attempt to understand Him, and that's certainly a valid view. Other rabbis feel that it is better to avoid the topic with the generation of the actual Holocaust sufferers themselves, since understandably their wounds are too fresh for them to accept any rationalization for what had happened. Many rabbis are of the opinion that since the next generation doesn't really have any of their own direct wounds or scars from the Holocaust, but are left with many unanswered questions that the Holocaust presents, it's a good idea to try to answer some of the questions with some valid answers. Now I'm sure that we won't do complete justice to this topic, but surely we will be of some help by giving a general understanding of the subject.[8] Therefore, we feel obligated to present a few important Torah principles which should go a long way toward understanding the Holocaust, and Jewish suffering in general.[9]

The truth is that the Torah itself clearly predicted that God will run our nation with doses of Jewish suffering. In a few different places,[10] the Torah emphatically impresses upon the Jewish people the great responsibility of being the Chosen People. The basic gist of those passages are as follows: If you'll keep the laws of My Torah, the special gift that I've given to you, the Jewish people — if you'll keep My *mitzvos* — then everything will go well. You'll have peace, security, and power. But, if you don't

---

8. Truthfully, if one has even the beginning of an understanding of what it means when we refer to the deeds of God, then he'd realize that it was pure arrogance to presume to be able to grasp and fathom God's deeds. As a parent and a teacher, I know how I feel when a child or student has "questions and doubts" about something I have done — especially when I did it with my child's or student's benefit in mind, and the student wasn't mature enough to understand this. Similarly, *l'havdil*, it's complete haughtiness and brazenness to think for even a fraction of a second that we can possibly fathom the reasons behind God's deeds. To do so is to forget Who God is.

9. I recommend two excellent books that deal extensively with the subject of human suffering in general, and the Holocaust in particular: *Shoah – A Jewish Perspective on Tragedy in the Context of the Holocaust*, by Rabbi Yoel Schwartz and Rabbi Yitzchak Goldstein (Mesorah Publications, 1990), and *Why Me, God? A Jewish Guide for Coping with Suffering*, by Lisa Aiken (Aronson Publications, 1997).

10. *Vayikra* 26:3–39, *Devarim* 28:15–69, 31:16–21.

listen to Me, and you go against the Torah, then things will not go well. You will have war, constant fear, and helplessness.

(Of course, we can't forget that keeping the Torah is also the main way to earn great reward in the World to Come, which is one of God's main purposes for giving us His Torah. It's only by sanctifying ourselves through the performance of the great mitzvah of the study of God's Torah, and the performance of God's mitzvos, that enables us to have the merit of basking in the Light of God's splendor in the World to Come. This is exactly the message of the Mishnah in *Makkos*, Chapter 3, *mishnah* 16: "God wishes to bring much merit [spiritual perfection] to the Jewish people, therefore God has given them an all-encompassing Torah, with many commandments [which we must learn, since it teaches us the will of God by instructing us what to do and what not to do].")

A natural reaction to that arrangement is surprise and wonder. Is God vengeful or mean? Is He like a human being who reacts harshly out of anger to someone who defies His will?[11]

The answer is that of course God is not vengeful, mean, or motivated by anger — not by any stretch of the imagination. Quite the contrary, it is precisely because of His great love for us that He does whatever is necessary to "keep us on the right track," and help us avoid adopting evil ways. An analogy to this would be of a parent who hits his child since his child ran wildly across the street without being careful. The child is upset since he wants the freedom to run around without restraints. However, the parent knows that for the good of that child, and for the good of any other children who may have also seen this child's dangerous behavior, he must be reprimanded. This will help keep this child, and other children, in line for their future safety. Of course, it's very possible that the child at his young age will not appreciate this lesson; nevertheless, we understand that he

---

11. See also Rabbi David Gottlieb, *The Informed Soul*, New York: Mesorah Publications, 1990, p.153.

must be punished regardless of the lack of his current appreciation level. The bottom line is, that he will be more careful in the future when he wants to cross the street, so the lesson was learned regardless of his appreciation of it. In the same vein, we can understand how people who are involved in eating harmful foods (non-kosher), or are caught up in immoral relationships (which are spiritually dangerous for one's soul), may also elicit a harsh reprimand from our Father in Heaven, either on an individual basis, or sometimes, when there's rampant spiritual breakdown among the Jewish people, on a communal level. But, it's all out of Fatherly love.

Therefore, it's only because God wants to keep us away from spiritual degradation and because He wishes us to act as His Chosen People — to act as a people who by learning His Torah bring spiritual light to themselves and to the rest of the world (through their observance of the Torah way of life) — that He holds us to a higher standard.

To bring this point home, I remind myself how several years ago, the papers were filled with the news that one of the Kennedys, who was a college student, was addicted to drugs. When the story first hit the press, I wondered: There are millions of college students taking drugs, so why do they just write about the Kennedy family? Then, I answered myself: True, but, after all, he's from the Kennedy family. We expect more from him — he's from an affluent, educated, politically successful family. We expect him to know better than to become hooked on drugs and mess up his life. (Eventually he died from an overdose.)

Princess Diana and Prince Charles of England were always in the news. Their courtship, their engagement, their marriage, their separation, and then Princess Diana's death. Why did they always get so much attention? They're regular people; they're made of the same flesh and blood as the rest of us are, so why the whole to-do? What's it our business? Who cares? The answer is: they're not regular people, they're special people. A Prince and Princess. Kingship. Sovereignty. They're special. We expect more from them. What they do means more.

It's the same idea (although there is obviously no comparison) with the Jewish people. God gave us special status for our benefit, but understandably, He expects more of us. Once again, to understand this we can use an analogy. Imagine a child of royal lineage, who is dressed in his finest, ready to attend a royal banquet. As the child is walking to the banquet, he gets a desire to play in some mud, so he bends down to play and starts to get himself all filthy. We understand that if someone who cared about the welfare of this child was watching, he would rush over as fast as he could to pull the child out of the mud. Now, even if the child already got a little dirty, still the quicker he gets pulled out of the mud, the easier it will be to get him cleaned up. Of course, the best situation would have been if beforehand someone would have explained to this child about his important royal lineage, and about how he must keep himself as clean as possible, and act in the appropriate manner, which is befitting for someone of his lineage. The better he understands his importance, the better the chance that he can overcome his normal childish desires to play in the mud. Of course, if the child refuses to accept the fact that he is from a royal family, if he refuses to lead a more refined way of life than those of his peasant neighbors, then he may very well get reprimanded. Ultimately, it's for the child's good. So too with the People of God. Yes, there are grave consequences for the wrong that we do, but these are consequences that are sent to us not out of hatred, God forbid, but to remind us who we are, and to get us back onto the right track. The intent is, as usual, for our ultimate good — to bring us back to God.

That's one general way of answering the question.

The next way is actually an extension of the first answer. It concentrates on why the righteous suffer, even though they keep up their part of the deal by behaving as good-standing members of the Chosen People who follow God's Torah and mitzvos. This answer relates to the teaching that when God gives permission to the Destroyer to wreak havoc, even the righteous are often not spared (*Bava Kamma* 60a). Why is this? Well we know that in a dictatorship, if anyone disobeys the rules of the dictator, it's "off with his head." Luckily, God does not usually rule us by this standard, which is called *middas ha-din* (the attribute of strictness or strict judgment). Rather, God usually rules us with the attribute of mercy, meaning that He temporarily overlooks our wrongdoings and gives us the chance to correct them. Nevertheless, there are various offenses which can trigger off this attribute of strictness. We know, for instance, that "baseless hatred" triggered the destruction of the Second Temple. If enough Jews stop acting with basic decency toward each other, and they allow themselves to get upset and angry over every little perceived wrong done against them, then God too becomes "angry" for every little thing done against Him, and decides to "collect the debt" owed on all their past and present misdeeds, which He had chosen to ignore in the past. Regardless of what it may be that triggers off the *middas ha-din* of God, one thing is for sure, it becomes dangerous for everybody; even the righteous are not safe, for they too have some sins — minor as they may be — and share the responsibility for the Jewish community at large.[12]

A third answer lies in the responsibility for the righteous to censure — in the correct way — and/or teach those who are straying from the path of the Torah the proper way to be a Jew. If they fail to do so, in a certain way they are held accountable for the sins of the wicked. Therefore, when the wicked suffer, many times the righteous must suffer too. See *Shabbos* 55a, b; 56b; 119a, and many other locations for discussion of this responsibility.

Continuing with our question, if God is running the world, then why do sufferings come upon His Chosen People? There's a fourth answer and it has to do with natural cause and effect,

---

12. Of course, not everybody who appears to be righteous is actually righteous. For all we know, this person may have many sins that he, or she, does in private. Also, even though one may be doing good deeds, it doesn't necessarily make them righteous. It could be that God, based on His knowledge of that person's capabilities, expects much more from him or her.

more than retribution and punishment. It has to do with a "deal," so to speak, which was made between God and the Jewish people. The Torah makes it clear how the Jewish people's covenant with God works in two directions. God says, "I will...distinguish [you] from the nations," and make you "...a holy people, a kingdom of Kohanim," and a "treasured people" (*Shemos* 19:5,6). The Jewish people's part of the "deal" involves distinguishing themselves from all the other nations through adherence to the Torah, in word and spirit. As long as we differentiate ourselves from all other peoples, God places us above normal historical processes. And therefore, even though we are a small nation, dispersed amongst other cultures which should guarantee that we will assimilate with the other cultures and get lost, God will raise us above the natural course of history and we will survive. However, the moment we begin thinking and acting as just another nation, then God lets our history take on the characteristics of any other nation. And according to the normal laws of history, a hated minority such as the Jewish people, living in a foreign land, simply cannot last for very long.

Unfortunately, it is not difficult to see that the Jewish people have at times not lived up to their end of the deal. *Shabbos* 119b records a long list of sins done by our people which led to the destruction of both the First and Second Temples. In more recent times, some historians have noted how only about half of pre-World War II Eastern European Jewry were Torah-observant.[13] The truth is that it was even less. The slide away from genuine Torah observance escalated greatly after World War I.

Rabbi Avigdor Miller, *zt"l*, a prominent Rabbi who resided in Brooklyn, New York, had in his possession pamphlets that were published after World War I, written by various Jewish communities for the sake of detailing their past. They speak of how they lived before and after World War I. The books tell how Chassidic

---

13. Rabbi Chaim Rabinowitz, in his famous commentary on the Bible called *Da'as Sofrim*, also makes these observations.

shuls were filled with Jews learning Torah and *davening* before the war. However, after World War I, there were great changes. By the 1930's, many parents were sending their children to gymnasiums (secular schools) for a "modern" education. These schools were usually run and supported by *maskilim*, "Enlightened" Jews, who openly expressed their feelings that Judaism and God's Torah were outdated. The *maskilim* claimed that a modern Jew should be well-versed in German, Polish or Russian, and should know the gentile works of literature. Pre-World War II German, Polish and Russian literature was modern. Torah? Old fashioned. Such was the atmosphere among an increasingly large segment of the general Jewish populace after World War I.

Rabbi Miller himself was in Europe in 1932, in Kovno, once a stronghold of Torah observance. He writes, however, that in 1932, on any given Shabbos, buses, departing every half-hour, would fill up with Jews going to work, openly desecrating the holy Shabbos. And in 1938, before he left Europe, buses were still filling up with Jews going to their jobs on Shabbos — except now the buses were leaving every five minutes! Assimilation had in fact escalated out of control. More and more Jews had begun acting like all the other nations, and so our history became like all the other nations'; it became subject to the natural historical processes that all other nations follow.

Rabbi Meir Simcha HaKohen (1843–1923), famous for his *sefer* entitled *Ohr Someyach*, saw the trend of assimilation well before 1932 and made a remarkable comment about it. His words, recorded in one of his most important works, *Meshech Chochmah*, published after his death in 1927, have a prophetic ring: "Those [Jewish] people who said that Berlin is Jerusalem and that German is the chosen language...[will see] those very people [i.e., the Germans] rise up like a stormwind [to destroy them]" (Commentary to *Vayikra* 26:44).

If we want to be like one of the nations, we will experience history like one of the nations. Only when we dare to be different, and remain true to God's Torah, do we merit to be lifted above natural historical processes. This is another approach to understanding Jewish suffering.

Regardless of how one wants to approach the subject (and it's certainly a delicate subject, and by no means have we exhausted the different approaches), the common denominator is that God has not abandoned us. (As we mentioned before, Mark Twain, and many others, have all recognized that the Jewish people's political, financial, and academic status in the world is way out of proportion to what it should be. Anyone familiar with the former top "honchos" in the white house in the year 2000 knows how true this is. Secretary of State — Madeline Albright, Secretary of Defense — William Cohen, former Secretary of the Treasury — Robert Rubin, Sandy Berger, Alan Greenspan, Senator Lieberman... the list goes on and on.) He is always there, always watching us, always protecting us, always nurturing us — knowing that there will always be a group of Jews who will show enough self-confidence and self-esteem to live as proud Jews who follow His Torah.

PERSONAL HASHGACHAH PRATIS

Just as God watches especially over the Jewish people as a whole, so too He watches over each individual. In fact, the first of the Thirteen Principles of the Jewish Faith (as enumerated in Maimonides) states: "I believe with perfect faith that the Creator, blessed be He, created and guides all creatures, and that He alone did, does, and will do all that transpires in this world." Everything which transpires to each individual comes about through God Himself.

In actuality, this idea shouldn't sound too surprising, since we know that regardless of how many children a person has, each one is important to the parent. Even more so, then, is it logical to believe that God pays particular attention to the needs of those who comprise the Jewish people, since He calls us His firstborn son (*Shemos* 4:2), whom He loves (*Devarim* 7:8, 23:6), and whom He disciplines like a father (*Devarim* 8:5).

Now, in truth, there are far too many verses laced throughout the entire Torah which teach the principle of individual providence, to try to mention them all.[14] And I am sure that virtually everyone can tell over personal stories which would sound unbelievable if not for the fact that they know firsthand that they're true. However, I would still like to close this chapter by relating two stories of individual *hashgachah pratis*, since it's the culmination of all that we've discussed in this chapter. The first story can be found in *In the Footsteps of the Maggid*, by Rabbi Pesach J. Krohn,[15] while the second is in *Candlelight*,[16] by Mr. Avi Shulman.

*   *   *

Rabbi Shimon Gutman,[17] a well-known *talmid chacham* who served for many years as a *rav* in New York and then as dean of a yeshivah in Jerusalem, is today the *mara d'asra* (Torah authority) in a community he founded in Israel.

In 1986, a young woman living in Tzefas, Mrs. Adina Efrat, came to visit Rabbi Gutman following a lecture he had given at Moshav Chilkiyahu. She had been married for eight years and had only one child. She was coming now to ask for a *berachah* (blessing) that she be able to conceive.

Rabbi Gutman, who has taught thousands of men and women throughout his life, explained to the young woman that giving a *berachah* for something of this nature was not within the purview of his normal activities. "I am a teacher. I study Torah with people. I discuss *hashkafah* (Jewish philosophy) with those who seek guidance," he said to the woman. "But for what you

---

14. Two of the more well-known verses include: "God is my shepherd, I shall not lack..." (*Tehillim*, Chapter 23) and "You open Your hand and satisfy the desire of every living creature..." (*Tehillim*, Chapter 145). There are many more.

15. New York: Mesorah Publications, 1992.

16. New York: Mesorah Publications, 1993.

17. All names appear as they do in *In the Footsteps of the Maggid*, where it is noted that they were changed by personal request.

seek, you must go to a very holy person, a *tzaddik* — someone known for his blessings and prayers, someone known to have been answered from Above."

The distressed young woman would not be put off. She insisted that because she had heard so much about Rabbi Gutman from his students, she wanted a *berachah* specifically from him.

Again and again he explained that *berachos* were a serious matter, laden with holy intensity and sincere prayers by those who offer them. "*Berachos*," Rabbi Gutman explained, "are not merely flippant wishes for good fortune and attainment."

His arguments were to no avail. Mrs. Efrat, who was a *ba'alas teshuvah* (one who had come to Torah Judaism of her own volition), said that she didn't know any *tzaddikim*, rebbes, or other prominent *Roshei Yeshivah* whom she could easily relate to or speak openly with. That is why she desired to receive a *berachah* from Rabbi Gutman.

He thought quietly for a few moments and then said to Mrs. Efrat, "I want you to know that I feel your anguish and I share your pain. I myself have a daughter living in Milwaukee, who has been married for more than ten years and has never borne a child. The Gemara (*Bava Kamma* 92a) instructs us: 'If one has a problem and prays for another who has the identical problem, he who has prayed will be answered first.' Let us make an agreement between us. You pray for my daughter and I will pray for you."

Now it was Mrs. Efrat who was struck by another's anguish. The personal pain that Rabbi Gutman had unexpectedly shared with her, and the unique suggestion that he proposed, bonded the young woman with the renowned individual who sat before her. She felt an inner serenity and knew that regardless of what the future held, her trip had been worthwhile.

Mrs. Efrat left the *moshav* and went back home to Tzefas. In the ensuing months Rabbi Gutman did not hear from her, nor did he discuss the matter with his own daughter, Mrs. Devorah Shain, in Milwaukee. In the course of time, Rabbi Gutman's daughter and son-in-law adopted a child.

Five years went by, but the incident with the young woman was on Rabbi Gutman's mind almost daily. And then he heard that his own daughter was expecting a child! The Gutman and Shain families were ecstatic as they anxiously awaited the great event. One day, Rabbi Gutman unexpectedly received a letter from Mrs. Efrat. She wrote that she had heard the good news that Rabbi Gutman's daughter was expecting a child. She wished to tell Rabbi Gutman that she, too, *b'ezras Hashem*, was going to give birth in a few months.

The doctors in Milwaukee had given Mrs. Shain the date they thought she would give birth, but her little girl was born two weeks later than the "due" date. Little Faige Elisheva arrived on the 15th day of Shevat (1991).[18]

A few days later, Rabbi Gutman received an excited call from Mrs. Efrat. The doctors had given her a "due" date but her infant son arrived earlier than expected. "He was born just a few days ago," she said excitedly. Rabbi Gutman asked her the exact date of birth, and was stunned by her reply. The boy's birthday was the 15th day of Shevat! Incredibly, the infant girl in Milwaukee and the newborn boy in Israel had been born on the same day!

According to human calculation the baby girl had come late and the baby boy had come early, but in reality their arrivals had been Divinely synchronized. Because of the prayers that had been offered, the children would forever be united by time as measured by a Divine clock.

*   *   *

A young rabbi who was learning in a Jerusalem *kollel* received a wedding invitation that puzzled him. Neither he nor his

---

18. As a teacher, I had tried one year to tell an inspiring story to my students every day. One night I just "happened" to turn to this story. When I came to this line, though, I got excited. The night that I just "happened" to read this story was Tu b'Shevat, the 15th of Shevat! Talk about *hashgachah pratis*!

wife recognized the names of the bride or groom, but since they had many guests at their home, and there was a possibility that either the *chasan* or *kallah* had been with them for a Shabbos, he decided to drop in during the wedding.

When he did, he was even more perplexed, not recognizing anyone there. As he was about to leave, chalking up the experience to a mistaken invitation, the *kallah* saw him and asked him to remain for the meal. He was, she explained, to a large extent responsible for the wedding.

The following story unfolded: The rabbi had been doing research in a library for a scholarly book on the Talmud. One day he brought along some sandwiches for lunch. After eating, he recited the Grace after Meals slowly, thoughtfully, and carefully. As he finished, a young librarian approached and said that she could not help overhearing him.

Although she was no longer religious, she confessed, she had fond memories of her father, an observant Jew who had *bentched* in much the same way as this young rabbi. However, there was one exception. In one of the blessings that we say after eating, we ask that the Almighty make us not needful of human gifts, but sustain us through His generosity so that we need not feel inner shame (*she-lo nevosh*) nor ever be humiliated (*v'lo nikalem*). When the rabbi was reciting the blessing, he added a third phrase, we should not stumble (*v'lo nikashel*), which she had never heard. Could he please explain why he included that phrase?

The rabbi looked at her in amazement. All his life he had been reciting *bentching* with the three phrases, and no one had ever questioned him. Since they were in a Hebrew library, it was easy enough to find *siddurim*, and he started to search through them. Each *siddur* had only the two phrases, but not the third. As this was the last day he was to be in the library, the rabbi asked the librarian for her address.

Several weeks later, a package arrived at the young lady's home containing a small *siddur* whose worn pages testified to years of constant use. A simple bookmark directed her to the disputed sentence in the Grace after Meals, and the Hebrew words *v'lo nikashel* were underlined. His point had been made, he had validated his three-phrase version.

What the young scholar could not have known, was the special day on which the package had arrived, and the effect it had had on the recipient.

For the past several months she had been dating a non-Jewish man. As their romance became more serious, the young man proposed and pressed her for an answer. Torn between her head and her heart, she couldn't make a decision. Her boyfriend, his patience wearing thin, had given her until the next Tuesday to decide.

Tuesday's mail brought the *siddur* with its clear message: *v'lo nikashel*, a fervent prayer that we not be allowed to stumble. Understanding this to be a signal from the Almighty, she broke off the relationship with her non-Jewish friend, re-evaluated her life, and became a *ba'alas teshuvah*, returning to her family's roots.

Almost a year later, she met the young man who that night became her husband.

Some call it serendipity. We Jews call it *hashgachah pratis*, the way the Almighty runs the world, with the well-being of each and every Jew in His "heart."

*   *   *

We would venture to guess that everyone has at least one of their own *hashgachah pratis* stories which would make for nice reading in a book. There are times when God wants each of us to know beyond a reasonable doubt that He is right there with us, so He leaves His mark more clearly than usual. Of course, even when *hashgachah pratis* is not openly evident, God is nevertheless always there overlooking and directing everything that transpires. It is up to us to try and see how His hand is behind everything going on around us.

Now even though we can't see or feel Hashem, that shouldn't hamper our knowledge that He is everywhere. Because let's face it, we know that there are radio waves radiating in every direction, and these waves can travel through and under almost anything, until they finally reach our radio. And even though we can't see or feel these waves, we know that they are there. Just break your antenna off and you'll see how the broadcast will be interrupted. Similarly, we know that there is the force of gravity on our planet which we can't see or feel, but we know it's there by seeing the results of its force. So if this is true for a physical manifestation of energy in our world, then surely we can understand that God, Who is completely removed from the physical realm, can certainly be present everywhere and at all times, and the lack of our ability to see or feel Him shouldn't negate our ability to believe that God is behind every event that transpires.

"His glory fills the whole world" (*Yeshayahu* 6:3; *Tehillim* 72:19). "Who is like Hashem our God, Who dwells on High, Who looks down on heaven and earth" (*Tehillim* 113:5). He sees everything that's going on. And He not only sees it; He's orchestrating it. And we see it clearly through the history of the Jewish people. And, if we look closely, I am sure that we will see it clearly in our own personal lives as well. God has reasons for whatever He does. As King David stated in *Tehillim* 92:16: "...God is just, my Rock, in Whom there is no wrong."

Our history, communal and personal, teaches us and the world that God exists, and that He's still in control. However, before teaching the world, we must teach ourselves that God is in control. It's true for the Jewish people as a whole, and it's true for every individual. *Hashgachah pratis* — individual, detailed Divine Providence. Relax, you're in safe hands.

Epilogue

We hope that this book has helped to increase the reader's faith in all the basic tenets of our religion. However, the author realizes that not all the evidence that's brought in this book may have proven to be satisfactory evidence to some people, and that can be understood. What may seem to one person as solid rational evidence, may not be so to someone else. However, even so, one has to be careful and respectful when dealing with a 3,300-year-old religion [the religion that the other two "competing" faiths both agree is of truthful origin.] The religion that the other two religions have copied from. A nation whose continued existence continues to baffle historians. A tiny nation which has made such amazing contributions to world society. Such a religion is not to be taken lightly. So, even if this book has not provided sufficient evidence to satisfy your honest search for the answers to your questions, still it shouldn't be an excuse to stop your search. (We recommend that you continue your research with *Permission to Receive: Four Rational Approaches to the Torah's Divine Origin*, by Lawrence Kelemen (see "Suggested Reference Materials"). It has a very detailed and highly intellectual discussion about the validity and origins of the different religions. Rabbi Kelemen also has a great book called *Permission to Believe*:

Four Rational Approaches to God's Existence (see "Suggested Reference Materials"). A third recommendation is *The Road Back*, by Mayer Schiller (Jerusalem: Targum/Feldheim Publishers, 2001). Chapter three brings many different proofs to boost our *emunah* which I felt were beyond the scope of this book. However, for the intellectual reader it brings to light many other angles of thought that prove our *emunah*. It also has chapters which guide a newcomer to the basics that one must know when one starts to embrace the daily laws that an observant Jew must follow, and it also provides guidance to help the reader ease his, or her, way back into Judaism, slowly but surely. However, even if you're still not convinced, after all is said and done, it's important to still realize the validity of our nation's laws and traditions. These are laws and traditions that were handed down from one generation to the next, going all the way back to the millions of people who witnessed the revelation of God at Sinai. In fact, we can literally trace the transmission of the Torah starting from Moshe, all the way to the end of the period of the Talmud, continuing down to the present day! (See the preface that Maimonides wrote to his *Mishneh Torah*.) Therefore, any present lack of understanding, or lack of belief on our part, doesn't give us license to abandon God's Torah, and the way of life it dictates that we follow.

However, I believe, based on the positive comments of the many people who have read this book while it was in manuscript form, that most of those who read this book will become quite convinced of the truths of Judaism. But beware — to the non-religious, and even the semi-religious, there's a very large obstacle that lies in the way, which makes it quite difficult to accept the truth of the Torah. It's the obstacle of having the subconscious, or maybe even conscious, fear of losing your freedom to do as you please. There's the fear of being tied down to a specific set of laws. There's also the fear of facing the very uncomfortable realization that you may have spent so many years of your life doing the wrong things. It's hard to admit that one may have been living his life in error for quite a long time. (Of course, in most cases you didn't know any better, and therefore you are not to blame. However, regardless of whether or not you are to blame, God always accepts one's repentance.) There's also a legitimate fear that a change in one's lifestyle may cause a major strain on one's marriage, or any other relationships that you may have or it may lead to the possibility of losing one's job.

(I recently read a great book entitled *Pathways: Jews Who Return*, by Richard H. Greenberg [New York: Jason Aronson, 1995]. It contains interviews that the author, himself a returnee to Judaism, had with thirty-one returnees to Judaism. Each one had an interesting story about what brought him or her back to practicing Judaism to the fullest. Each returnee discusses the many difficulties that they encountered on their "trip back," and how they dealt with those difficulties. I truly believe that this is a must-read for anyone who believes in their hearts that they should fully embrace practicing Judaism, but have outside obstacles in their way. Another great book with the same theme, which also has many personal accounts of *ba'alei teshuvah*, is entitled *Anatomy of a Search: Personal Drama in the Teshuva Movement*, by Akiva Tatz [Mesorah Publications, 1988].)

Bearing all of the above in mind, it sometimes takes great character for one to embrace the truth, come what may, but what won't we do to finally get the truth. So be aware that because of these and other reasons, one may subconsciously reject what is otherwise very sound evidence to the truths of the Torah. In fact, it has been observed in many scientific studies that if there is some knowledge, which if accepted, will be too disturbing to our tranquil lives, then *any* evidence brought, no matter how substantial it may be, will automatically be subconsciously dismissed before it can be seriously evaluated.[1] True honesty is not easy to find. Therefore, I would like to suggest to those who do realize that they have found the truth, but are possibly afraid to

---

1. See Michael J. Behe, *Darwin's Black Box: The Biochemical Challenge to Evolution*, Free Press, 1996, Chapters 10–11; and Gershon Robinson and Mordechai Steinman, *The Obvious Proof*, C.I.S. Publishers, pp. 15–40.

make a full commitment to the Torah way of life all at once, to just start off slowly, taking on new laws of God's Torah a little bit at a time, and slowly but surely you will see that it's a lot easier to keep the Torah than you think. It would be a good idea to get in touch with an outreach professional (we list different organizations, along with their phone numbers, at the end of this book) who can help you with any of the aspects of becoming a fully committed Torah Jew.

Of course, there's no end to the pursuit of increasing the conviction of one's faith. In fact, it would be of great benefit to review this book once in a while, or at least the parts that you felt strengthened your faith the most, just to keep the evidence fresh in your mind. Better yet, if you feel that this book isn't enough, then look for other kosher books that deal with these topics. (I say kosher, since there are many books written by unscrupulous authors who intertwine heretical thoughts in their writings, and therefore such books obviously must be avoided.)

Truthfully, much more could have been written on each of the topics that I have discussed; however, for the sake of brevity I minimized my writing wherever possible. Hopefully, with our renewed faith, we will all go on to serve God better. I mean, since God created us, and He gave us His Torah, and He endowed us with an eternal soul, then it should be obvious what He had in mind. So let's use our lives in a more Godly way, by studying His Torah and by keeping His commandments, Amen.

Feldheim Publishers published a great book entitled *After the Return*, by Rabbi M. Becher and Rabbi M. Newman, which guides the newly observant into a religious lifestyle and gives advice on how to maintain good family relationships. It also gives practical advice on many issues, such as dealing with parental requests that are contrary to Jewish law, the way to attend parties and ceremonies that are conducted in non-Orthodox settings, and — probably one of the most difficult problems a returnee faces — how to deal with *Kashrus* dilemmas. This is certainly a book that will help you smooth out the "transition stage" that *ba'alei teshuvah* often go through. But don't worry, you are in good company, because tens of thousands of Jews have already successfully gone through this "transition," and they all end up adjusting quite well. Of course you can be assured that God will be with you at all times, helping you adjust as well. It's a well-known principle (*Masechet Makos* 10b) that God helps those who have chosen to help themselves, so you're in good hands!

If you have any comments, pro or con, please forward them to the publisher, who will then forward them to me. Thank you.

Appendix A
The Oral Law

It is a fundamental principle of our faith that together with the Written Law, which is the *Five Books of Moses,* God also gave an Oral Law. This Oral Law supplied all the details necessary to understand the Written Laws as they are found in the Torah.

As we said earlier, the Written Law can be compared to "reminder notes." A speaker often jots down some notes on a little piece of paper which act as a reminder to him of the many details he wishes to speak about. For any given topic jotted down in his notes, the speaker might easily be able to talk for ten or fifteen minutes. So, too, all the laws that are in the Written Torah have a tremendous amount of detail associated with them, detail which was handed down orally from God, to Moshe, to all of Israel, and from generation to generation, as presently found in the Talmud. This is a general explanation of what we mean when we refer to the Oral Law.

Indeed, anyone who objectively reads the Torah cannot help but admit that the Written Laws must have come along with some oral interpretation. Otherwise it would simply be impossible to properly know how to apply the laws in practice. There are numerous examples which testify to this; however, I'll only cite a few very basic ones.

Shemos 16:29 states: "See! God has given you the Sabbath; that is why He gives you, on the sixth day, a two-day portion of bread. Let every man remain in his place; let no man leave his place on the seventh day."

The question is, what does it mean that you are not allowed to leave your place? Can I get up from my chair? Can I leave my room? Can I leave my house? How far does one have to go for it to be considered as "leaving his place?" There is absolutely no explanation given for this in the Written Torah. This verse thus indicates that there must have been an oral explanation transmitted along with these words to explain their meaning. And there certainly is; it is to be found in *Eruvin* 51a.

Another example, in *Shemos* 31:15: "For six days work may be done; the seventh day is a day of complete rest and is sacred to God. Whoever does work on the seventh day shall be put to death!"

Now, doing work on the Sabbath is a very serious matter. If someone were about to do "work" on the Sabbath, and there are witnesses who warned him not to do the "work," under the threat of death, and still he did the work, then he gets the death penalty. However, there's just one problem — what's the definition of "work?" Is carrying a feather out from a private domain to a public domain considered "work?" Is carrying a 300-pound sofa up a flight of stairs considered "work?" What exactly is considered "work?" Obviously there has to be some Oral Law that explains exactly what "work" is. Indeed, the entire Talmudic tractate *Shabbos* deals with the laws of the Sabbath.

In *Vayikra* 16:29: "This shall remain for you an eternal decree. In the seventh month on the tenth of the month you shall afflict yourselves and you shall not do any work, neither the native nor the proselyte who dwells among you."

What exactly does it mean to "afflict yourselves?" And this is a particularly serious law because one who is lax about it, and doesn't "afflict himself" is deserving of *kares*, getting "cut off" (*Vayikra* 23:29). There are different interpretations as to what we mean by *kares;* however, all agree that it is a severe punishment. Obviously then, there has to be some definite meaning to "afflict yourselves," and we again see that there has to be some Oral Law to explain this. See *Yoma* Chapter 8, which deals with this subject.

Then we have also in *Vayikra* 23:40: "You shall take for yourselves on the first day, the fruit of a citron tree *[pri etz hadar],* the branches of a date palm, twigs of a plaited tree, and brook willows; and you shall rejoice before Hashem, your God, for a seven-day period."

We know through tradition that this verse refers to the citron tree *(esrog),* yet in actuality the words of the Torah state nothing more than, *"pri etz hadar,"* which literally translates, "the fruit of a beautiful tree." It does not explain which tree "a beautiful tree" refers to. Obviously, in order to fulfill our requirements of this commandment a specific tree must be meant. Moreover, there are no specifications given here pertaining to the actual fruit itself. For instance, if something's a little wrong with the fruit can we use it? How about if it's slightly blemished, or if a small part of it is cut off, or if there is a tiny hole in it — is it still permissible to be used for the mitzvah? We need more details. We need the Oral Law. Here too, we find that the Oral Law supplies all the answers. See *Sukkah* Chapter 3, where it deals extensively with these laws.

Then we have a few verses later (verse 42): "You shall dwell in booths *(sukkos)* for a seven-day period; every native in Israel shall dwell in booths."

We know that the booth is the *sukkah,* but without the oral tradition how can we be expected to fulfill this commandment? The Written Torah gives us no details as to how many, how high, what length, and what width the walls of the *sukkah* should be. Nor does it tell us what it should be made of, what it shouldn't be made of, with what it should be covered, etc. No explanations! Obviously, there must be an Oral Law which gives detailed explanations for all the requirements needed to fulfill this Divine commandment. Here too, see tractate *Sukkah,* in the first and second chapters, where it deals with these topics.

In *Bemidbar* 29:1: "In the seventh month, on the first day of the month, there shall be a holy convocation for you; you shall do no laborious work, it shall be a day of shofar-sounding for you."

The verse does not explain what sounds we are supposed to make. It doesn't even explain what we're supposed to blow! And it doesn't tell us how many sounds we should make. No details are supplied! There must be an Oral Law to supplement this commandment. Once again, if we will look to our Oral Law, we will find the details in tractate *Rosh Hashanah* 33b–34b.

One of the most important commandments is *tefillin*. We read in *Devarim* 6:8: "Bind them as a sign upon your hand and let them be ornaments [*totafos*] between your eyes."

What are we supposed to be binding as a sign on our hands? And where do we bind them on our hands? And with what do we bind them — are there straps? Are there boxes? If so, what should be in the boxes? Do the boxes have compartments? How many? And what are these *totafos* that we are supposed to put between our eyes? This unusual word is not found anywhere else in the Torah.

Of course, we should point out that despite the complete lack of detail, throughout history, no matter where Jews were found, *tefillin* always consisted of black leather straps and black boxes — one compartment in the hand box, four compartments in the box that goes on the head — and in these boxes were parchments with specific verses from the Torah written on them. Yet, not a word of explanation appears in the written text! Only the Oral Law explains it to us! See *Menachos* Chapter 3 for all the pertinent details.

One last example. In *Devarim* 12:21 it reads: "If the place that Hashem, your God, will choose to place his Name will be far from you, you may slaughter your cattle and your flocks that God has given you, as I commanded you, and you may eat in your cities according to your heart's entire desire."

Now no matter where you'll look in the Written Law, you

won't find *any* commandment supplying details about how to properly slaughter an animal! So what does it mean "as I have commanded you"? It's obviously referring to the oral explanation that God gave Moshe regarding the details of slaughtering animals.

One more point. We find that some words in the Torah have an especially large, small, or upside down letter as part of the word. Obviously, all these "abnormalities" are there to teach us something. There are countless examples of words that are doubled, such as *shaleiach t'shalach* (*Devarim* 22:7) — translated as you shall surely send, and *hasheiv t'shiveinu* (*Shemos* 23:4) — translated as you shall surely return it. What was God trying to convey to us by writing in a double fashion? Furthermore, many words are written with an extra letter (*malei* — full), and sometimes the same word is written in a different location missing that letter (*chaser* — missing). The problem is that the Written Torah doesn't explain anywhere what these lessons are. Thus, there must have been some oral explanation that was given to tell us the meanings behind all these departures from the standard. And there was — it's the oral explanation that God told Moshe, which elucidates every aspect of the Written Torah.

There are numerous other examples. However, the main point here is that we see clearly that the Written Torah must have an oral explanation to accompany it. And it does. The *Talmud Bavli* and *Yerushalmi*, along with all the midrashic works, contain all the missing links and explanations that go hand in hand with the Written Torah. This is true beyond any reasonable doubt.

Appendix B
The Unity of Hashem

Shema Yisrael...Hashem Echad. "Hear O Israel...God is One."
(*DEVARIM* 6:4)

Belief in God's Oneness is another fundamental tenet of the Jewish faith. Therefore, in order to help us fortify our belief in this fundamental principle, God has set up this world in a fashion which clearly shows us His Oneness. In fact, the study of science can help us in this endeavor.

Science has a branch called ecology. Ecology is the study of the various ecosystems as they exist on our planet. An ecosystem is the interaction of plants, animals, and their environment, which produces an integrated system that makes it possible for all life to exist.

For example, the sun initiates the rain cycle through the process of evaporation. The water which evaporates rises to the sky in the form of vapor, where it eventually condenses to tiny droplets and starts to form rain clouds. However, there's a little problem. The clouds form mainly over large bodies of water, since that's where most of the water vapor comes from. But what good are rain clouds to land life, if they hover only over water? All they will do is rain the water back into the oceans. That's where wind comes into the picture. The winds blow these clouds over dry land where eventually they will rain, thereby causing food to grow. The excess water flows downhill in rivers, above and below ground, back to the sea. And the cycle continues.

At the same time that the rain cycle is at work, bacteria, earthworms, and many other insects are busy tilling the soil so that when it does rain, the soil will be in optimum shape to cause food to grow from the seeds that were planted in it. This is the rain cycle which brings about the food cycle.

The food cycle continues when small insects feed off the newly grown vegetation. Then larger insects feed off the vegetation and the smaller insects. Small animals and rodents then feed off the larger insects. Larger animals feed off those smaller animals, with even larger animals feeding off those medium-size animals.

This food chain culminates with human beings at the top of the cycle, since humans eat and utilize even the largest of animals. We eat their meat, use their skins, ride on them, drink their milk, etc.

And so we see how all these different entities — the sun, water, wind, trees, soil, bacteria, worms, insects, vegetation, animals, and humans — are all part of one big plan, ensuring the production and maintenance of life. No accidents could produce such harmony between so many diverse systems. Accidents do not cause unity. Rather the unity found in nature which keeps the life cycle going clearly reflects the unity of one great plan set up by One Great Planner.[1]

Let me point out one more way to recognize the Oneness of God, by once again utilizing science and the phenomenon of our universe. If we study the building block of all matter — the atom — we shall again see that God is One.

There's a chart which lists all the basic elements of our uni-

---

1. For more details about this study see *Rejoice O Youth*, pp. 83–104.

verse. It's called the periodic table, and it lists over 100 different elements. Upon closer scrutiny, however, we see that as different as these elements are from each other (oxygen, hydrogen, gold, silver, uranium, etc.), at their core they are exactly the same. Each of the elements consists of atoms, which in turn are made up of three basic components: protons, neutrons, and electrons. What primarily differentiates one element from another is just the number of protons, neutrons, and electrons that there are in each element. However, in essence, everything in the universe is made up of the exact same building block: an atom that has some protons bound together with some electrons and neutrons.

Again we see the oneness of the system. If this world were a result of millions of accidents then it would be highly unlikely for such an awesome, unified system to have developed by itself! This is God's way of telling us, "If you look into the world that I created you will see My Oneness." Truly, *Hashem Echad*, God is One.

Appendix C
Mashiach

Another very basic doctrine of our faith is the belief in the coming of the Jewish Messiah (*Mashiach* in Hebrew) who will bring about our final Redemption. When we say Redemption, we mean that the Jewish people (those who are worthy) will all go up to the Land of Israel and be freed from the yoke of physical rule and anti-Torah influences which the nations impose upon us. We will be free to pursue *avodas Hashem* (the service of God) to our heart's desire.

However, sometimes in the back of our minds, we may find ourselves thinking: How could it ever happen? After all, we live in a world of nuclear superpowers, so how will we ever be able to overpower the rest of the world? And why should our generation, of all generations, deserve this?

In response to the first question all we need to know is some basic Jewish history. The Jews in Egypt were there 210 years. The harsh slavery had been going on for many years and the people thought it would never end, in spite of the fact that they were told a prophesy by Yosef that they would be redeemed. How could they ever get out from under the yoke of this enormously powerful Egyptian civilization?

But when the proper time came — Boom! — ten plagues and good-bye! And then, just a few days later they were up against another brick wall — surrounded by the elite of the Egyptian army on one side and the waters of the Red Sea on the other. What now? No problem. God split the sea and the Jewish people went across while the Egyptians ended up drowning.

Since that time, there have been many other cases where God caused miraculous victories and quick salvations. (For example, the battle against Jericho in the time of Yehoshua (*Yehoshua*, Chapter 6), and the battle against the army of the Assyrian King Sancherev in the time of King Chizkiyahu (*Melachim* II 19:32–36).) In our very recent history (as discussed in Chapter 5) we had the miraculous victories of the 1948 war, the 1956 war, the Six Day War, the Yom Kippur War, and the Gulf War. Moreover, our Sages tell us that the miracles which happened in Egypt will be but little when compared to the miracles which God will perform when the time to bring *Mashiach* arrives. So, the first step is to remind ourselves that nothing is impossible for God to do.

As for the question of how we, of all generations, can possibly merit the coming of *Mashiach* when all previous generations did not merit his coming, there are many explanations. We will cite just a few. First, imagine a balance scale which we are trying to tip over by placing grains of sand on the pan, one at a time. Eventually, all it will take is one grain of sand to finally tip the scale. Similarly, all the generations before us piled up great amounts of merits to put onto the "scale" in order to tip it over, but it isn't enough yet. Who knows how many "grains" of merit remain necessary to put onto the scale until we will finally tip it and merit *Mashiach*?[1] At some point, only one mitzvah is all that will be needed. Therefore, there's no reason why that can't happen in our generation.

Next, perhaps precisely because we are in such dire straits,

---

1. This adds a new dimension to our responsibility to do as many mitzvos as possible in order to hasten the coming of *Mashiach*.

living in a generation faced with so many tests of virtue and or-
phaned of the great leaders of the past, that the little that we actually do may be extremely precious in the eyes of God. Add to
that, that even in this generation there are those who strain
themselves to excel in the service of God, making our merits all
the more precious in His eyes. It's well-known that the Arizal
(who lived about 500 years ago) told his student Rabbi Chaim
Vital that (in his days already) if a person just gives a sincere
sigh because he feels bad about whatever sins he may have done,
it's considered in heaven as if he went through a thorough process of repentance done by the great Jews of the previous generations. Well, if that was true 500 years ago, then certainly today
every little bit of sincere effort that we apply to serve God and to
repent of our misdeeds is inestimably valuable in His eyes.

So again, we really don't know who we are. Maybe our generation, with its rebuilding of Torah in America and Eretz Yisrael, is considered very worthy in the eyes of God. And surely
the Jews in Israel who sit and learn with great physical sacrifice
are bringing great merit to our generation. Who knows, maybe
we are under estimating the greatness of the "simple" Jew of our
generation.

One final thought on this matter: consider the fact that in
Devarim 9:45 the Torah states that the main reason that the Canaanites were expelled from the Land of Israel was because of
their wicked practices — the Torah specifically writes that the
righteousness of the Jews was *not* the reason for the Canaanites'
expulsion. Thus, when we consider the evil prevalent in certain
gentile circles today, together with all the reasons mentioned
above, it becomes a lot easier to understand how *Mashiach*'s arrival could happen imminently despite the seemingly diminished
status of our generation.

Appendix D
Techiyas Ha-Meisim

Techiyas Ha-Meisim is Hebrew for "The Resurrection of the Dead." It's the last of the thirteen pillars of our Faith which the Rambam writes about. *Sanhedrin* 90b brings many verses from the Torah from which we derive the message concerning the Revival of the Dead.[1] That should of course suffice as evidence to this belief, since by now, at the end of this book, one would assume that we are all believers in the truth of the Divine origin of the Torah. However, let me offer a little analogy in order to help us better grasp the possibility of the dead being resurrected. (This analogy of a caterpillar is cited by Rabbi Yisroel Lipshitz, zt"l, a scholar of the 1800's and author of the *Tiferes Yisrael*, a scholarly work on the Mishnah.)

One summer, I was staying in the Catskill mountains in upstate New York at the camp owned by the Yeshivah of Staten Island. I had a bungalow that had a closed-in porch in front of

---

1. Concerning what that era will be like, see *Da'as Tevunos* by Rabbi Moshe Chayim Luzzatto, paragraphs 66-81. See also *Sha'ar HaGemol* by Nachmanides, Chapters 9,10.

the bungalow. I had noticed that there were many caterpillars by the edges of the walls of the porch. A few days later the caterpillars were gone but I noticed that on the bottom of the ledge that went all around the porch were little white silky packages about the size of the top part of a thumb. Inside each of the "silky packages" was a former caterpillar in the midst of the most amazing and truly miraculous metamorphosis. It was changing into a moth! I decided to do a little scientific research, and I came out with the following as the general idea of what is happening during this metamorphosis.

The caterpillar starts off by spinning silk around itself. This is what turns it into a cocoon. While inside the cocoon, the caterpillar sort of dies — it turns into a thick liquid. There isn't the slightest trace of the caterpillar that was just there. It's completely "melted." And then (as one book put it) the magic of "Nature" takes place. (How an accident can perform magic is beyond my comprehension!) This liquidy glob turns into the most dainty, exquisitely colored, most petitely shaped, moth or butterfly. The appearance, lifestyle, and eating habits of the butterfly are completely different from that of the caterpillar.

This is truly a miracle. The *Tiferes Yisrael* tells us that one of the reasons that God created such a phenomenon is to help us comprehend and perceive how even after a person dies and his body decomposes, it's still possible for his body to arise again, at a later date during the period called *Techiyas Ha-Meisim*. And just as when the caterpillar emerges from the cocoon it emerges with the most sublime changes, so too will miraculous changes happen to previously decomposed human bodies at the time of *Techiyas Ha-Meisim*.

The same phenomenon, by the way, is found when a seed is planted into the ground. The seed also decomposes and rots — and then sprouts, eventually turning into an enormous tree giving forth its fruits and leaves, etc. This, too, teaches us the same lesson. A simple look at nature will strengthen our faith that God can take the most rotted, decomposed matter and turn it into whatever He so wishes. That is *Techiyas Ha-Meisim*.

Appendix E
Torah and Nature Working Together

Our Sages tell us that God "looked into the Torah and created the world."[1] In other words, Hashem created nature to work in harmony with the laws of the Torah, not the other way around. There are numerous laws by which we can actually see this principle demonstrated.

Consider Shabbos, for instance. The concept of complete rest from work for a seventh of one's life was once looked upon as an excuse for laziness. Today, however, it's generally accepted as a very beneficial practice. Many professionals have started to take "sabbaticals," which means they take a vacation every once in a while. Of course, in this day and age, where there are so many broken homes, one does not need to be a sociologist to see how a whole family sitting and eating a sumptuous meal together in an atmosphere of serenity, at least three meals a week, has a tre-

---

1. *Midrash Bereshis Rabbah*, in the beginning; *Zohar* (*Toldos*); *Zohar* (*Chadash*); *Pirkei d'Rabi Eliezer*, Chapter 3; and many other places.

mendously stabilizing effect on the family structure.

Another natural benefit of the Torah, which doctors and marriage counselors today are first beginning to acknowledge, is the benefit of keeping the laws of family purity. Physically and psychologically, they naturally help create a healthy, well-balanced marriage.

Or consider *kashrus*. At many times and in many places throughout our history *shechitah* (ritual slaughter) has been considered inhumane, and efforts were made to ban it (as recently as the 1980's in England). However, an amazing phenomenon has recently been discovered. The flow of blood to the head in *kosher* animals (called ruminants) is physiologically different from the flow of blood to the head in *non*-kosher animals! *Shechitah* done on kosher animals — and only kosher animals — immediately stops the blood flow to the brain, causing instant death.

Non-kosher animals have vertebral arteries which run up through their vertebrae, and continue into the "Circle of Willis" (a part of the brain), and since the laws of *shechitah* do not permit cutting through the spine (*shechitah* isn't performed by chopping off the animal's head; rather it's performed by the swift, accurate slitting of its throat, which immediately cuts off the blood flow from the jugular vein and the carotid artery, from going up into the brain), it would seem that *shechitah* would not stop the flow of blood to the brain since it doesn't cut all the way through the spine to those arteries. Amazingly, it has been discovered that in kosher animals vertebral arteries do not go up to the "Circle of Willis"; rather, they merge with the carotid artery, which is completely severed in the *shechitah* process, thereby causing the animal to die instantly. (After a little while the animal starts to twitch, but this has nothing to do with pain. The animal is dead, and feels no pain; just the tissues go into a spasm because of a lack of oxygen.) "God created the world based on the blueprints of the Torah."

Or consider *bris milah*, circumcision. In some circles it was once thought of as a barbaric act. Today, however, it is well-known that circumcision prevents many diseases. The American

Academy of Pediatrics quoted in an article from the *Los Angeles Times*, entitled "Health Concerns Prompt Circumcision Comeback," which says: "Far stronger, those experts said, were studies showing a link between non-circumcision of boys and dangerous urinary tract infections, including some with life-threatening complications."

Interestingly enough, the strength of the child on the eighth day can be understood with regard to the child's coagulating factors which classic medical studies have discovered to be at a peak around the eighth day of life. Factors of coagulation which are synthesized in the liver, include plasma thromboplastic component (PTC), plasma thromboplastin antecedent (PTA), and prothrombin. Normally, in the full-term infant, these factors are slightly below normal at birth. In the period between the second and sixth days of life there occurs a further, though temporary, fall in prothrombin, with the minimum levels occurring during the first forty-eight to seventy-two hours of life. A gradual rise then begins to take place, and by the eighth day the prothrombin level has not only reached the birth level, but it has surpassed it to above normal levels. Thus circumcision on the eighth day, with regard to blood coagulation, would seem to be the optimum time.[2]

The laws of *tznius* require both men and women to dress in a modest way. Besides the obvious social benefits of these laws, it has recently been discovered that overexposure of the skin to the sun's rays greatly raises the likelihood of contracting skin cancer.

Shemittah (the laws of letting the land rest every seventh year). The fact is, that agriculturally speaking, it's very good for the land to have a sabbatical. However, it's interesting to note that in the recent past we have documented accounts of many open miracles that have happened to those farmers who kept the laws of *shemittah*. The Ridvaz documents how the first farmers to settle in the Land of Israel did not keep the laws of *shemittah* for

---

2. Rabbi Paysach J. Krohn, *Bris Milah*, Mesorah Publications.

four *shemittos* in a row. And so from 1889 to 1917, in each year following the violated *shemittah* year, great catastrophes happened to the fields — to the extent that in 1918 a third of the population had to leave Israel. On the other hand, it's documented that in 1972 there was a disproportionately higher growth of produce only in the fields which were preparing to keep *shemittah* the next year, just as the Torah promises (*Vayikra* 25:20–22). No natural causes were able to explain it. It would seem that nature and the Torah were once again working together.

Appendix F

The Amazing Traditions of Our Sages

We have shown in Chapter 4 how the prophesies of the prophets were, beyond a reasonable doubt, of Divine origin. Now we will briefly show how the traditions of the Sages also had to be of Divine origin — starting with Moshe who received them from God. We'll give three examples.

THE JEWISH CALENDAR

The Torah tells us (*Devarim* 16:1) that we must make sure that Passover always falls in the springtime (since that is the time of the year that the Exodus actually occurred). We also find (*Devarim* 16:13) that the holiday of Sukkos must fall at the time of the year that people harvest their grain — which is usually between the end of the summer and early autumn. Likewise, we know that a Jewish month is calculated according to the moon's movement (*Shemos* 12:2). Now, in order for Passover, Sukkos, and our other holidays to fall at the correct times, the calculations must be exact, taking into account the difference between the lunar and solar calendars. (That's why we have leap years, where a thirteenth month is added to the year.)

This presents a very serious problem if the calendar is to be a product of human intellect. The Moslems, for instance, set their holidays according to the lunar calendar, with each new moon signifying the beginning of a new month. Since the lunar year (354 days) is approximately eleven days shorter than the solar year (365 days), their festivals fall out in entirely different seasons every few decades. Over time, a given Moslem festival will fall out during each season of the year and then begin cycling throughout the seasons again. The Torah, however, says that Passover must *always* be in the spring and Sukkos in the late summer/early autumn. The lunar month must be calculated precisely, and coordinated with the periodic addition of a leap month, in order for this to happen.

The Sages in *Midrash Sod Ha-Ibbur* tell us that the moment when Moshe was told about making the calculations of the months by the lunar calendar, God told him the precise rules of how to calculate the new moon. These calculations were handed down generation to generation, to the greatest Sages of Israel, but weren't revealed to the multitude. The new-moon date was determined each month by the testimony of witnesses. However, after the destruction of the Second Temple the Torah leaders felt that these teachings had to be taught to the multitude or else they would be forgotten.

The Talmud records (*Rosh Hashanah* 25a) that Rabban Gamliel told the Sanhedrin (Great Court) that he had a tradition going back to his grandfather's house that the renewal of the moon took place not before 29 days and 12 hours, plus two-thirds of an hour and 73 parts. (The hour is divided into 1080 parts — each second has 18 parts to it. Two-thirds of an hour is 720 parts plus 73 parts which equals 793 parts. Thus we find that the new moon occurs every 29 days, 12 hours, and 793 parts.)

[According to this tradition, every 29.530594 days the moon is renewed. Only recently did NASA (National Aeronautics and Space Agency of the United States) come up with their computerized calculations of the time between one new moon and the next. And their calculation is almost exactly as ours! (Just for the record, they say it's every 29.530588.)[1] How is it possible? How could a human being have come up with such an accurate calculation without the benefit of modern, scientific equipment? The answer is that the traditions of the Sages go all the way back to Moshe, who received them directly from the Divine source.

FINS AND SCALES

There is another amazing scientific "discovery" that the Sages knew thousands of years ago. However, unless they were very, very sure of themselves, they should never have divulged to us this "discovery" since it could easily have been disproved at a later time. The only reason they weren't afraid to share it with us is because it wasn't a "discovery." It was an old scientific tradition that God Himself told Moshe.

What scientific discovery are we referring to? The Torah (*Vayikra* 11:9) tells us that the only fish which we may eat are those that have fins and scales. Two thousand years ago, our Sages, when writing down the Oral Law in the Mishnah, wrote as follows (*Niddah* 6:9): "Any fish which has scales has fins, but there are some fish with fins that don't have scales." We derive the following halachic ruling from this Mishnah. (See Maimonides, *Mishnah Torah*, Laws of Forbidden Foods, 1:24.) Any fish you find which has scales on it — even if it doesn't have fins at the moment — may be eaten. You're allowed to assume that either it had fins and they fell off, or it would eventually grow fins — but one thing is for sure, if it has scales, it's a fish with fins, and it can be eaten.

Now, how could our Sages possibly have known this as a fact? Maybe on a different continent there would be found fish that have scales, but don't have fins? But no one has ever discov-

---

1. Ridpath, *Dictionary of Astronomy*, Oxford Press, 1997.

ered such a fish. The Sages didn't say that their law was based on any aquatic studies — they based it on pure tradition going back all the way to Moshe, who heard it directly from Hashem.

THE WESTERN WALL

Another tradition regards the *Kosel Ha-Ma'aravi*, the Western Wall. Our Sages make a fascinating comment on the verse in *Shir HaShirim* 2:9: "[God is] standing behind our wall, looking through the windows and peeking through the cracks...."

In the plain allegorical sense, the verse is telling us that no matter how bad things seem for the Jewish people, God is constantly watching over His people from the distance. Another *midrash*, which relays a comment on this verse in the name of Rav Acha, states that God's presence will never depart from the Western Wall: "The Divine Presence (*Shechinah*) will never depart from the Western Wall, as it is written, 'Behold He was standing behind our Wall'" (*Midrash Shemos Rabbah* 2:2). The Sages make an even stronger statement in yet another *midrash*[2] on this verse: "'Behind our wall' [means] behind the Western Wall of the Temple. Why? Because God swore that it will never be destroyed."

Now, we know that the Torah predicts that the Land of Israel will become desolate (and our Sages actually lived when the land was already desolate), meaning that we Jews will not be in Israel in order to stop anyone from trying to destroy the Western Wall. In fact, many attempts were made to destroy it. But to no avail. Indeed, the Midrash[3] tells how the Roman general Vespasian assigned the destruction of the four walls of the Temple to four generals. The Western Wall was given to a general called Pangar. As much as he tried, he wasn't successful in destroying it, for, the Midrash tells us, "It had been decreed by

2. *Midrash Shir HaShirim Rabbah* 2:22.
3. *Eichah Rabbasi* 1:31.

heaven that it will never be destroyed." Why not? "Because the *Shechinah* dwells by the West [Wall]."

Why would our Sages go out on a limb and make such a bold statement, that the Western Wall will never be destroyed? Wouldn't it have been safer to simply look for other reasons why the Wall wasn't destroyed yet in their time? Why say with such conviction that it's a decree from heaven that the Wall will never be destroyed? Obviously, they had a tradition from the best sources that God will never let it be destroyed. And so it is until today.

The Downfall of the Theory of Evolution

After giving much thought as to whether or not I should write about the main problems with the theory of evolution, I decided that this type of book would be sorely lacking if it would virtually ignore the topic, and just rely on Chapter 1 as the sole rebuttal to evolution. And I'm sure that for many of our readers, Chapter 1 was enough to show that our world must have been created by God, and they will have no need to read this chapter, which is just fine. In fact, for such people it is halachically questionable if they are permitted to read this chapter, since they have no need for it. (See Maimonides in *Mishnah Torah*, Laws of *Avodah Zarah*, 2:1-3.) That's the reason why we haven't included this appendix as one of the main chapters of this book, even though it's close to the size of a regular chapter. We specifically made it as the last appendix of the book, because it's not meant for everyone to read. However, it's quite obvious that for many of our readers, Chapter 1 alone will not suffice to remove the heretical doubts that the theory of evolution has put into many of our minds. Whether we read about it in a school textbook or in a local newspaper, heard about it through the media, or possibly all of the above, such — what seems to be — national acceptance surely has made a deep impression on many of us. (As to how evolution snuck into the public school curriculum, that's a separate story; for a little background, read *What Are They Teaching Our Children?* by Mel and Norme Gabler [SP Publications, Inc., 1985], Chapter 2.)

Before we begin, we must clarify a few important points. I have spoken with a number of true, bonafide scientists, and they have made it quite clear that belief in evolution does *not* automatically make one anti-religious. One can believe in *certain aspects* of evolution and still be a firm believer in God. To understand this seeming contradiction one must first understand the basic differences between two important terms. There's *micro*evolution and *macro*evolution. They may be spelled similarly, however, in their essence, they are quite different.[1]

Microevolution is when *small* genetic evolutionary changes take place in a specie. These small genetic changes can sometimes lead to a new *variety*, all within the original framework of this certain specie. For instance, changes in the shape of the shells of a snail, or the changing of color on the skin of different vegetables. These aren't intrinsic changes in the complete specie, they're just slight variations from their previous state.

Macroevolution is a much more serious step in the process of evolution. Macroevolution is when there's a *major intrinsic change* that occurs in an organism. It's when one specie, supposedly, suddenly turns into *a completely different* specie without any trace of in-between, transitional changes. For instance, evolutionists claim that a massive change took place and reptiles turned into birds through the process of macroevolution. This is very difficult to accept, since we do not find any transitional changes be-

---

1. The information that I write here was taken from the book, *Not by Chance! Shattering the Modern Theory of Evolution*, by Dr. Lee Spetner, The Judaica Press, 1997, 1998, Chapter 3.

tween reptiles and birds anywhere in the fossil record, and the differences between the two species are massive!

Now a thorough knowledge of the makeup and function of genes, with regard to the changes in the nucleotide of a gene, certainly leads us to conclude that there's a possibility of *micro*evolution occurring. Indeed, microevolution is a scientific fact which is easily seen all over nature. It makes perfect sense that God created the world with species that have pre-programmed genes with the future ability to develop many, many, variations, all within that same specie. However, the belief in *macro*evolution has lots of problems. First of all, macroevolution does not explain the fundamental origin of the first species. It does not explain how the first organic (live) matter came about. The jump from inorganic matter (matter that never had any life to it — like a rock) to organic matter, is the most difficult jump for macroevolution, since the vast complexities of the live cell are too great a hurdle for it to have happened *randomly*, through any possible series of mutations, and as we shall soon see, the fossil record is missing all the transitional stages between each specie.

In fact, recently, I've spoken with a molecular scientist, who is involved on a daily basis, with *micro*evolution. He is constantly "toying" around in his laboratory mutating various strains of bacteria. He told me that even though we find an abundant amount of bacteria mutating (some being beneficial mutations, but many of them harmful), with all of these mutated bacteria differing in some small, and sometimes essential way from its parent bacteria, nevertheless, they *always* remain with the general makeup of the original specie, just with some slight variations. However, he stressed that *never* has there been found that one specie of bacteria could change enough to actually acquire such a different structure that it could be called a new specie. Never would a bacteria that for instance causes strep, change enough to start causing tuberculosis, which comes from a different strain of bacteria.

To fully appreciate these bacterial studies, we must understand the advantages that studying bacteria affords the scientist.

It can potentially provide the scientist with great knowledge and evidence about the evolutionary process, since bacteria divide very, very quickly. Bacteria, under optimum conditions, can divide every 20 minutes, equaling 72 generations in a 24-hour period! In human terms, 72 generations, assuming a generation to be 20 years, would equal 1,440 years! Furthermore, one milliliter of bacterial culture (which is approximately one three-hundredth of an ounce) contains about one *billion* individual bacteria. Therefore, it's possible to observe a sequence of mutations that technically could possibly lead to *macro*evolution, even though there's such a very low probability. Still, with bacteria it has a very good chance of occurring given the vast amount of individual bacteria being studied, and the enormous amounts of generations that can be observed in such a relatively short time. Yet it has never been recorded to have happened! Now, although it technically can happen, we see it hasn't happened even on the smallest levels, so it's only logical that it didn't happen in the more complex creatures as well. We shall soon see how even the fossil record shows that macroevolution has never happened, and we shall also see how it's almost mathematically impossible for it to have taken place.

Now, to understand why scientists are still involved with this theory, we must understand what science is all about. All scientists, even those who believe in God, are trained to study all types of data, artifacts, and natural events, past and present, with the intention of eventually coming up with some type of *natural* scientific explanation for them. Any supernatural explanation, as appropriate as it really seems, is out of the realm of *science*, and therefore, although the scientist himself (or herself) may truly believe, based on current scientific data, that special creation by a Creator is really the answer to the mysteries of our universe, he can't, and won't, mention this solution in the halls of science since it's inherently not scientific. Scientific explanations must be based on provable, visible facts. This is why we find many scientists, religious and non-religious alike, who are scientifically opposed to macroevolution.

(The theory of the survival of the fittest, and of natural selection, is completely outdated, since it only attempts to explain how certain *already existing species*, (that "somehow" were created) survived over other species. However, it does not explain how the original vastly different species came about. The more recent theories of evolution deal with the concept of mutations.)

On the following pages we will elaborate more on the above points, and we will provide scientific sources that state why macroevolution is highly unlikely; in fact, some state that it's virtually impossible.

Before we begin, I feel that it's important to point out again that we don't mean to minimize the importance of science in any way, shape, or form. However, with regard to this most important topic of belief in a Creator, we found it important to bring quotations from evolutionists themselves who state in the strongest of terms how they honestly don't believe that macroevolution could be possible. Since these quotations aren't well-known, we have taken the liberty to bring quite a few of them, in order to break the magic spell that belief in evolution has over so many people. Evolution, even to this day remains but a theory, far from ever having been proven factual!

We begin. It's interesting to note that in the 1980's many professional scientists decided to accept the facts as they saw them, and the facts clearly pointed to a God. So they developed the "anthropic principle" which suggests that the universe is "man-centered," created by God, with one of man's functions being the responsibility to recognize the amazing design that God put into the universe.[2] So we see that the trend is slowly turning. However, we must first realize that to disprove the theory of evolution to a scientist is not going to be so simple. In fact we find a number of evolutionists who have stated (admitted) that it's only because of their refusal to have to face their Creator — which would require them to start doing a lot of soul-searching — that

---

2. G. Robinson and M. Steinman, *The Obvious Proof*, CIS Publishers, 1993.

they rationalize and hold on with their dear lives to this far-fetched theory. (See Chapter 1, Note 3.)

The theory (*theory*: the Random House dictionary (1985) tells us that this is an explanation that has not yet been proven true) of evolution started in the 1870's, and let's see what Darwin himself, the originator, really felt about his own theory.

While Darwin was attempting to convince the world of the validity of evolution by natural selection, he was admitting privately to friends, to moments of doubt over its capacity to generate very complicated adaptions or "organs of extreme perfection," as he described them. In a letter to Asa Gray, the American biologist, written in 1861, just two years after the publication of *The Origin of Species* [the book that Darwin wrote which pushed the theory of evolution] he acknowledges these doubts and admits that "The eye, to this day, gives me a cold shudder."[3]

And truthfully there has always been a quiet voice of top-quality scientists who have been very skeptical about the theory of evolution.[4]

The intuitive feeling that pure chance could never have achieved the degree of complexity and ingenuity so ubiquitous in nature has been a continuing source of skepticism ever since the publication of *The Origin*; and throughout the past century there has always existed a significant minority of first-rate biologists who have never been able to bring themselves to accept the validity of Darwinian claims.

And now, some 125 years later, scientists have a much keener awareness of the complexities of the universe, down to the smallest particles such as the DNA found in one's genes and the tiniest particles found in an atomic nucleus, and many scientists have come to the realization that this world could never have

---

3. C. Darwin (1860), in a letter to Asa Gray, in *Life and Letters of Charles Darwin* (1888), 3 vols., ed. F. Darwin, John Murray, London, Vol. 2, p. 273.
4. Michael Denton, *Evolution: A Theory in Crisis*, London: Burnett Books, 1985, pp. 326–329.

come about by accident no matter how old the world supposedly is.

(A fabulous book has been published on the subject of the validity of evolution. It's called *Darwin's Black Box; A Biochemical Challenge to Evolution*, by Michael J. Behe, Free Press, 1996. In this book, the author brings many amazingly complex mechanisms that are found in the human body, which Darwin hadn't the slightest idea about, and he comes to the inevitable conclusion that this world had to have been designed by a Great Designer. See Chapters 8–11 where he talks about the reluctance of scientists to face the obvious truth of the universe, i.e., it was created by a Great Designer. In Chapter 8 (page 182), he writes about a survey taken of thirty biochemistry textbooks which have been used in major universities over the past thirty years. It showed that most of the textbooks barely mentioned evolution, and a number of them ignored the subject completely. Evolution, on the molecular level, is just glossed over as a given, without any scientific studies to back it up. The author claims that there are no bonafide scientific writings that attempt to show how molecular evolution, in a real, intricate, complex biochemical system, may have occurred through Darwinian evolution. This book is a must-read for someone who wishes to get an up-to-date, thorough discussion on this topic. In fact, for those that have access to the Internet, I am told that there is a website, which is run by a number of highly qualified scientists, that post their latest findings on this topic, and they respond to personal inquiries as well! The address is www.arn.org, and I recommend you look it up for their most recent discoveries. I'm also told that they get into religious topics when discussing the age of the universe. It is halachically questionable whether such discussions may be read, since they may contain very heretical translations of the Torah, and therefore, it is not advisable to read those parts of the website.)

We will now quote some of the evolutionists who agree to the impossibility of evolution to have taken place, yet they hang onto the theory like a religion.

> All of us who study the origin of life find that the more we look into it, the more we feel it is too complex to have evolved anywhere...And yet we all believe as an article of faith that life evolved from dead matter on this planet. It is just that its complexity is so great that it is hard for us to imagine that it did.[5]

Amazing double-talk.

> Our faith in the doctrine of evolution depends upon our reluctance to accept the antagonistic doctrine of special creation.[6]

> The reasonable view was to believe in spontaneous generation [evolution]; [for] the only alternative, is to believe in a single, primary act of supernatural creation. There is no third position. For this reason many scientists a century ago chose to regard the belief in spontaneous generation as a "philosophical necessity."[7]

A necessity indeed.

Britain's most eminent astronomer, Sir Francis Doyle, documents "howling" problems with the theory of evolution and concludes that the theory survives only because "[It is] considered socially desirable and even essential to the peace of mind of the body politic."[8]

So we see clearly that some evolutionists cling to the theory of evolution not because of any evidence that they may have, but merely because they are afraid to face their Creator.[9]

Let's start to analyze some of the main branches of evolution and we'll see that the theory has nothing to stand on.

---

5. Professor Harold C. Urey, Nobel Prize winner in chemistry, *Christian Science Monitor*, Jan. 4, 1962.

6. L. T. More, of the University of Cincinnati, *The Dogma of Evolution*, Princeton; Princeton University Press.

7. George Wald, Nobel Prize winner in biology, "The Origin of Life," *Scientific American*, Vol. 191, No. 4, p. 46.

8. Fred Hoyle and Chadra Wickramasinghe, *Evolution From Space*, London: J.M. Dent and Sons Co., 1981, p. 148.

9. See *The Obvious Proof*, which deals at length with this topic.

MUTATIONS

The following is an almost exact reprint from the book *The Obvious Proof,* pp. 88–90, with permission from the publisher (CIS).

Darwin began his theory by proposing that the agents [causes] behind the live "systems" that we find today in nature are blind chance, inheritance of acquired characteristics and natural selection. However, the science of genetics and heredity contradicted this idea, and upon the discovery that cells undergo mutations, scientists finally proposed the "synthetic theory." According to synthetic theory, the cause of evolution was mutation.

What exactly is a mutation? All life forms are made up of cells. Within the nuclei of all cells are genes, each a compact, computer-like code of information about any certain trait that could be found in this live entity. One sheep gene, for example, might carry within it the code for the thickness of its wool. Other genes would be for other body traits.

The cells of plants and animals constantly renew or reproduce themselves by means of "cell division." In cell division, a plant or animal's entire genetic code is reproduced. A copy is made. When, every now and then, at random, the genes do not copy correctly, the result is a mutation. These mutations can sometimes even be passed on to their offspring. According to the synthetic theory, the offspring with the beneficial or "positive" mutations are "selected" by the environment to survive. Over billions of years, long chains of beneficial mutations in successive offspring are said to lead not only to changes within a species but also to the formation of entirely new species.

However, there's a major problem with this theory; the offspring resulting from mutated cells almost always end up unhealthy. They are weak, diseased, and often deformed. In other words, copying mistakes usually generate offspring that natural selection would eliminate. The synthetic theory is based on a faith that mutations moved life "forward." The fact is however, that mutations, in an overwhelming number of cases, are steps backward, not forward. Indeed, Nobel Prize winner Dr. Ernest

Chain has declared:

> To postulate that the development and survival of the fittest is entirely a consequence of chance mutations seems to me a hypothesis based on no evidence and irreconcilable with the facts. These classical evolutionary theories are a gross oversimplification of an immensely complex and intricate mass of facts, and it amazes me that they are swallowed so uncritically and readily, and for such a long time, by so many scientists without a murmur of protest.[10]

Now just to strengthen this point, I will bring you quotes from other sources as well.

> In 1966 there was an inconclusive and often ill-tempered two-day symposium at the Wistar Institute of Anatomy and Biology in the University of Pennsylvania entitled "Mathematical Challenges to the Neo-Darwinian Interpretation of Evolution." Here it became clear that doubts among biologists were doubled and redoubled by physicists, mathematicians and engineers, some of whom were openly incredulous at the lack of a testable scientific basis for evolutionary theory.

> Computer scientists, especially, were baffled as to how random mutations alone could possibly enrich the library of genetic information. A mutation, they repeatedly pointed out, is a mistake — the equivalent of a copying error. And how could copying mistakes build up into a new body of complicated ordered information?[11]

Here's an excerpt from an article entitled "What Do Mutations Achieve?"[12]

> The first major objection to genes being the sole and sufficient

---

10. "Was Darwin Wrong?" *Life Magazine*, April 1982. From Francis Hitching, Ticknor and Fields, *The Neck of the Giraffe: Where Darwin Went Wrong*, London: Pan Books, 1982.

11. Francis Hitching, Ticknor and Fields, *The Neck of the Giraffe: Where Darwin Went Wrong*, London: Pan Books, 1982, p. 82.

12. Ibid., p. 59.

driving force for evolution is that practically every mutation is obviously harmful, and puts the organism at a disadvantage rather than an advantage. Two of the most powerful causes of mutation are mustard gas and X-rays. A moment's reflection on the horror of Hiroshima children born with deformed limbs and bodies, or blood disorders condemning them to premature deaths, is enough to show that they were unlikely candidates, to say the least, to win the struggle for existence in a life game where survival of the fittest is the governing rule.

C.P. Martin of McGill University's biology department, once compared the way that X-rays work on the body's metabolism to a person being kicked and beaten in a random, mindless manner — it was impossible for X-rays to cause anything but damage, he said, even if the damage was subsequently somewhat repaired. 'It is quite possible that the violent knocking about might dislocate a man's shoulder and that continued knocking about might actually reduce a previous dislocation,' he continued. 'No sane person would cite such a case as this to prove that the result of knocking a man about are not injuries; nor would anyone refer to the result as evidence that knocking a man about can produce an improvement over the normal man.'

So he concluded that a mutation was a pathological process that had nothing to do with evolution, and that the rare occasions when one proved helpful had been isolated flukes that did not constitute a general evolutionary mechanism. Even Theodosius Dobzhansky, while coming to the opposite conclusion, admitted the problem: 'A majority of mutations, both those arising in laboratories and those stored in natural populations, produce deteriorations of viability, hereditary disease, and monstrosities. Such changes, it would seem, can hardly serve as evolutionary building blocks.'

Another important point about mutations. In all experiments where scientists caused gene mutations there was always a limit as to how much larger, smaller, or how defective the object would become. Never did the object change into something really new or different, as we see from the following excerpt:[13]

> In a remarkable series of experiments, mutant genes were paired to create an eyeless fly. When these flies in turn were interbred, the predictable result was offspring that were also eyeless. And so it continued for a few generations. But then, contrary to all expectations, a few flies began to hatch out with eyes. Somehow, the genetic code had a built-in repair mechanism that re-established the missing genes. The natural order reasserted itself. There are also built-in constraints. Plants reach a certain size and refuse to grow any larger. Fruit flies refuse to become anything but fruit flies under any circumstances yet devised. The genetic system, as its first priority, conserves, blocks, and stabilizes.

FOSSILS

The next refutation of the synthetic (mutation) theory revolves around fossils. What are fossils? Fossils are any portion of an animal or vegetable organism which has undergone a process of petrifaction (turns hard like stone) and lies embedded in the rock strata. (A stratum is a layer of rock.) According to the theory of evolution, we should find in the lowest strata fossils of very simple forms of life, since the lower strata should have the most "ancient" fossils in them, and gradually in the higher strata, we should find fossils of increasingly complex organisms, which would supposedly indicate a slow process of evolution, brought about through mutations over a large passage of time. However, there are two major problems that have been discovered over the years, and the evolutionists (called paleontologists, since evolution is called paleontology) have tried to hide these findings.

1. Even in the lowest strata we find fossils of the most complex living forms which according to evolutionists couldn't have been there since they hadn't evolved until a much later date. We find mixtures of simple and complex fossils in places where only

---

13. Ibid., pp. 57, 61.

simple fossils should be found.

A well-known paleontologist notes: "It is indeed a well-established fact that the (physical-stratigraphical) rock units and their boundaries often transgress geologic time planes in most irregular fashion even within the shortest distances."[14]

> The boundaries between eras, periods and epochs on the geological time-scale generally denote sudden and significant changes in the character of fossil remains.[15]

2. There are absolutely no transitional (in-between) fossils to be found anywhere on planet Earth.

> If gradual, consecutive, positive mutations in offspring are the agents by which species have emerged and evolved, [then] the slow steady progress of evolution should be recorded in the rocks for all to see. There should be fossils corresponding to each "rung" in evolution's "ladder." Concerning any species alive today, it should be possible to find fossil records not only of distant ancestors, but also of the many "transitional" forms in between. [Author's note: For instance, as wings were supposedly developing, we should find millions of fossils of underdeveloped wings, as they slowly develop into fully developed wings. However, they are nowhere to be found.]
>
> When Darwin was alive, he admitted that the fossil record did not "yet" provide evidence that evolution has actually taken place. The record was packed with "missing links" in the alleged evolutionary chain. The "ladder" lacked rungs. Darwin was confident, however, that if paleontologists would dig in the right places, the "missing links" would certainly turn up. However, after a century of digging [scientists have] not uncovered the fossils to support Darwin's claim. Paleontologists have devoted entire

---

14. J. A. Jeletzky; "Paleontology, Basis of Practical Geochronology," *Bulletin, American Association of Petroleum Geologists*, Vol. 40 (April 1956), p. 685.
15. "Fossil Changes: 'Normal Evolution'," *Science News*, Vol. 102 (September 2, 1972) (Reporting International Geological Congress at Montreal), p. 152.

careers to finding fossils that would show gradual changes in life forms over time. [However,] the search has been in vain. Indeed, for evolutionists, not being able to find the "missing links" in the alleged chain of development is "a professional embarrassment."[16]

Hoyle writes: "It is not hard to find writings in which the myth is stated that the Darwinian theory of evolution is well-proven by the fossil record. But one finds that the higher the technical quality of the writing, the weaker are the claims that are made."[17]

Although some of the quotations that we have selected, out of an enormous amount of material that was available to choose from, seem to be outdated, nothing has changed. The fossil record remains a mystery.

Now some more revealing quotes.

Statistically, the absence of any traces of transitional forms proves that there never were any.[18]

*   *   *

The [supposed] evolutionary transition from invertebrates to vertebrates must have involved billions of animals, but no one has ever found a fossil of one of them. Invertebrates have soft inner parts and hard outer shells; vertebrates have soft outer parts and hard inner parts — skeletons. How did the one evolve into the other? There is no evidence at all.

*   *   *

The "earliest" vertebrates were certain orders of fish, the Osteostraci and the Heterostraci...Dr. A.S. Romer of Harvard University has written [in *Vertebrate Paleontology* (Chicago: University of

---

16. *The Obvious Proof*, pp. 90–91.
17. *Evolution from Space*, p. 148.
18. D. Dewar, H.S. Shelton, "*Is Evolution Proved?*" London: Hollis and Carter, 1947, p. 61.

Chicago Press, 1966), p. 15]: "In sediments of late Silurian and early Devonian age, numerous fishlike vertebrates [of the "early" type] of varied types are present, and it is obvious that a long evolutionary history had taken place before that time. But of that history we are mainly ignorant."[19]

Why is it "obvious"? Not because of any evidence, but because they are missing the links between the invertebrates and vertebrates, such as these fish. What invertebrates turned into these vertebrates? "Of this we remain mostly ignorant."

The origin of birds is largely a matter of deduction. There is no fossil evidence of the stages through which the remarkable change from reptile to bird was achieved.[20]

The study of paleobotany has been even more disappointing to evolutionists than that of ancient animal life. One of the outstanding paleobotanists of modern times was Professor C. A. Arnold, of the University of Michigan. In his authoritative treatment of this subject he noted this fact as follows: "It has long been hoped that extinct plants will ultimately reveal some of the stages through which existing groups have passed during the course of their development, but it must be freely admitted that this aspiration has been fulfilled to a very slight extent, even though paleobotanical research has been in progress for more than one hundred years. As yet we have not been able to trace the phylogenetic history of a single group of modern plants from its beginning to the present."[21]

Likewise, Professor Corner of the Botany Department of Cambridge University, though an evolutionist himself, has said: "...but I still think that to the unprejudiced, the fossil record of

---

19. *Scientific Creationism*, San Diego, California: C.L.P. Publishers, p. 82.
20. W.E. Swinton, *Biology and Comparative Physiology of Birds*, A.J. Marshall, ed., New York: Academic Press, 1960, Vol. 1, p. 1.
21. C.A. Arnold, *An Introduction to Paleobotany*, New York: McGraw-Hill, 1947, p. 7.

plants is in favor of special creation."[22]

> This regular absence of transitional forms is not confined to mammals, but is an almost universal phenomenon, as has long been noted by paleontologists.[23]

This is an amazing and a very revealing statement by a noted evolutionist!

Professor N. Heribert-Nilsson of Lund University, Sweden, after forty years of studying the subject, summed up in his book *Synthetische Artbildung*, "It is not even possible to make a caricature of evolution out of palaeobiological facts. The fossil material is now so complete that the lack of transitional series cannot be explained by the scarcity of the material. The deficiencies are real, they will never be filled."[24]

In 1980, at a scientific convention that was held in Chicago, the secret was let out [that] "the fossil record not only does not support the theory — it refutes it." This conclusion was then unanimously acclaimed by all the participants there. Professor Stephen J. Gould from Harvard University calls this the "trade secret of paleontology":

> The advent of the theory of punctuated equilibrium and the associated publicity it has generated have meant that for the first time biologists with little knowledge of paleontology have become aware of the absence of transitional forms. After this revelation of what Gould has called "the trade secret of paleontology" it seems unlikely that we will see any return in the future to the old comfortable notion that the fossils provide evidence of gradual evolu-

---

22. *Scientific Creationism*, quoting E.J.H. Corner, *Evolution in Contemporary Botanical Thought*, A.M. MacLeod and L.S. Cobley, eds., Chicago: Quadrangle Books, 1961.
23. George Gaylord Simpson, *Tempo and Mode in Evolution*, New York: Columbia University Press, 1944, p. 106.
24. Quoted in *The Neck of the Giraffe: Where Darwin Went Wrong*, p. 22.

tionary change.[25]

*   *   *

Scientists are largely responsible for keeping the public in the dark about these in-house arguments. When they see themselves as beleaguered by opponents outside the citadel of science, they tend to put their differences aside and unite to defeat the heathen. The layman sees only the closed ranks.[26]

From these latter two quotations we get an idea of how the fear of meeting up with their Creator has made some scientists seem to be somewhat dishonest, but there's another area where their dishonesty has come out into the open. You may remember having seen at a display in a museum, or in a science textbook pictures of the supposed gradual development of a small dog-like creature, turning into a full-grown horse. We were also shown drawings of bent over men that looked like hairy apes, gradually "straightening out and turning into" modern men. However, it's well-known that many museums have been forced to take down those exhibits since it had been discovered that they were pure falsifications based on wishful thinking but they weren't backed up with any evidence at all. As the following quotations will show us:

> The great majority of all the diagrams in the best biological text-books, treaties and journals would incur in the same degree the charge of "*forgery*," for all of them are inexact and are more or less doctored, schematized and constructed."[27]

*   *   *

25. S. J. Gould, *The Panda's Thumb*, New York and London: W. W. Norton and Co., p. 181, as quoted in *Evolution: A Theory in Crisis*, p. 194.
26. Tom Bethell, "Agnostic Evolutionists — The Taxonomic Case Against Darwin," *Harper's* Magazine, February 1985, pp. 51–52.
27. Ernest Haeckel, Assmuth (1914), p. 63, quoted in *The Neck of the Giraffe: Where Darwin Went Wrong*, p. 204.

Some anatomists model reconstruction of fossil skulls by building up the soft parts of the head and face upon a skull cast and thus produce a bust purporting to represent the appearance of the fossil man in life. When, however, we recall the fragmentary condition of most of the skulls, the faces usually being missing, [it] leaves room for a good deal of doubt as to details. To attempt to restore the soft parts is an even more hazardous undertaking. The lips, the eyes, the ears and the nasal tip leave no clues on the underlying bony parts. You can, with equal facility, model on a Neanderthaloid skull the features of a chimpanzee or the lineaments of a philosopher. These alleged restorations of ancient types of man have very little, if any scientific value and are likely only to mislead the public.[28]

MATHEMATICAL PROBABILITIES

The next stop would be to delve into the mathematical probabilities that vastly complex organs such as the brain, the eyes, etc., could have developed by themselves. But before we begin, I'd like you to be able to fathom what the numbers that we will be giving you represent. It has been estimated that in 30 billion years there would *only* be 10^{18} seconds. Scientists estimate that in our entire universe there are *only* 10^{80} electrons (that's a 1 with 80 zeros after it). So I guess we would agree that 10^{100} is a number that's pretty much impossible for us to truly comprehend. With this introduction, hopefully we'll be able to properly appreciate the upcoming quotations.

Ilya Prigogine, chemist–physicist, recipient of two Nobel Prizes in chemistry, wrote: "The statistical probability that organic structures and the most precisely harmonized reactions that typify living organisms would be generated by accident, is zero."[29] That's right — zero!

---

28. E.A. Hooton (professor of Anthropology, Harvard University), "*Up from the Ape*," New York: Macmillian, 1947, p. 329.
29. I. Prigogine, N. Gregair, A. Babbyabtz, *Physics Today* 25, pp. 23–28.

Professor Francis Crick, awarded the Nobel Prize for the discovery of DNA, wrote:

> An honest man, armed with all the knowledge available to us now, could only state that in some sense, the origin of life appears at the moment to be almost a miracle, so many are the conditions which would have had to have been satisfied to get it going.[30]

> The trouble is that there are about two thousand enzymes, and the chance of obtaining them all in a random trial is only one part in $(10^{20})^{2,000}=10^{40,000}$, an outrageously small probability that could not be faced even if the whole universe consisted of organic soup.[31]

> In terms of complexity, an individual cell is nothing when compared with a system like the mammalian brain. The human brain consists of about ten thousand million nerve cells. Each nerve cell puts out between ten thousand and one hundred thousand connecting fibers by which it makes contact with other nerve cells in the brain. Altogether the total number of connections in the human brain approaches 10^{15} or a thousand million million. Numbers in the order of 10^{15} are of course completely beyond comprehension. Imagine an area about half the size of the USA (one million square miles) covered in a forest of trees containing ten thousand trees per square mile. If each tree contained one hundred thousand leaves the total number of leaves in the forest would be 10^{15}, equivalent to the number of connections in the human brain! Despite the enormity of the number of connections, the ramifying forest of fibers is not a chaotic random tangle but a highly organized network in which a high proportion of the fibers are unique adaptive communication channels following their own specially ordained pathway through the brain. Even if only one hundredth of the connections in the brain were specifically organized, this would still represent a system containing a much greater number of specific connections than in the entire communications net-

---

30. Crick, F., *Life Itself,* New York: Simon and Schuster, 1981, p. 88.
31. *Evolution from Space,* p. 24.

work on Earth.[32]

George Wald, leading evolutionist, wrote:

> Organic molecules therefore form a large and formidable array, endless in variety and of the most bewildering complexity. One cannot think of having organisms without them. This is precisely the trouble, for to understand how organisms originated we must first of all explain how such complicated molecules could come into being. And that is only the beginning. To make an organism requires not only a tremendous variety of these substances, in adequate amounts and proper proportions, but also just the right arrangement of them. Structure here is as important as composition — and what a complication of structural. The most complex machine man has devised — say an electronic brain — is child's play compared with the simplest of living organisms. The especially trying thing is that complexity here involves such small dimensions. It is on the molecular level; it consists of a detailed fitting of molecule to molecule such as no chemist can attempt.[33]

GETTING VERY DESPERATE

We continue. After scientists discovered the vast complexities of the DNA code, and that these codes are to be found in even the most simple forms of life, they started to see "scary visions of a God." Its massive complexities clearly pointed to a Great Designer, and that was no good. So they made up a new far-fetched theory which in essence was saying — we see that there must be a God, but we do not want to acknowledge Him, so we must place God somewhere else and are saying the following theory. However, before we tell you the "latest theory" we must first tell you that this theory is taken seriously by many in the scientific world, even though the ones that expounded it really didn't believe it themselves. (We'll speak about this shortly.) The second

---

32. *Evolution: A Theory in Crisis*, p. 330.
33. G. Wald, "The Origin of Life," *Scientific American*, Vol. 191, No. 4.

thing is, that you must know the credentials of the ones that said this theory, and they have great credentials. First, let's hear a little about Sir Francis Crick. Sir Francis H.C. Crick, a noted biologist, is the one who deduced the double-helical structure of DNA, for which he, together with his partner James Watson, later received the Nobel Prize. Crick went on to contribute to the elucidation of the genetic code. In short, he is a very respected scientist. And what led Crick to give the following view was the feeling that it's virtually impossible for the origin of life to have been undirected (an accident). So Crick, together with noted chemist Leslie Orgel (who are trained scientists, who always look for naturalistic explanations to their problems — and to admit to a God wouldn't be scientific) said the following wild theory. And mind you that this theory was proposed in 1973, and reaffirmed in 1983 when Crick wrote it in a book called *Life Itself*, and reaffirmed again in 1992 during an interview in *Scientific American*.[34] The wild theory is as follows. They say that some extraterrestrial civilization of another solar system, because of the fear of extinction, decided to "seed" other planets with the essence of their live matter. So they sent frozen bacteria out into space, and eventually it reached earth. While on earth, it was these live bacteria from outer space that evolved into life as we see it now. This is their theory. And this wild theory was necessary, since it helped explain a hurdle that couldn't be made. They, as well as many other scientists, couldn't explain how an inanimate object could turn into even the most simple of life forms, bearing in mind the vast complexities that are found in all life forms. So "necessity, the mother of all inventions" led them make up this story, which supplied them with instant life, without having to recognize God. Pretty wild, huh? Really desperate. This is the theory of Drs. Francis Crick and Leslie Orgel.[35] Now you know what weight the word "theory" has.

---

34. See *Darwin's Black Box*, pp. 248–49; and *The Obvious Proof*, pp. 77–78.
35. "Directed Panspermia," *Icarus*, Vol. 19, 1973, p. 341.

But astronomer Sir Fred Hoyle, together with Chandra Wick-ramasinghe, in *Evolution from Space*, said that just as it's impossible for life to have developed by chance in our solar system, so too there could never have developed intelligent life anywhere else in our entire universe as well. Hoyle wrote as follows: "Biochemical systems are exceedingly complex, so much so that the chance of their being formed through random shuffling of simple organic molecules is exceedingly minute, to a point where it is no different from zero... For life to have originated on earth it would be necessary that quite explicit instructions should have been provided for its assembly."[36] So Hoyle is certainly agreeing that at the top, is God. But even so Hoyle tries to pull off an interesting trick. He says that really the theory of seeding (which in scientific terms is called panspermia) is correct, but of course there had to be a Higher Intelligence which created those outer space creatures that eventually sent down the seeds. So Hoyle, in order to avoid God, says the same far-fetched "theory" as Crick and Orgel, in order to take care of the problem of having to meet up with this Higher Intelligence. Hoyle said that it's the creatures from outer space that have the obligation to serve this Higher Intelligence, since it's them who the Higher Intelligence created, and not us, so we earthlings have no obligation to serve Him. So even though Hoyle was at least scientifically honest, as was Crick, by agreeing that life could never have evolved from inorganic (dead) matter, he still wasn't brave enough to face the God that he really admitted existed. But *Newsweek* couldn't handle what Hoyle said, for ultimately, according to Hoyle, you still have to face a God somewhere at the top of the line, and this frightened them.

> Tongue in cheek, *Newsweek* (March 1982) says only that "Hoyle has actually performed the improbable feat of reinventing religion...[and has been] led to exactly the same view that seemed prevalent in the Middle Ages: that life did not arise spontane-

---

36. *Evolution from Space*, p. 30.

ously on earth." Apparently, when Hoyle the scientist is led to God, *Newsweek* is irritated.[37]

As mentioned before, Crick confided to Professor Robert Shapiro[38] that he personally wasn't really sold on the theory, and his real purpose in espousing this new theory was to get people to drop all previous theories that they held as true (such as the chemical soup theory, and the mutation theory, etc., all of them built on the idea that live matter can evolve from dead matter, which he held can't be true) and give them an idea which they can relate to, such as unmanned rockets with live bacteria in them, to hold on to. Not that he really believed this story, but it was to help people understand that this world could only have developed from live matter, and it could never have developed by accident from dead matter. So even though in public Crick says that he still believes his theory to be "reasonable," in private he told Shapiro otherwise.

> Nothing illustrates more clearly just how intractable a problem the origin of life has become than the fact that world authorities can seriously toy with the idea of panspermia.[39]

Desperate people indeed. After hearing such "theories," one sees the staunch loyalty these scientists have to "science," for the sake of science. But it would be more honest if they would express more openly the problems that they face, and maybe, just maybe, suggest that there is an alternative solution to the origin of our universe — God.

THE AGE OF THE UNIVERSE

Finally we come to our last topic, the age of the universe. It's a

---

37. *The Obvious Proof*, pp. 103–104.
38. R. Shapiro, *Origins: A Skeptic's Guide to the Creation of Life on Earth*, New York: Bantam Books, 1986, pp. 227–228.
39. *Evolution: A Theory in Crisis*, p. 271.

topic that many mistakenly think is a proof to evolution, when it's anything but that. I'll explain. Let's assume for a moment that scientists are correct in their evaluation that the world is a few billion years old. We must understand that this doesn't in any way prove the theory of evolution — it's just important to scientists since they must try to establish that our universe is billions of years old in order for them to further promote their theory. This is because if the world is relatively young, then even evolutionists would have to agree that no process of evolution could ever have been able to evolve into the super-complex world as we see it. Of course, we have already shown that macroevolution could never have happened even if the world is as old as the scientists claim. So for all I care, let the world be as old as they want; macroevolution could still not have taken place.

It's also interesting to note that it has been shown that the methods that scientists use to date different material, such as carbon dating, etc., have many inaccuracies. There is also evidence that implies that our universe is a lot younger than evolutionists claim; however, these discussions are really beyond the scope of this book, and as we shall soon explain, they are really irrelevant with regard to the discussion of the truth of evolution. However, they are very relevant to the subject of the truth of our Torah.

If one were to calculate the age of the universe starting with the creation of Adam and Eve, then following the detailed chronology that is found in the Torah, one would come up with a world that is less than six thousand years old. How can we reconcile the age of the earth as found in our Torah, with the age that the scientists claim — or can't we? It's really quite simple.

If one would look at the first chapter of *Bereshis*, where the creation of Adam and Eve is related, one will find that they were created in a mature, fully functional state, and the world that they were created in was also already fully functional. We see that Adam found himself in a fully grown garden with fully grown trees. At night, Adam was already able to see rays of the stars, even though they were coming from millions of light years away, since the world was created in a fully mature way with the light already visible. Insects that live off of decayed matter had food for themselves right away, since the world was created with pre-decayed matter, from which these insects can live. The world was created as if it was an old world. Therefore, the fact that matter and other materials that scientists study in the laboratories seem to be quite old does not contradict the chronology of the Torah, since according to the simple interpretation of *Bereshis*, Chapter 1, the world was created "old." Also, there are those who explain that the first six "days" of creation may have spanned a very, very long time, being days that God counts as days, not the regular 24-hour day that humans consider a day.

The chronology of the Torah starts with the birth of Adam, and not with the creation of the world, and therefore, the materials of this world may actually be old. Therefore, the fact that scientists claim our world to be quite old, does not in any way cause problems with the calculations that we find in our Torah, even assuming that their calculation of the age of the universe is correct. So an old world doesn't scare me, because it doesn't disprove our Torah, nor does it prove evolution in any way, since no matter how old this world is, it's still not possible for macroevolution to have taken place — based on the complexities that we find in all organic matter, and all the links between the various species that are so glaringly missing, as we have explained above.

*   *   *

Hopefully we have brought enough material to do a good job in discrediting the theory of evolution. However, if you feel the need to further pursue the study of the downfall of evolution it would be recommended to read the books I've quoted in this chapter, such as *"Evolution: A Theory in Crisis"*, or *"The Neck of the Giraffe: Where Darwin Went Wrong"*, or *"Darwin's Black Box"* — or any of the other books which I bring in the Bibliography, specifically the books by Rabbi A. Miller *zt"l*, who brings many quotations by the *evolutionists themselves* that admit to the extensive problems of evolution.

I'll end with a quote from *Time* magazine, Feb. 5, 1979: "For the scientist who has lived by his faith in the power of reason [meaning, only following logical proofs], the story ends like a bad dream. He has scaled the mountain of ignorance; he is about to conquer the highest peak; [and] as he pulls himself over the final rock, he is greeted by theologians who have been sitting there for centuries."

And so, we hope we have shown how it's quite reasonable to believe in a Supernatural Creator. It would be beneficial to society, religious and non-religious alike, if the scientific community would be more straight-forward in revealing their severe lack of evidence to prove that the world (in the macroevolutionary sense) came about through random macroevolutionary mutational changes. Which of course is why it is still called the *theory* of evolution, since it has yet to be proven scientifically.

I believe that one of the main reasons that this theory has stuck so well is because there is some truth to it. We saw that on the microevolutionary level there is an "evolutionary" process taking place. Therefore, once there is some truth to an idea, on any level, it has a good chance of being accepted on all its levels, as opposed to an idea that is a complete lie, which is usually easily refuted. This is especially true if the difference between the different levels are not well-known, as in the differences between microevolution and macroevolution. Of course, there is also the "wishful thinking" involved, since it seems so much easier to live our lives without the need to be accountable for our actions.

After all is said and done, it's quite clear that you don't have to feel that it's unscientific to believe in a Creator, since science itself, in certain ways, leads us to this conclusion.

So why not believe??!

Jewish Organizations

The following organizations offer help and answer inquiries about Judaism and its practices.

AISH — NEW YORK
313 West 83rd Street
New York, NY 10024
Tel.: (212) 579-1388

Jewish Renaissance Center
210 West 91st Street
New York, NY
Tel.: (212) 580–9666; 1–888–CLASSES

Project Chazon
731 Montauk Court
Brooklyn, NY 11235
Tel.: (718) 648-4555

Priority One
33 Frost Lane
Lawrence, NY 11559
Tel.: 1–800–33–FOREVER

Yeshivas Ohr Someyach
244 Route 306
Monsey, NY 10952
Tel.: (845) 425–1370; 1–800–431–2272

NJOP – National Jewish Outreach Program
485 5th Avenue
New York, NY 10017
Tel.: (212) 986–7450; 1–800–44–TORAH

The Hineni Heritage Center
232 West End Ave.
New York, NY 10023
Tel.: (212) 496–1660

Partners in Torah
(A Project of Torah Umesorah)
(212) 227-1000

Recommended Jewish websites:
www.chozrim.net   Click on Jewish links.
www.jdstone.org/truth/pages/intro.html
www.beingjewish.com   Click on Jewish links page.

For websites with strong anti-missionary information:
www.outreachjudaism.org
www.drazin.com
www.jdstone.org/truth/pages/anti.html

Suggested Reading

The existence of God through the examination of nature:

1. Miller, Rabbi Avigdor, *Rejoice O Youth* (1962), paragraphs 62–71 in Day One.

2. ——, *Sing You Righteous* (1972), Chapter 7, paragraphs 265–412.

3. ——, *Awake My Glory* (1983), Chapter 17, paragraphs 903–959.

4. ——, *The Universe Testifies* (1995).

5. Gewirtz, Rabbi Eliezer, *Lehavin U'lehaskil*, pp. 31–44, Jerusalem: Feldheim Publishers, 1980.

6. Kelemen, Lawrence, *Permission To Believe: Four Rational Approaches to G-d's Existence*, Jerusalem: Targum/Feldheim Publishers, 1990.

7. Kanievsky, Rabbi Y.Y., *Chayei Olam* (in Hebrew), Vol. 1, Chapter 1; Vol. 2, Chapters 2 and 3, published in Bnei Brak, Israel, 1961.

8. Schwartz, Rabbi Yoel, *B'emunaso Yichyeh* (in Hebrew), Chapter 5, pp. 46–59, Dvar Yerushalayim Publications, 1978.

9. Behe, Michael J., *Darwin's Black Box: The Biochemical Challenge To Evolution*, Chapters 1–7, Free Press, 1996.

10. Robinson, G., and M. Steinman, *The Obvious Proof: A Presentation of the Classic Proof of Universal Design*, CIS Publishers, 1993.

Evidence showing the Divine origin of the Torah:

1. Schwartz, Rabbi Yoel, *B'emunaso Yichyeh* (in Hebrew), Chapter 7, pp. 69–82, Dvar Yerushalayim Publications, 1978.

2. Gewirtz, Rabbi Eliezer, *Lehavin U'lehaskil*, pp. 86–94, Feldheim Publishers, 1980.

3. Shafran, Rabbi Avi, *Jew Think*, Chapter 4, Sepher-Hermon Press, N.Y., 1977.

4. Zohar, Rabbi Uri, *Waking Up Jewish*, pp. 73–162, HaMesora Publications, 1985. One of the greatest secular actors in Israel tells of his debates which he had about the truth of the Torah, and which ultimately led to his turning religious and embracing the Torah's way of life.

5. Priority One offers 3 audiocassettes (in Yiddish) of lectures given by Rabbi Zilberman which give many proofs to the truth of the Torah. They can be contacted by mail at Priority One, 33 Frost Lane, Lawrence, NY 11559; or by telephone at 1–800–33-FOREVER.

6. Aish HaTorah, an outreach organization, has a tape called "The Seven Wonders of Jewish History," on which Chapter 4 of this book was based.

7. Coopersmith, Y., *The Eye of a Needle*, Jerusalem: Feldheim Publishers, 1993.

8. Kelemen, Lawrence, *Permission To Receive: Four Rational Approaches to the Torah's Divine Origin*, Jerusalem: Targum/Feldheim Publishers, 1996.

9. Miller, Rabbi Avigdor, *Awake My Glory* (1983), Chapter 7.

Judaism compared to other religions:

1. Miller, Rabbi Avigdor, *Rejoice O Youth* (1962), paragraphs

2. ——, *Sing You Righteous* (1972), Chapter 3, pp. 22–40.

3. ——, *Awake My Glory* (1983), Chapter 6.

4. Levine, Samuel, *You Take J, I'll Take G-d: How To Refute Christian Missionaries*, Hamoroh Press, P.O. Box 48862, Los Angles, CA. 90048. This book doesn't bring evidence to prove the Torah, but it does do what the title says.

5. Kaplan, Aryeh, *The Real Messiah? A Jewish Response to Missionaries*, National Conference of Synagogue Youth/Union of Orthodox Jewish Congregations of America (NCSY/OU Publications), 1985.

6. Scalamonti, John David, *Ordained To Be A Jew: A Catholic Priest's Conversion to Judaism*, New York: Ktav Publishing House, Inc., 1992.

7. Drazin, Michoel, *Their Hollow Inheritance: A Comprehensive Refutation of Christian Missionaries*, Safed: GM Publications, 1990. Distributed by Feldheim Publishers.

Evidence that there must be a World to Come:

1. Kanievsky, Rabbi Y.Y., *Chayei Olam* (in Hebrew), Vol. 1, Chapters 2–10. Published in Bnei Brak, Israel, 1961.

2. Miller, Rabbi Avigdor, *Rejoice O Youth* (1962), paragraphs 159–209, specifically 187–209 in Day Two.

3. ——, *Sing You Righteous* (1972), Chapter 1, paragraphs 1–12.

4. Menasheh ben Israel, *Sefer Nishmas Chayim*, Chapter 1 in the fourth *Ma'amar*, published 1652. Recently it has been republished by Saphograph Corp., NY.

5. Tuchachinsky, Y.M., *Gesher Ha-Chayim: The Bridge of Life: Life as a Bridge Between Past and Future*, Chapters 6–7, New York: Moznaim Publishing, and Etz Hayim Publishers in Israel, 1983.

6. Eliyahu ben Shlomo, Rabbi. A great article entitled "Life After Death and the World to Come" was written on this subject. It can be found in the book entitled *Return to the Source: Selected Articles on Judaism and Teshuvah*, pp. 130–141, Jerusalem: Feldheim Publishers, 1984.

7. Shain, Ruchoma, *All For the Best*, chapter called "Highlights from Heaven," pp. 179–192, Jerusalem: Feldheim Publishers, 1995.

Evidence of Divine Providence:

1. Schwartz, Rabbi Yoel, *B'emunaso Yichyeh* (in Hebrew), Chapter 6, pp. 63–68, Dvar Yerushalayim Publications, 1978.

2. Gewirtz, Rabbi Eliezer, *Lehavin U'lehaskil*, pp. 73–78, Jerusalem: Feldheim Publishers, 1980.

3. Kelemen, Lawrence, *Permission To Believe: Four Rational Approaches to G-d's Existence*, Chapter 5, Jerusalem: Targum/Feldheim Publishers, 1990.

4. Aish HaTorah, an outreach organization, has a tape called "The Seven Wonders of Jewish History," on which Chapter 4 of this book is based.

Problems with the theory of evolution:

1. Miller, Rabbi Avigdor, *Rejoice O Youth* (1962), paragraphs 24–61 in Day One.

2. —— , *Sing You Righteous* (1972), Chapter 5, paragraphs 149–152; Chapter 6.

3. —— , *Awake My Glory* (1983), Chapter 2, paragraphs 20–61; Chapter 3, paragraphs 62–98; Chapter 4, paragraphs 99–139; Chapter 5, paragraphs 140–173.

4. —— , *The Universe Testifies* (1995).

5. Gewirtz, Rabbi Eliezer, *Lehavin U'lehaskil*, pp. 46–57, Jerusalem: Feldheim Publishers, 1980.

6. Kelemen, Lawrence, *Permission To Believe: Four Rational Approaches to G-d's Existence*, Chapter 4, Jerusalem: Targum/Feldheim Publishers, 1990.

7. Morris, Henry M., Ph.D., *Scientific Creationism*, San Diego, CA:, C.L.P. Publishers, 1974.

8. Behe, Michael J., *Darwin's Black Box: The Biochemical Challenge To Evolution*, Free Press, 1996.

9. Greenberger, Josh, *Human Intelligence Gone Ape*, National Conference of Synagogue Youth/Union of Orthodox Jewish Congregations of America Publications, 1990. Very humorous.

10. Robinson, G., and M. Steinman, *The Obvious Proof: A Presentation of the Classic Proof of Universal Design*, CIS Publishers, 1993.

11. Carmell, Aryeh, and Cyril Domb, *Challenge: Torah Views on Science and Its Problems*, Jerusalem: Feldheim Publishers, 1988.

12. Slifkin, Nosson, *The Science of Torah: The Reflection of Torah in the Laws of Science, the Creation of the Universe, and the Development of Life*, Jerusalem: Targum/Feldheim Publishers 2001.

13. Pollack, Louis, *Fingerprints on the Universe*, Shaar Press, 1994.

Glossary

The following glossary provides a partial explanation of some of the Hebrew and Yiddish (Y.) words and phrases used in this book. The spellings and explanations reflect the way the specific word is used herein. Often, there are alternate spellings and meanings for the words.

ALIYAH L'REGEL: the pilgrimage to the Holy Temple in Jerusalem on the Festivals of Pesach, Shavuos, and Sukkos.
AVERAH: a transgression.

BA'AL TESHUVAH: one who returns to Jewish practice and observance.
B'EZRAS HASHEM: "with G-d's help."
BECHOR: firstborn.
BEIS HA-MIKDASH: the Holy Temple in Jerusalem.
BENTCH: (Y.)to recite a blessing; to recite the Grace after Meals.
BITACHON: trust in God.

CHAMETZ: leavened foods that are prohibited during Pesach.
CHASAN: a bridegroom.
CHESED: kindness; compassion.

DAVEN: (Y.)to pray.

EMUNAH: faith and belief in God.
ESROG: the citron fruit; one of the Four Species taken on the Festival of Sukkos.

HASHGACHAH PRATIS: Divine Providence.
HASHKAFAH: Jewish philosophy; outlook.
HASHPA'AH: influence.

KALLAH: a bride.
KASHRUS: the Jewish dietary laws.
KLAL YISRAEL: the Nation of Israel (the Jewish People).
KORBAN: a sacrificial offering.
KOSEL HA-MA'ARAVI: the Western Wall.

MEZUZAH: a rolled parchment containing the prayer *Shema Yisrael*, affixed to doorposts in Jewish homes.
MIDDAH: a character trait; a Divine trait.
MITZVAH: a Torah commandment.

OLAM HA-BA: the World to Come.

RASHA: an evil person.

SHA'ATNEZ: a garment which contains a mixture of wool and linen, the wearing of which is prohibited by the Torah.
SHECHITAH: ritual slaughter of animals for food.
SHEMITTAH: the Sabbatical year.
SHIR HASHIRIM: the Song of Songs.
SHLITA: a Hebrew acronym for "May he live long and happily".
SUKKAH: a temporary hut dwelt in during the Festival of Sukkos.

TAHARAH: ritual purity.
TAHARAS HA-MISHPACHAH: the laws of family purity.
TEFILLAH: prayer.
TEFILLIN: phylacteries; four Scriptural sections written in parchment, enclosed in black leather boxes, and worn by men on the head and arm during morning prayers.
TUMAH: ritual impurity.
TZITZIS: fringes knotted in a special way and attached to four-cornered garments worn by males.
TZNIUS: modesty.

ZT"L: a Hebrew acronym for "May the memory of a righteous one be for a blessing."

נר תמיד

מזכרת נצח

לזכר ולעילוי נשמת

ר׳ **צבי יעקב** בן ר׳ **שמואל** ז״ל

ליברמן

איש תם וישר, מוכתר בנימוסין ובכל מידה נכונה

רודף צדקה וחסד, צנוע בכל מעשיו ומסתיר כל פעליו

משכיל אל דל לעזור ולסייע נצרכים בכל יכולתו

קבע עתים לתורה, ונשא ונתן באמונה ביושר ובאמת

נלב״ע י״א ניסן התשד״מ

ת.נ.צ.ב.ה.

נדבה ע״י משפחתו

In Memory of

R' Naftali Jacobs, z"l

By the Jacobs and Hasenfeld families

Our voices are silenced
and our hearts are pained.
Mere words cannot express the deep loss
of our dear Rov זכרונו לברכה

מו"ר הר"ה יצחק בן יהודה ארי' לייב הכהן Isbee זצ"ל

His warmth, noble character, and dedication
to the Klal will never be forgotten.

It is a beautiful legacy that will surely be
a source of inspiration to his dear Rebbetzin
and their children.

We pray that we will have the wisdom and strength
to emulate all that he personified
during his short and incredibly rich life.
May he be a מליץ יושר for his entire family,
for his kehillah, and for כלל ישראל

Avrohom (Bumy) and Shaevy Schachter
Shmuli, Shragi, Asher, Shaindy and Yaakov Simcha

תהא נשמתו צרור בצרור החיים

תנו לה מפרי ידיה
ויהללוה בשערים מעשיה
לע"נ

שיינדל בת שמואל

מאת
בן ציון אברהם Papernik

In honor of my nephew
Rabbi Shmuel Waldman

In memory of my parents
אליה בן זאב וואלף Teitelbaum
פייגע מינגע בת מאיר שבתי

Nina Teitelbaum Waldman

משה בן אברהם חיים
Roberts

לזכר נשמת

בעלי ואבינו היקר

אברהם חנוך בן דניא–ל דוב

ובני ואחינו היקר

ישעי'ה פישל בן אברהם חנוך

ממשפחת שולץ

לזכר נשמות הורינו היקרים
In revered memory of our dear parents

David and Rebecca Zelikovitz ע"ה

דוד ב"ר יהושע ז"ל
רבקה לאה בת בנימין זאב ז"ל

תהא נשמתם צרורה בצרור החיים

לז"נ

אברהם בן שמואל

לז״נ הרב משה אהרן בן הרב צבי הירש זצ״ל

לז״נ הרב יחזקאל יהודה בן ר׳ אהרן זצ״ל

לז״נ מרת נחמה בת ר׳ מאיר הכהן ע״ה יוסלובסקי

From a friend

לעלוי נשמת יטה חי׳ בת זלמן מרדכי ע״ה

לעלוי נשמת אשר אנשיל בן שלום זעליג ע״ה

לז״נ יהודה ארי׳ בן אברהם יקותיא–ל ע״ה

לז״נ יוסף מרדכי בן שלמה אהרן הכהן ע״ה

לז״נ רפאל בן ארי׳

לז״נ טובי׳ה בן יהודה ארי׳ לייב

לז״נ ר׳ צדוק מנחם בן חיים יוסף Green

לעלוי נשמת התינוק יאיר חיים ע״ה בן מאיר הלוי נ״י